the PRESENT:
a gift from
the DIVINE

A JOURNEY *by*
KANCHANA KRISHNAN AYYAR

Kanchi
Books

Published by:
Kanchi Books

Kanchi
Books

http://www.kanchibooks.com

Copyright © 2013 Kanchana Krishnan Ayyar
All rights Reserved.

ISBN-13: 978-0-9838765-3-3
ISBN-10: 0983876533

Library of Congress Control Number: 2012923553

Edited by Nandita Bhardwaj
Page Lay-out by Sudipto Basu
Cover design by Feroza Unvala
Author's photograph by Daljeet Singh

To my Guru H.H. SriSri Ravi Shankar

Your presence is my strength,
Your words, my inspiration,
Your smile, my love,
Your love, my compassion.
And your life, my meaning.

Contents

Keynote Message

The key concept of the Vedanta is that there is an all pervasive divine consciousness, Brahman, which pervades the entire cosmos. It pervades all that has been, that is and that will be forever. The Upanishads have beautiful definitions of the Brahman, although it is essentially beyond verbalization. The second concept is that all human beings encapsulate a spark of the divine that we call the Atman, regardless of race, religion, sex, nationality or any other classification. And the third is the philosophy and methodology of joining the Atman and the Brahman, known as Yoga in its broadest sense. While there are hundreds of yogic practices, they fall broadly into four categories – Jnana Yoga, the way of Wisdom; Bhakti Yoga, the way of Devotion; Karma Yoga, the way of Dedicated Action; and Raj Yoga, the way of Psycho-spiritual practices.

It is in this background that the presence of a teacher or guru assumes great significance. The guru is defined as one who removes the darkness and shows the path to the disciple, although the actual inner work has to be done by the disciple himself or herself. India has a rich heritage of gurus going right back to the great Upanishads, which are the high watermark not only of Hindu but of a world philosophy. In recent times, towering figures like Sri Ramakrishna, Swami Vivekananda, Sri Ramana Maharishi and Sri Aurobindo made a profound impact upon millions of people and continue to shine like beacon lights amidst the surrounding darkness.

One of the most influential and respected gurus today is SriSri Ravi Shankar. Through his Art of Living Movement and his extensive writings, he has spread the message of yoga not only around India but in distant lands across the legendary seven seas. Constantly on the move himself, he has opened centers of the Art of Living on five continents and continues to be a source of inspiration and devotion for his followers.

One of these is Kanchana Krishnan Ayyar, who in her book '*The Present: A gift from the Divine*' has narrated in detail her interaction with her guru. In the process, she has thrown light on a number of practical issues relating to happiness, positive and negative consciousness, as well as the yoga itself. I am sure this book will be of interest and value not only to devotees of SriSri Ravi Shankar but also to all those around the world who are sincerely involved in the spiritual quest.

Taranling

Padma Vibhushan Sri Karan Singh
Member of Indian Parliament
05.01.2013.

Foreword

As someone who has spent the last fifteen years on something of a voyage of spiritual discovery, I am always on the lookout for insights and perspectives that help me better define my own spiritual path. As such, when I was approached by Kanchana about giving my opinion of her latest book, *The Present: A Gift from the Divine,* I was hopeful I'd find another kindred spirit to share my journey with. Not surprisingly, I was not disappointed.

Kanchana is one of those rare writers who manages to write from the heart using a straight-on approach uncommon in books of this nature. Her life experiences and willingness to talk to literally hundreds of people and hear their often painful and always informative personal stories attests to her dedication to furthering the cause of spiritual enlightenment and global awakening so vital to people today and for the world of tomorrow. Her perspectives are told in a way that manages to be both enlightening and entertaining, and should serve those seeking their own path to spiritual enlightenment well. What I found especially appealing about *The Present: A Gift from the Divine:* she is obviously a woman who heralds from an eastern background, yet possesses a keen awareness and innate understanding of how the western mind works. This allows her to bring eastern concepts to those who didn't have the opportunity to grow up steeped in those traditions, further bridging the ever shrinking gap between east and west. While many of her ideas have been explored in the writings of Eckhart Tolle, Neale

Donald Walsch and Wayne Dyer—among others—her unique voice infuses those ideas with a new vibrancy that many who are looking for a way to make sense of their life and its many challenges will appreciate. All-in-all, I found *The Present: A Gift from the Divine*, to be an important book that fits well on any bookshelf dedicated to spiritual growth, and a work I am only too happy to endorse.

Best of luck to you, Kanchana, and may the present moment be your gift from the Divine.

Namaste.

J. Allan Danelek
Author of "*Mystery of Reincarnation*"
April, 2013

Author's Note

A Journey

I decided to write this book three years ago in pure gratitude, as dakshina to my Master. I have met H.H. SriSri Ravi Shankar several times and even had the opportunity to cook for him when he visited Florida. Deep within me I accepted him as my Guru. I feel in my heart that he knows me and we share a common bond beyond verbal communication. His knowledge and *sutras*, (aphorisms) are the guiding principles by which I live. Like everything else about him, the knowledge and practices he teaches are simple yet profound. They are all about being in the present moment where there is only love and joy. I knew I had to write a book about my experience but had no idea where to begin. So I began with the present moment.

What the Master really wants the world to understand is, above all, we need to be here right now, in the bliss of the present moment. The present moment is your only choice, your only chance to be truly happy. Being blissful in this moment entails dispassion and awareness of world delusion, which ensures that you are not cheating yourself of your solitary, inalienable duty; the right to be happy.

I am a devotee who has rediscovered divinity, moved from the form to the formless and begun my journey inward. I have presented to you in this book as a student on a path, what I have learned through my own experience and through the eyes of many other devotees. I have interviewed over a hundred people who are following and have benefited from Art of Living techniques and related practices. With each interview I learned something new. I spoke to people from different religions, age groups, continents and countries, socioeconomic backgrounds and ethnicities. Some were well-off, others struggling, some had bad health, and others had overcome financial issues. But the one common denominator was that each and every one was happy. Each and every one lived in the moment and was able to surpass problems with a smile.

In this book, I have touched on some of the knowledge points that stand out as impediments to happiness. Issues that touch people, regardless of their background, in a way that takes away the present moment from them. I have spoken about the knowledge and practices that worked with me in bringing happiness and peace in my life. I am not an expert. Like you, I too, am on a journey and my transformation has been so stark that all I want is to share my experiences with the world.

Throughout the book I refer to the Master as SriSri or Guruji. Art of Living has the acronym AOL which is also the basic course, sometimes referred to as Part-1 and also called the Art of Breathing. The Advanced course is called Part-2 or the Art of Silence course. The Art of Living was founded by the Master three decades ago and works as a handbook to develop effective skills to live in this world, combating life's struggles with minimum effort and maximum happiness. It is an aid to the essential inward journey which celebrates the present moment. In the coming pages you will learn about the movement which is sweeping continents and gain insight into the knowledge and practices which bring about ground breaking transformations in the lives and paths of seekers. The quintessence is the practice of *Sudarshan Kriya*, the brainchild of the Guru, adapted from ancient pranayama or breathing exercises, as well as the practice of *Sahaj Samadhi*, a mantra meditation, both of which have helped thousands find peace worldwide.

When I called for interviews, people opened their hearts and shared very personal experiences. Some had no problems using their real names and others asked for their names to be changed. I am deeply grateful to all of whom willingly participated in this project and hope I have justified their confidence in me. They are my Gurus, it is through them I have learned and am able to share the benefit of their collective wealth.

It is my hope that after reading this book, you begin that inward journey, bringing mindfulness and awareness into your life. It is my prayer that the experiences of others resonate somewhere in your heart and you choose this life as your opportunity to move from the head to the heart.

Prologue

Whenever you are in love and feel joyous, your mind is in the present. At some level, to some degree, everybody is meditating without being aware of it! There are moments when your body, mind and breath are all in harmony. That is when you achieve yoga. The art of living lies in being in the present moment.

—H.H. SriSri Ravi Shankar

If you have picked up this book, you are probably on a spiritual path and might wonder what is inside its pages. The Present Moment for me is truly a gift from the Divine, which assists in the inward voyage to a place of lasting happiness.

Harry Kahn from my local Satsang group once recounted a story which I believe aptly describes my endeavor; in reminding one about some of the obstacles to self-discovery and search of Truth in your internal journey.

He was at a talk by Guruji and for the very first time was actually in the presence of SriSri Ravi Shankar. After the Master had spoken, someone in the audience stood up and asked him a very potent question.

'Who are you?' he posed in all earnestness.

There was palpable silence in the hall and everyone held their breath waiting for the Master to reply.

SriSri paused and looked at the audience, and with his customary compassionate smile replied in invaluable words.

'When you know who you are…then you will know who I am.'

1

The Present Moment

*In the present moment you are new again, pure and clear. In the
present moment—making the mind be there, now—makes you like
a child, innocent, and still with a lot of wisdom and depth.*
                                    —H.H. SriSri Ravi Shankar

At the core of every living person, there is a longing to get
out of *Maya*—delusion, a need to know the Truth, to answer
the universal questions of *'Who am I? Why am I here? Where
did I come from? Where will I go? What is life and what exists
beyond it? Why do I suffer? Am I the body, the mind or the
intellect? Will living in the world answer my questions? Will it
lead to happiness?* In this eternal quest there arises the concept
of Divinity and God. The Present Moment is a gift from
the Divine. In that moment at one level, nothing exists yet
everything does. At another, nothing matters yet everything
does, nothing happens yet everything does. It is the present
moment that determines your future. It is in the present
moment that you rid yourself of ghosts from the past. You can
be truly happy and experience that shift in your consciousness
from the mind to the heart.

The Present Moment is your chance to renew yourself,
make new choices, switch perspectives and reinvent your goals.

Every instant is a chance to die to the past and look ahead with enthusiasm and vigor. Having what Guruji refers to as a '*childlike innocence*' makes you ready to accept the present moment with whatever it brings and still have the capacity to be enthusiastic about the future. It is a brief yet complete vision of divinity.

Pawan Mulukutla, an AOL teacher, believes you cannot see the present moment for what it is until your mind settles. You have to catch a glimpse of stillness amidst all the mental and physical activity around you, within all that buffets you, in the hub of everything that simultaneously pulls you in different directions.

'*If your mind is settled, being content in the moment is being with the divine. Having a childlike innocence, I still have a long way to go but I think I am on the right track. It's alright to have goals and work towards it. Once Guruji said "Every moment in itself is a goal, it is your hope, don't wait for things to pan out, don't rush, just enjoy the journey." There is nothing to achieve, every moment is a goal, and every moment is your destination.*'

Life around you is so fast-paced with so many demands on your time that there is no opportunity to pause and reflect. This need to succeed, the very definition of success, makes us think that even a miniscule halt in the flow of constant thought and action is detrimental to progress.

Goran Popovski from Macedonia believes this is what takes you away from the present moment: '*A discerning mind needs to discover that the present moment is so precious and powerful. Very little is needed to live in the present moment.*'

In the space of the present moment all you need is a fistful of gratitude, courage and faith. When you halt the runaway train, then life stops being a struggle and you can pause in the moment and actually enjoy the journey because there is no past and there is no future; it all happens in the now. As Meenakshi Srinivasan, an AOL teacher from California perfectly encapsulates, '*Life becomes a celebration moment to moment.*'

Personal identity for most of us is limited to our physical body, the image we see in the mirror and from this we develop our self-esteem, depending on whether we like what we perceive or wish to modify it. For many others, identity is our academic qualification, the job or position we hold and what we value as success, given our limitations and abilities.

Guruji identifies seven layers of existence: Body, Breath, Mind, Intellect, Memory, Ego and Self. The problems we face can be at any one of these layers and this defines our lives, our state of well-being and happiness. Meenakshi laments that we limit our identity merely to our body and situations, when in reality our identity encompasses all seven layers of existence. For her, identity was embedded in her ideology; her opinions and values. This is what defined who she was and what she was doing in this world. She realizes that if it's not the body it's the mind; the thoughts of past and future, or the intellect with judgments and opinions and with negative memories. Failing that, the ego dominates with '*how dare you?*'

'*With the seven levels of the Self we get stuck in one and lose the others. It's what is going on at this moment and how we deal with it. When we live in the moment, the world becomes Kailash. Then we see everything as the play—Leela of the Divine.*'

Embrace this moment: it is all you have. Examine what you feel right now and experience it totally. Whatever your situation know that '*it is what is,*' and choose your present option. Then each moment gets converted to grace, acceptance and surrender and you can bask in divine glory. As Umberto Sartori reaffirms: '*The present moment is inevitable. Everything that happens, good or bad is what it is, and in order to make it work for you, you have to surrender to it. It is what it is; good or bad. Embrace everything as an honored guest without getting too excited about it. Accept and work with everything.*'

To understand the importance of the present moment you have to know what takes you away. And it all begins with an understanding of the mind.

2

The Birth of the Mind

The present moment, making the mind be there now, makes you like
a child, innocent but still with a lot of wisdom and depth.
                                        —H.H. SriSri Ravi Shankar

At the moment of birth, the mind as we know it comes into existence and brings with it world delusion. It breaks away from eternal consciousness with the sole purpose of controlling and directing your actions, your emotions and your happiness.

From then on, time becomes linear and phenomena around us measurable. Thus emerges the delusion of the world existence; of life, emotions, problems and solutions.

As we are born in this world, we are weaned away from true reality and drawn into a world perceived and enjoyed by the five senses. In this process begins the cycle of desires, the denial of which leads to sorrow. In the pursuit of desires, the ego balloons and becomes all-consuming and in the interplay of the ego and the mind, life happens.

Even as a child nurses at its mother's breast it is taught separateness. '*I am your mother, this is your father and you are our child.*' Yet the memory of the true Self is so strong, it persists through childhood and often into adolescence. In good faith, always with the child's welfare at heart, good deeds are rewarded and bad ones punished. Parents smother a child with hugs and kisses when she utters her first word and simultaneously attend to her needs the moment she wails. This reinforces in the child at a very early age, notions of good and bad, right and wrong, pleasure and pain. Happiness, to the socialized child stops becoming her true nature and gets deeply connected to the world around her. She stops acting naturally and is governed by outward manifestations of reward and punishment. Yet her true nature surfaces at times and as she experiments with the world, these notions get set in concrete. When her wayward behavior is punished, she develops worldly concepts of acceptability; in that moment, notions of fear, anxiety and guilt creep into the psyche and shrouds her true nature in stress.

The nature of the mind is drawn to the negative and she is thrown into a clash of opposites—pleasure and pain, happiness and sorrow, feverishness and peace and so on. The self gets shrouded in ignorance and forgets that '*I alone am the Brahman* (Eternal consciousness).' Eastern philosophy views opposites as being on different ends of a continuum rather than in airtight black and white compartments and this lends itself to more acceptances of things as they are, rather than labeling them straight away as right and wrong, good and bad.

Vicodin, a prescribed pain medication in the US is useful to a patient recovering from knee surgery, yet should not find its way into the hands of a teenager looking for a high. The ability to see things as they are get clouded by societal labeling. And the moment the word '*Vicodin*' is mentioned, alarms in the head go off and the mind thinks that this is bad. Ignorance shrouds your perception, leaving you with the inability to see that a person, object or situation is what it is. Vicodin is neither good nor bad, it is a chemical combination. How it is used is open to judgments of good and bad. It is only through awareness that you can train yourself to be more objective, dispassionate and nonjudgmental.

Parents, in an attempt to teach the child skills for survival, inadvertently encapsulate the Self in a deep, dark place—there it remains, till ignorance about its true nature reveals itself as the person chooses to get back onto a spiritual path of inquiry and knowledge.

Your true nature is love and your sole responsibility is to be happy. When you begin the journey inward, practices of breathing and meditation take you from the head to the heart and an internal transformation takes place. In that shift of consciousness your concept of Divinity switches from being an outward object of prayer to an inward affirmation of happiness and in that beautiful moment you realize, you are the happiness you seek.

3

From Complaints to Happiness

I tell you, deep inside you is a fountain of bliss, a fountain of joy. Deep inside your center core is truth, light and love. There is no guilt there, there is no fear there. Psychologists have never looked deep enough.
— H.H. SriSri Ravi Shankar

A consequence of modern-day living is stress. There exists an urgent need to fit in, to acquire and to be successful. In order to accomplish, you constantly act, your mind is on overdrive, with thoughts rushing in a million a second. Life then becomes an endless struggle; a fruitless attempt leading to unrequited love, unattainable goals and unsatisfying achievements, while the body rushes around in circles, chasing ghosts of reality. Small successes lead to temporary happiness as fleeting and non-possessed as a flash of lightning in the sky. That resultant happiness leads to an upsurge of new quests, desires and ambitions. In this pursuit you forget your basic nature and completely lose sight of your real purpose in life. Dr. Neelam Raval from India believes:

'Behind everything is the play of ego which makes you want material things, attention, fame, success, getting things done your way and this play of ego makes you unhappy.'

Worries and fears become large monsters, making you obsess about unreal and unimportant matters like *'what will happen if my boyfriend breaks up with me?'* and *'what if I never get married?'* and *'when will I earn as much as he does?'* Between the rushing and fears, worries and futile action, existence becomes a burden, an endless monologue of complaints.

Raji Swaminathan from Chennai, India, believes that we take things too seriously. She recalls being splashed, once, with muddy water by a passing bus while walking down a street in Kolkata with her mother.

'Typically, I should have lost my cool. My mom did. But I just laughed and asked her to get over it. Looking at me, my mom laughed, too, and did feel better. People don't laugh enough. We are so grave as if the whole world's responsibility is on us. When you laugh, the bodily stress gets released and you just feel the happiness.'

Mental care was a non-issue while I was growing up in India. People relied principally on familial support, which unfailingly helped them sail through life and deal with their issues. Solutions were based on maintaining harmony in the family and society, and as long as they conformed and accepted this, there was mental peace. Mental asylums were for mad people; and only 'mad' people went to Psychologists.

The realization that regular people need psychologists came to me later in life, after I moved to the West. Nuclear families deprived the individual of that emotional support, so far provided by an extended family. This vacuum was now filled by regular visits to mental health counselors. It was less of a burden to the immediate family if one complained to a psychologist who was paid to listen. Later on, when I became more involved in the American school system, I saw that even young children were not spared. Disruptive children were diagnosed with ADHD, or ADD, and not admitted back into the classroom until they were medicated. Pure mischief had become a legend of the past. Prescribed medications to combat depression are now consumed as commonly as multivitamins.

While such drugs alleviate symptoms of anxiety, lack of concentration and depression, they do not eliminate the underlying cause. Many psychologists do not delve deep enough to reveal your true essence, instead they attribute your behaviors to fear, guilt and blame; all byproducts of modern-day living. And for the lay person the burden of life gets alleviated by complaining.

4

Complainers

When your mind is not complaining, you are responsible, courageous, confident — and hollow and empty. You are inexplicably beautiful.
—H.H. SriSri Ravi Shankar

The purpose of a spiritual journey is to move away from complaining mode and find joy in everything around you. As Guruji says we need to be *'hollow and empty'*.

I see three broad categories: people who complain constantly, those who *think* they never complain and finally those that actually never do. These are not watertight compartments but spaces between which we move depending on our *prana*, (subtle life force) state of mind and environment.

Everyone has had some experience of people in their workplace or neighborhood who complain incessantly. Either the boss is ineffectual or overbearing, the children incompetent or ungrateful, the weather too hot or too cold, and friends too nosey or distant. Nothing is ever just right. Such chronic complainers create an aura of negative energy around them, making you instinctively avoid excessive contact with them. Just being in the company of such complainers makes you question your own circumstances. *'Maybe my children are also ungrateful, and perhaps my boss shouldn't*

have said that to me, and possibly she should mind her own business.'
Doubts such as these germinate in the mind, possibly flowering
into full blown phobias and obsessions over time. The very act
of being around such people depletes your own positive energy,
allowing unconstructive, deflating thoughts to surface.

Lekha Chari from Chennai, has been on the path for several
years; she knows one can't escape complainers, especially when
they are closely connected to you and one has to interact with
them regularly. She, instead, uses the complaints to her advantage:
to monitor her own behavior and comments and ensure she is
not a chronic complainer. *'You can't run away from such people, you
have to hear them. They really don't want a way out. No person is free
of worries and problems, it's just that they can't handle it and so they
complain, whereas perhaps I can handle them, hence I complain less. It
makes me introspect to see if I do the same thing.'*

According to Bhushan Deodhar from Washington D.C. *'It is
a state of mind — if your system is low, you tend to complain more,
because your prana (subtle life force) is low. Realizing it and being
aware of what you say and do, gives you a more positive outlook.
If your complaint is coming from awareness it is alright, because
something needs correction and it makes other people move.'*

Guruji (SriSri) declares that negative energy has no real
existence and is nothing other than a lack of positive energy.

Chronic Complainers

When I lived In Mexico I joined a social club and decided to
attend local *'coffee mornings'*. I later realized this was largely a
group of North Americans coming together to complain about
the locals. After the first few *'mornings'* I realized my enthusiasm
about the meetings waned, and within a few weeks I decided not
to attend at all. Instead of deriving pleasure from local cuisine,
friendly people, help that was inexpensive and easily available
and pristine beaches, where luxurious holidays were affordable at

throwaway rates, these people focused on the negative. Somehow they could not help but compare their present situation to the perceived perfection of living back home. Expatriate salaries, first-class fares home and maids around the clock were what kept them there. No matter where they are and what they do; such people will always look for things that are lacking in their life. They are not interested in solutions, they want to complain and they want you to listen and commiserate. At this point I wondered if complainers would always be complainers. Was it possible to change?

SriSri narrates a charming anecdote about Mullah Nasiruddin to drive the point home. Mullah Nasiruddin is a mythical character who has novel experiences that are sometimes comic, and sometimes tragic, but are always parables mirroring common satirical situations we face daily, stories we immediately identify with.

In the anecdote, Mullah Nasiruddin had economic problems as his crops failed year after year, because of a drought. Weighed down with his problems, his face wore a constant expression of woe. *'Oh what will happen? Oh my plight is terrible. Oh why does God make me suffer?'* All the words that left his mouth were designed to complain about life which was treating him so harshly.

Well, the rains arrived and the following year the Mullah's fields were overflowing with grain. A passerby saw him sitting near his fields and shouted out, *'Mullahji, you must be very happy, your fields look beautiful and you are sure to earn well this year.'* But then he came closer and noticed the Mullah still sported a woebegone expression. Astounded, he asked, *'Why are you sad now? Everything is fine, the crops are growing, and you should be beaming with joy.'* To this the Mullah replied, *'Oh you don't understand, now I have to do all this work to cut the grain, make bundles and then cart it to the market to sell. All these years I was free, now I am overwhelmed by this burden.'*

Complaining becomes so much part of their character that inertia prevents them from seeing beauty and bounty all around. They complain whether things are good or bad. It's just the way they are, it's just the way they perceive things. They do not seek a solution, they really never hear your advice, they are happy just being the '*victim*'.

Aspiring non complainers

The second category of people are those who think they are above complaining. This group of people takes every opportunity to complain about complainers, whom they supposedly abhor. As I mentioned earlier we tend to drift between these groups depending on our prana, situation and mindset. In moments of lucidity you don't want to be a complainer but there are times when you slip into complaining mode without your own cognizance.

People grouped in this category enjoy the good things of life at least for some of the time and don't have much to complain about. Unlike chronic complainers these folk use complaints as a safety release valve. Having comfortable lives, the opportunity to complain does not present often but a nice moan every now and then is good and at times even necessary. They are fortunate enough to police their verbal communication and realize that complaining allows the negative side of their nature to surface and then are able to pull themselves out of complaining mode.

Such people may not complain unremittingly, but thrown into a group denouncing someone or something, will be quick to take sides, condoning their complaints in the sanctuary of '*group think*'. If all my friends feel the same way about the wealthy, for example, then what I feel is not really a complaint, it is just my opinion. Aspirer's are not perfectly content because of a lack of complete awareness and may have not have considered walking down an introspective spiritual path.

The mind works in devious ways to rob you of happiness which is your true nature. But you need the mindset to pause and examine the mechanics of the mind as it presents obstacles like the ego, a spirit of competitiveness, expectation and social etiquette, all of which stand in the way of connecting with your true self; one that in SriSri's words is a *'fountain of truth, bliss and pure joy'*. They are happy because for the most part because life is comfortable and no threat to the ego is perceived. What stands out starkly in this group of complainers is the paucity of spirituality.

Non complainers

Which brings me to the last category of people; those who do not complain. Very early in their spiritual journey, such people decided to be happy no matter what. Continually existing in bliss, they found nothing to complain about.

Steve Sperber, a teacher from South Florida, boasts that once upon a time he was a great complainer! *'I'm from New York. If you don't complain and you're from NYC, you are not happy. It's one of the ways people deal with stress. I grew up complaining, but as you get older, it starts to be a drag.'*

The need to be happy transcends everything. What is the worst-case scenario? *That I might die? Everyone dies, so why should I worry? Till such time I will be happy.* Such an attitude bypasses the mind, raising the self above the complaining mode. A person on a spiritual path is steeped in consciousness and able to recognize divinity in others. They realize that the light that shines within, which makes them who they are, is the same light shining within me and him and everyone else. They do not make any differentiation between good and bad, rich and poor, worthy and worthless.

How is that possible? Does that not describe a truly enlightened person; a Master? Isn't that out of reach of ordinary persons? Aren't emotions and feelings important? And the answer is yes to all the above. The great Masters are enlightened souls who see divinity in everyone. But this divinity is the same consciousness that exists within you and I. Once this realization sinks in, you have taken the first step onto the spiritual path.

- One where you the Self, begin to stand apart from temptations, sensations and judgments.
- Where you the Self, realize that the body, mind and intellect are essential tools in self-discovery.
- Where you the Self, rise above petty fears and anxieties, aligning yourself with the essence of the universe.
- Where you the Self, come closer to the core of your being, where nothing but pure peace, joy and happiness exist.
- Where you the Self, know that you are more than complaints, weaknesses and shortfalls. And that your only entitlement is to be happy.

That is the day you take the decision that no matter what, today, I will be happy. Life can come at me with full force and present any problem, and I will face it. I will live my life but most of all, I will be happy.

5

The Happiness Decision

Happiness depends on the mind. When the mind is free of past impressions and future cravings, happiness is there.
—H.H. SriSri Ravi Shankar

This realization of happiness in the present is momentous, because as soon as the decision is made, a huge burden lifts off your shoulders. You suddenly become aware of the beauty and perfection around you, which earlier was overshadowed by the ugliness of blame, guilt, fear, hatred, expectation and anxiety. You also become sharply aware of the present moment. Suddenly, time stands still, while earlier there was no time for you between shuttling the kids to school, soccer practice, work and the gym. Unexpectedly, you find yourself staring at a wild flower nestled in a corner of the soggy grass, admiring the wonder of creation and the beauty of its miniscule petals and its resilience to survive and bloom. Without your own volition, you are drawn into swirling divinity that cradles you and consciousness that embalms your soul. Gone is the irritation that made your rip your hair out and hurl verbal abuse. In its place, now, there is patience in thought and fortitude in action. It is a moment of deep gratitude for the chance to live in a beautiful world.

One person who readily comes to mind when I talk of making this decision to be happy is my dear friend Steve Sperber. All those who live in South Florida are familiar with him and one thing makes him stand out in a crowd. He has a beaming smile on his face—Always. At a very young age even before his path drew him to Guruji, Steve decided to be happy.

Steve was only five years old when he made that decision. His mother's pet, Steve grew up in Long Island, brought up in the Jewish tradition. He learned TM (Transcendental Meditation) propagated by Maharishi Mahesh Yogi and in 1979 he met Guruji.

Not only has Steve kept his promise to himself but he has undertaken to spread this knowledge, teaching courses all over South Florida, training several as they learn the breathing exercises incorporated in Sudarshan Kriya.

Ru Wan who currently lives in China understands clearly that the decision to be happy should not be postponed until some elusive event takes place. It needs to be taken right now. Once you take that decision events do not shake you. For many like Ru Wan the ability to make the happiness decision was like turning on a light bulb. It just happened.

'It's not that we have to wait for a specific time to be happy. In one moment a vision appears and your specific mission becomes clear. It can be momentous. Time nurtures the knowledge. Enlightenment can happen at any moment.'

But the tendency to complain for most of us (myself included) does not stop immediately. It raises its ugly head ever so often, forcing you to become conscious of this thought pattern and will yourself to return to your core. This requires practice. Once you know that your first fundamental right is to be happy, then you practice being happy. Every time you face a challenge, (*note that I use the word challenge and not problem*) you tell yourself, *'I will deal with it and while I do that, I will be happy.'* There are many moments of frustration when the mind struggles to regain supremacy, for complete control of your life, and sometimes you are drawn into a quagmire of emotions and stand at a crossroad where choices torture the soul. At those times, yielding to temptation, you blame yourself and others for your predicament, rescinding your earlier promise of happiness that brought you into the realm of divinity. That is the time to remember what the great Master says, '*that your true nature is a fountain of bliss,*' and you tell yourself I will be happy, and I will smile, even if I have to fake it.

6

What is Happiness?

When love glows it is bliss. When it flows it is compassion.
When it blows it is anger. When it ferments it is jealousy.
When it is all "No!" it is hatred. When it acts it is perfection.
When love knows, it is Me.

—H.H. SriSri Ravi Shankar

Ravi Pathak is very clear when he states that *'happiness is in the mind. It's all about translation. If a child calls you a donkey you may say, "Yes, I am a donkey, I am a monkey and you make funny faces," but if your boss uses the same word, you would say, "How dare you?" It's all a state of mind, a matter of perspective.'*

This means that happiness is a deliberate choice you make and it is possible to be happy no matter what comes your way, as long as your internal interpretation or perception of the situation is positive, and you don't see the external stimulus as threatening, harmful or insulting. By taking responsibility for one's own emotions, positive or negative, you can better influence or determine your own mental state. When we don't take responsibility for our own emotions we often blame the situation or others for the way we feel. By doing this we are actually giving away the power for our own state of mind to an external force or situation.

'*Responsibility*,' according to Reshma Kurup, '*is taken not given. Responsibility increases your power. Most people take care of themselves; their home, their family, their needs. People are self-centered. The moment you take responsibility and move outside yourself, there is a subtle shift in consciousness. You gain inner strength and it gives you more benefit than it takes from you.*'

Reshma Kurup believes the way we react to situations is often based on whether we take responsibility for it and that determines our state of happiness. The spiritual path allows you to move out of yourself and view your emotional responses dispassionately. The present moment whether good or bad, is what is, and the ability to see it in all its purity comes from taking responsibility. This is when you can be happy whether a situation is good or bad.

Happiness is that deliberate choice where you take responsibility for your own state of mind, and doing so empowers you to determine how to engage in any situation, good or bad. In the Art of Living course (Part-1) the very first knowledge points revolve around this principle. '*The present moment is inevitable*,' yet it is not until you begin the practices of breathing and meditation does the profound insight of this sentence crystalize in your brain. Till that happens we continue to live in the world, mired in delusion, believing it will provide us with happiness.

Timothy Wong from Hong Kong, believes that we develop our individual mental notions of happiness. '*Concepts of what constitutes happiness are what prevent people from being happy. Job, position, money, relationships, everyone defines it differently, but once you realize it, then you come into that space that it's just me ... I don't have to prove anything to anyone; it's all about just being.*'

Based on our situation we prioritize what constitutes happiness. Such happiness is short-lived because its existence depends on outside influences and people and these factors are always subject to change. This results in huge mood fluctuations.

Once the realization dawns that the feeling of happiness originates inside me, it is how I feel, there is a shift from this dependency and you tap into yourself for that limitless fund of happiness.

Guruji, while responding to a question on getting hurt in relationships, asked why we want to postpone happiness to a point in the future when the other person chooses to apologize. *'You are waiting for that one word; Sorry. Just pretend he said it and go about your life.'* If only I had learned this valuable lesson 25 years ago! I might have been spared hours and nights of anguish as I waited for my husband to realize he had hurt me and apologize. Today, I don't flinch when anyone says anything hurtful. I merely pretend they didn't and carry on doing whatever I am busy with. The apology is unnecessary and even superfluous. Whether they repent or not, I continue to be happy. By the same token, I apologize immediately if I feel I have said or done something I shouldn't have. The word *'sorry'* doesn't demolish my self-esteem or pride. In fact it builds on it. I feel a sense of accomplishment and learning when I can immediately realize how others are affected by me.

One of the main reasons we get hurt in our relationships is because we look outside for love. When we find that love in a person then we believe we are truly happy. We relegate love to an emotion and the hallmark of a well tread spiritual journey is the discovery that you are the love you seek. It is not a mere emotion but your very essence.

SriSri truly believes that everything is love. It is all around you, it embalms your soul, and it is present in the positive and the negative. It exists even when you are bubbling with rage. It does not matter which of the seven layers of existence (explained earlier) you are stuck in, love flows through them all. It is said in the *Upanishads* that from a germ of love the human form was created. Love is embedded in the core of your existence. It is the world delusion that forces you to look for it outside yourself. It is your mind that convinces you that happiness lies in a past memory or as a mirage in the future. Happiness exists now and is within you. It is how you feel.

Once you take responsibility and that decision to be happy, everything else slides into place. Problems become challenges, fermenting relationships interesting and even abuse can be viewed with compassion. After everything you have said and everything you have done, once you have ranted and raved and complained till the cows came home, what you really wanted to say was that '*I Love You.*'

In order to say that, you first have to love yourself. Once you honor yourself and free your mind of all the cobwebs of hate, envy and disillusionment then love will grow within you and you will realize you are the happiness you seek.

7

Six Indices of Happiness

Your desire for pleasure or happiness makes you unhappy.
—H.H. SriSri Ravi Shankar

Gross National Happiness (GNH)

The term '*gross national happiness*' was coined in 1972, by Bhutan's fourth Dragon King, Jigme Singye Wangchuck. Bhutan is one of the only countries in the world where spiritual growth is a national government-mandated policy. Although the indices used are qualitative in nature, happiness is a subjective concept and no measureable value can be put on it. Based on the interviews conducted over this past year, I have deduced that there are about six indices that govern happiness.

#1 Physical well-being

Your body belongs to this world and this world will take care of it.
You belong to the Divine and the Divine will take care of you. Make
this distinction that you are really separate from the body, you belong
to the Divine. Then your smile becomes a permanent feature.
—H.H. SriSri Ravi Shankar

In order to be happy in spirit, the body needs good health. There
is a close body-mind connection and if you pay attention to your
state of mind you will notice an elevated level of turmoil and
disturbance a few days before the onset of illness. Yet, in spite
of the body going through suffering, the mind need not. You
can continue to be calm and peaceful, present in the moment
with hope for the future. Anirvachan from Bengaluru, India,
was doing extremely well in college, which he totally attributes
to his practice of Sudarshan Kriya. He was in his third year
of college when he noticed a swelling in his lower abdomen,
but paid no attention to it. One day he blacked out and was
rushed to the hospital. The diagnosis was cancer. After surgery
he needed five sessions of chemotherapy, during which he lost
all his hair. His mother was devastated and cried continually,
unable to bear the thought of losing her son. But Anir never
lost his smile and never felt he was approaching death. Instead,
he felt strong and full of hope. He was so positive, he ended up
counseling his counselor! The hospital staff was amazed and said
they had never before encountered such a patient. Today Anir is

an emissary of SriSri in Nigeria and is doing well. The cancer is in remission and he lives happy in the present moment.

Pia Lahdenpera the National Coordinator for AOL Sweden, lives in Stockholm. A couple of years before taking the course, Pia was diagnosed with cancer and at the age of 34 had to have her uterus removed, which meant she had no hope of bearing her own child. Naturally coupled with an imbalance of hormones and the thought of never being able to conceive made her very depressed, and she was crying all the time. But her experience with Sudarshan Kriya was incredible and she was able to find her balance amidst all her pain.

'My whole body was shaking and shivering. Something very deep resonated. It was very physical and beyond physical and I was howling and screaming and laughing. It was as though my sorrow was dragged out of my body as I wailed. It was such a relief. Then I felt pure bliss.'

Petar Mollov lives in Bulgaria and in March, 2009, was diagnosed with Multiple Sclerosis (MS) which attacks the immune and muscular systems. Prior to this, he was youthful and indulgent doing the usual; parties, bars, alcohol, cigarettes, a little marijuana and ecstasy sometimes. This was his life; working as a realtor and in his free time, partying. When the MS set in he couldn't even brush his own teeth and certainly couldn't write or even walk. *'I couldn't move more than 100 meters without exhaustion,'* he held.

With the diagnosis confirmed, Petar was at first shocked, wondering how he was going to survive this. Knowing the limitations of traditional medicine he knew he had to try something different. On a friend's recommendation he saw an herbalist, who put him on a combination of natural herbs and a rigorous diet.

Between the rehab and MRIs he was utterly depressed, scared he would have to live the rest of his life handicapped and dependent on others. The cortisone controlled the symptoms but his life was far from normal. Still, Petar was slowly improving and had hopes of getting back to his earlier physical state. The therapist working with him suggested yoga, but to Petar, who could barely walk without pain, it was a distant dream.

Soon after, he saw the picture of a bearded man who was to do a practical seminar with yoga and wisdom, so he decided to attend and see what he had to say.

'I didn't really care about who was teaching. I didn't know who that bearded guy was, but I was convinced that I would get the right information there. I just wanted to find out more about yoga and now was happy to hear it from the source—that smiling guy from India.'

SriSri was a dot on the stage but Petar looked at him on the screen and he seemed childlike and innocent and so loveable. In a few minutes the hall was alive with smiles and laughter. He spoke about the power of the breath, demonstrated *Sukshma Yoga* of the face and ended with a guided meditation. *'After the meditation I was amazed how relaxed I was. It was a new sensation, one I had never experienced. I felt that each of his words was coming to a new, totally clear and fresh state of mind. I was basking in the amazement of this new experience. I then decided to do the course for sure and enrolled for one the next month.'*

After the course, the regular practice of Sudarshan Kriya worked a miracle and he recovered rapidly. Few months later, Petar spent some time doing *Seva* (service) in the International AOL center in Germany and noticed that his body was craving the medications.

On Guruji's birthday a few months later the thought entered his mind that he didn't need any more medication and that he would use the breath to heal himself. He knew he was taking a risk and the pain would get worse before improving but he had so much faith in the Master and was willing to surrender to him. He pleaded to Guruji, '*You take care of me, I'm stopping medications and if things are going to get worse, it's your problem.*'

For a few weeks the body desired the medicines and there were crippling symptoms but then he started improving and has been medication free for a year and a half. Petar knows in his heart what helped him. '*I believe it was Guruji, I surrendered everything to him. I am here for him, for his work.*'

Today he is perfectly alright. He not only walks, runs, but is also a full-time YES+ and Art of Breathing teacher, leads many introductory talks and yoga classes. What seemed to be a dead-end street, a distant dream in the past, transformed to an awakened reality and a vast sky of possibilities.

Samir Desai is an aspiring writer and spends his time between India and USA. He had done the AOL course but was not very regular with his Kriya. While visiting his brother in Michigan, he mentioned a lump he had detected earlier and his brother being a doctor, recommended they operate. They removed a few suspicious cysts but did not confirm a diagnosis of cancer. Samir before his return to India, did a Part-2 course in Canada and met Guruji for the first time. At the time there was not a lot of concern but he mentioned it to Guruji who said nothing, just half nodded. When Samir went back to Michigan he had another biopsy. This time they confirmed that it was cancer and he would need at least six months of chemotherapy. Samir was in denial and sure it was going to be a false alarm. As time passed the reality of his prognosis hit him. But his earlier meeting with the Master had kindled confidence in him. He began reading *Yoga Vashishta* at night before sleeping and the knowledge became part of his existence. Samir could not share this news with his parents because they were older and cancer meant death to them. But his faith was resilient and his connection to the Master strong. The night before he got his first clear scans, he saw Guruji in a dream. On his return to California he took a nine-day Silence course which was life transforming for him. That was the day he gave up eating meat and drinking.

Whether it was Guruji, the Universe or their karma, one thing is certain; that the breath has a powerful role in healing the body especially when it is coupled with intention and gratitude. When physical illness strikes, you are so grateful for living one more day, it becomes easy to slip into the present moment. Instead of filling that moment with doom, the practices of breathing and meditation change your outlook, replacing fears and worry with hope and enthusiasm.

Goran Popovski was diagnosed with cancer. He had a tumor— adenoma of the pituitary gland. Doctors advised him radiation therapy and surgery, but it was an expensive proposition. For two years Goran continued with the treatment although his inner feelings were telling him to stop. Then one day he decided to discontinue everything and only stay with the practice of the breathing techniques, the program and Sudarshan Kriya.

'A few weeks ago, after two years without therapy, only regularly practicing the program, my inner feeling was proven as truth. I did an MRI, a very tortuous process, which showed that the tumor had gone, it no longer existed.'

The breath can heal and that coupled with intention, makes for miracles. Either way it is possible to be centered and happy in spite of sickness. These stories are inspiration for all who suffer from physical illness. The lesson to learn is that the mind and the self need not suffer when the body is tormented. It is possible to smile through it all.

8

#2 Mental Stability

The technique for being depressed is sitting and thinking, "What about me?" Be active, be dynamic—but not feverish. That is the root cause of depression. Underneath the depression is a lingering desire.
—H.H. SriSri Ravi Shankar

There are several reasons people succumb to mental illness. Some are predisposed to it; others are forced into it because of their situations. Both Ignacio Escribano and Marco DiGiano are from Buenos Aires, Argentina, and while they suffered from depression their stories are different.

Ignacio was treated for a year and a half with anti-depressive medication. But the prescriptions could not alleviate the pain in his soul; it could not fill the vacuum created by emotional turmoil, and it certainly did not guide him into a space of peace.

Ignacio even as a child, felt a sense of isolation from his immediate environment. His short career as a medical doctor brought him face to face with disease, desolation and death at a very young age. He wanted to specialize in psychiatry. '*I felt I knew human suffering from up close and that I could, as a war veteran in those hidden paths of the soul, lend a helping hand to those who needed it the most.*' Disillusioned with traditional medicine he quit without hesitating or looking back. He wandered into journalism and that is what brought him face to face with the Master. In April 2001, he got a call from an editor of *La Nación*, the most prestigious daily in Buenos Aires, offering an interview with '*a spiritual and humanitarian leader from India.*'

'*Yes, I accept, I will interview him,*' he said immediately, not knowing why he agreed, and even less, how that meeting would change the direction of his life radically and forever. A chance meeting brought him face to face with the one who would lift him out of his misery. These are Ignacio's beautiful words.

'*Meeting Guruji (SriSri Ravi Shankar) has been the most precious gift I have received in my life. What I for sure can assert today, is that I feel truly blessed. It makes me laugh now to think that ten years back I didn't even imagine that one day I'd have a spiritual master...and from India! And that I would be filled with infinite love and devotion towards him.*

But life, thank God, surprises us at every step...

I came to this world, like everyone else, without any form of instruction on how to live. Guruji's spiritual guidance has saved my life from falling into deep cracks on the path and it's very likely, that without him I would have ended up taking my life—he has also helped me mature, be stronger, understand that life is a celebration, cultivate my talents more and more (I'm currently recording my fifth music album), give myself to others without expecting anything in return, feel useful in this world, walk with less weight, feel happy without a reason, be closer to my parents whom I love so much, live moments of indescribable appeasement, harmony and happiness. I have learned not to give up and how to move from the mind to the heart...'

Ignacio did not become a doctor but as an Art of Living Teacher, armed with a guitar and a melodious voice, he instead became a '*healer of souls*'. On Guruji's direction he created a project called *Indra Mantras* aimed to popularize ancient Sanskrit chants.

Marco was a lawyer for eight years and had been taking pills for depression, anxiety, as well as sleeping tablets for several years. He was always consumed by feelings of doom and could not smile. Though he continued to work, the psychiatrist told him he had a chemical imbalance and his brain was not producing the happy hormones, so he put Marco on a combination of anti-depressants and sleeping tablets. Although the symptoms waned, he was not really happy. His mind continued to chatter and a sense of agitation and imminent calamity stayed with him at all times. It was at this point, on a friend's recommendation that Marco took the first Art of Living course. He waited for a miracle to take place but nothing happened. Then, four days later, he began sleeping again, eating better and in due course, also stopped the sleeping tablets. In Marco's words:

'I am really happy and I continue with my sadhana. In eight months I was able to stop all medications and feel content, happy and safe. Now I can function normally at work and I feel the world is a beautiful place. I was able to recognize opportunities around me to grow as a human being.'

While medication is crucial in the initial stages of depression, once that shift in consciousness takes place and you move out of the space of *'Why me?'* into *'What can I do for others?'* the symptoms of depression lessen.

Depression is always a result of anxieties and fears about the past and the future. The practices of Sudarshan Kriya and meditation allow the awareness of the present moment to exist and in the bliss of the moment, all other worries pale into insignificance. Marco and Ignacio had a life changing experience; under their doctors' observations, they were able to discontinue medicinal treatment for their depression with change in attitude and lifestyle and still be happy.

9

#3 Economic Sufficiency

A poor man celebrates the New Year once a year. A rich man celebrates
each day. But the richest man celebrates every moment.
                                        —H.H. SriSri Ravi Shankar

I read an interesting article in *The New York Times* on how much
money is needed to be happy. The team of Elizabeth Dunn and
Michael Norton said that in the United States that magic number
is around $75,000. Using Gallup data collected from almost
half a million Americans, researchers at Princeton found that
higher household incomes were associated with better moods
on a daily basis—but the beneficial effects of money tapered off
entirely after the $75,000 mark. Yet even though we cross that
magic number, we toil hard and do anything to earn just a little
more. According to their data with a national-level sample of
Americans, based on a theory that double income leads to double
the happiness, they were surprised to find out that people who
earned $55,000 were just 9 per cent more satisfied than those
making $25,000. The research was also correlated to what was
spent by the household and clearly showed that acts of charity
were much more rewarding than spending on themselves.

Using the above premises, when we reach the magic number
we should ideally coast along, completely satisfied with what we

have. But that is not what happens to most people. The need to earn and save just a little more makes them take unnecessary risks and when a business deal goes bad or greed is overriding, the results can be disastrous. Recent Wall Street exposures show many wealthy, educated men taking unnecessary, unethical risks, resulting in financial ruin and shame for the economy and the business. One moment of greed, of being unmindful, of not being happy with what is, leading to a lifetime of repentance.

Arjuna Salih led a blessed life. Born into a traditional Muslim family in the south of India, he was raised with core Indian values of caring and sharing. His nature was one of true happiness. No one could spend five minutes in his company without laughing helplessly. He saw beauty and joy in everything and though he was unaware of it, he was in the present moment. He moved from his village in south India to the busy metropolis of London and began his apprenticeship in the family business. Although there was discord in the family over the choice of his wife, he still remained happy after finding the love of his life. Being a close friend of our family, we met at least once a year and always looked forward to these reunions, as we did to his phone calls.

But two years ago we received a call that didn't sound right. Arjuna seemed very distressed. My husband was reassuring him, when I insisted on grabbing the phone and speaking to Arjuna directly. The man at the other end of the line didn't sound like the Arjuna I knew and loved. What had happened to change things so much in his life? I did not ask about his situation, it was not important. I needed to reassure him about life and make him aware of what he was contemplating. I kept telling him that it didn't matter, that everything was transitory and though he listened, I knew he was in so much pain, he couldn't hear me. My fear at that moment was he was at such a low point in his life, that doing something risky was a definite possibility. My husband was on the Internet searching for an AOL (Art of Living) teacher in London and found a course beginning in the city that weekend. In the meantime I asked Arjuna if he was willing to try the breathing and, thankfully, he was open to it. Fifteen minutes after our conversation, the teacher in London contacted him and the rest as they say, is history. At the course there was that fundamental shift in his consciousness, a spontaneous release of pain and an instant connection with the self.

The workings of the Universe are very mysterious. At precisely a crucial juncture Arjuna called us and there was a course happening in London, which he took, so making a pivotal difference in his life. I later learned that a business deal gone badly triggered a series of events where his business, everything he worked for, including his reputation, was at stake. The fear of losing it all plummeted him into a steep downward spiral. Everything has worked out for Arjuna and he is back to his corny jokes. What a reversal of fortune!

Secure Employment

Having a lucrative job is extremely important for obvious reasons, the most basic, being able to provide for your family and yourself. At the turn of the century with the downward spiral of the economy, many families suffered as one or both members lost their jobs. Unable to find employment, they depleted their rainy day savings. This was a sure cause for unhappiness but for some, the insecurity and anxiety about what the future held became a source for depression.

Sunil K. lived in Kansas City, and had for many years a very successful career in a multinational company, with a jet-setting lifestyle, spanning continents. He was married with two children and his wife was a homemaker, while he remained the principal breadwinner, an arrangement that worked well for twenty years. Fearing a job loss, since several departments in his organization were liquidated, Sunil was relieved to be called by a recruiter for an excellent position in Charlotte N.C. With a hefty severance check in his pocket, he moved, while his family remained in Kansas City hoping to join him at the end of the school year. In the beginning it was exciting, but many unforeseen circumstances shifted his mindset. Although he had taken the AOL course, he was not regular with his practice. His mother passed away in India and he had to make several overseas trips. A new office environment, quite unlike the global outlook he was accustomed to, began taking a toll on his psyche as he had to constantly prove himself to his bosses each day. A month's leave of absence didn't shed good light on his commitment, added to which was the drain of returning to an empty apartment, and the stress of weekend flights to and from Kansas City. He was going through the motions without any interest and soon the serotonin (the happy chemical) stopped kicking in.

His wife, Sarita noticed a lackluster glossiness in his eyes but, never having encountered depression, relegated it to grief over his mother's death. Over the next few months he became somewhat like a zombie, not talking much, unable to sleep or focus. It became clear he would have to leave this job but when he interviewed for a new position, he couldn't answer any question with lucidity. The transformation that took place was like night and day. A year ago this man, the backbone of the family, to whom everyone looked for guidance and support, became like a child, helpless and resigned to a future that spelled doom. Sarita was at her wit's end. She knew that finding a job was meaningless. It would take her away from home and a starting salary would never even meet the mortgage payments. All she could do was support him constantly, reassuring him that it was going to be fine, that he needed to have faith; that the economy was to blame and that he needed to be strong.

In her heart there was an ounce of fear. In private she cried and begged God to find a way. She could not sleep restfully when right next to her Sunil thrashed in fitful sleep. All night his body would twitch, interspersed with heartrending moans. Sometimes he would awaken in the middle of the night to check his bank balance and recalculate when his money would run out. Head-hunters were not responding. The few interviews that came ended up as disasters and life began crumbling for this family.

Sunil was clearly clinically depressed but the combination of anti-depressants and Benadryl to help him sleep destroyed his system and he became completely nonfunctional. As a last resort, his wife spoke to the local Art of Living teacher who came immediately and made Sunil do some breathing. He told him to attend the weekly satsangs even if he had to crawl there. Sunil was willing to try anything, even laugh artificially at his image in the mirror, as the teacher said it would fool the body into thinking it was happy.

Providence heard him and he enrolled in a Part 2 (Advanced or Art of Silence) course with Guruji. He didn't know what to expect but six days of '*Hollow and Empty*' meditations created a shift. There was a definite change in his outlook. He stopped the sleeping tablets and in a month asked to be weaned off medications. A week after his return, a job interview came up and six grueling interviews later he was finally hired.

A strange phenomenon occurred, in that he forgot that dark period of his life. Instead, his mind surged forward unwilling to relive the pain of the past. Whether this return to normalcy was because of Guruji's Grace or a tryst with the mysterious ways of the Universe, memory loss of the pain is common among several people who have undergone emotional trauma. It is the way the Self preserves itself. What ultimately matters is that he is fine and his family once again has their strong, caring, generous and supportive father, whom they love.

Sunil was fortunate to have the support of his family at this crucial juncture in his life that occurred as a twist of karma.

I have met many families that split up when one or the other member lost their jobs. A single event like job loss can trigger unhappiness which drags you from that place of security into a quicksand of depression and hopelessness. Sometimes this manifests as physical illness.

Divya Mehta from California, had problems at the workplace. Working with numbers, her job entailed a lot of data analysis and mind numbing number crunching and it didn't help having supervisor who appeared to be a bully. At the same time her home front was not a happy place. She was in an abusive marriage with no commitment from her husband. The dual pressures started building up within her, resulting in carpal tunnel syndrome. The pain became so severe that she could not cook or use her fingers for simple tasks like cutting vegetables or opening doors. But she had to continue with work and in an altercation with her supervisor noticed a sharp throbbing in her collar bone. As the stress built up and she was unable to vent, it converted into symptoms of pain in her shoulders and hands. *'I was ready to do anything to get rid of the pain, and even willing to try something different or even weird, anything to be free from pain.'*

Destiny brought her to the Art of Living course. After the first Sudarshan Kriya at the course, she felt the pain in her shoulders and collar bone and a sudden alleviation, almost as if someone had pulled a 50 lb. weight off her. On the second day during Sudarshan Kriya, along the nerve affected by the pain of carpal tunnel syndrome, she felt a shock of lightning. She thought nothing of it and left to drive home. *'I went to my car and with dread reached for the car door, expecting the pain in my hand but to my astonishment, I had no pain. I literally jumped in exhilaration! What was happening? I had gone to physical therapists numerous times and had even contemplated surgery on my carpal nerve and I was putting it off for more than a year and now it was absolutely gone. I was speechless that in the 20th century, such magic could take place. Then I remembered the sensations during Sudarshan*

Kriya. There was no doubt in my mind that Kriya had faithfully done its job.'

The stress had manifested in her hand and during the process of Sudarshan Kriya the pressure was released and in Divya's case, once the stress went away, the pain vanished.

How stress manifests

The subconscious is a bottomless reservoir of impressions brought in for storage through the senses. There it is deposited but never lost, and from there in random order, it is able to reach the surface where it becomes manifest, confirmed by the ego that says, *'This is mine,'* and affirmed by the mind that says, *'I agree'.* There are no guarantees which impressions will rise, which will get apparent in behavior, which will become the ego and how the mind will contort it. The end result is a distorted reality that pries you away from your true nature and mires you in delusion. All of us manifest stress and our symptoms range from irritability all the way to psychotic behavior.

When stress takes over your life nothing works out the way it is supposed to. Your mind is not on work and as a result your business suffers. All relationships become fraught, as people around you sense the shift in your mood and react to it.

Ramakrishna lives in South Africa and in May 2008, was going through a very difficult time; things were spiraling totally out of control. He was unaware of his surroundings and pleaded with the Universe for help.

'I couldn't manage and I had never experienced this. All I wanted was inner peace; not family, job or money. I was suffering.'

His life was misery and he made the mistake of confiding in his business partner who was a close friend, or so he thought. Looking out for himself the partner wanted out, and for the next few months the two were involved in a financial deadlock. Once he realized Ramakrishna was in mental shambles, the relationship of seventeen years broke up. *'I was 45 but I looked 85,'* declared Ram recalling the physical ramifications of his mental state.

Then the recession arrived and the feelings worsened; the advice he got from all quarters regarding his business was to throw in the towel. His partner had lost faith in Ramakrishna and wanted out. Of the two companies they jointly owned, one was making profit and the other was in financial ruin. Of course, the partner wanted the profit-making company and there were tense negotiations which aged Ram considerably. By chance he took the Art of Living course and after his first Sudarshan Kriya felt relief immediately.

'I knew there was something in the breathing, something about this knowledge made me feel that it's not new. There has been a connection somewhere and I felt the presence of the Master whom I now know as a Guru.'

The day after the course he met his partner for a final meeting with his lawyers. During the course he learned about surrendering to the moment, and that affected him deeply. In that meeting he applied the knowledge, surrendering to the will of the Universe. With that came freedom. He was liberated after months of bondage to the fears of economic security.

'I allowed them to take what they wanted and the meeting that should have taken 30 months lasted 30 seconds. My partner was in tears. They were expecting a fight and I did nothing. It was a miracle. There had been so much animosity and bad feeling and it was gone in a flash.'

Ramakrishna let go of a flourishing business without looking back. He wanted no more bad feelings, no more fights and bitterness. He was armed with what he refers to as the antidote to stress and with that he was empowered and felt invincible, ready to face any challenge. He wanted and needed nothing in that moment and knew that he would be provided for. His business which had an overdraft of US $50,000 with a turnover of $40,000 and a staff of 18, ballooned. Because his mind was in a safe and comfortable place and he did not have a feverish fear about money, what followed him, was abundance. Now he hires 40 people and the business has an annual turnover of $150,000! And all his employees have taken the Art of Living workshop.

Sunil, Divya and Ramakrishna were fortunate to tap into resources provided by the Art of Living before their lives were ruined. Many others are not so fortunate. Guruji says it is impossible to treat the mind with the mind: you have to descend to the level of the heart. The practice of Sudarshan Kriya and meditation does exactly this and when you are safe in the present moment, when the underlying stress is released, only then can you truly appreciate the space you are in and experience the happiness which is your birthright.

Arjuna Salih's economic situation had not changed but his attitude to it had. He didn't feel the burden of his problems and was in a space where the future was full of possibilities. The trick is to feel a sense of abundance no matter how much you have. As Marco DiGiano says, '*When I was a lawyer I never had economic problems but I never had abundance. Now I have not much money but I feel abundance, I feel like a millionaire.*'

10

#4 Interpersonal Relationships

Let love be. Do not give it a name. When you give love a name it becomes a relationship and relationships restrict love.
—H.H. SriSri Ravi Shankar

With partners:

Having a strong, enduring relationship with your partner is very important in life, because you have someone to share your experiences with. When that relationship sours, it destabilizes you and you feel as though the whole world is crumbling. What happens in most relationships/marriages is a lot gets invested in the partner in terms of economic and emotional support; and when that is ruined, the focus moves away from the core. Many of us are unaware that we treat our relationships like transactions ... *what I get out of it ... what I get in return... what I deserve ... what is expected.* Love often becomes a red-herring in relationships. In ignorance we understand love to be an emotion when in fact it is your very existence.

Dr. Neelam Raval from Gujarat, India, says that in the groups she works with, people are not in a space of love and they drift into relationships to find that love which is missing within themselves.

'If you are secure and confident in love there is no room for unhappiness. There is always someone who cares for you. Some people have everything but they feel as if they lack something. This makes them unhappy and then they spread their misery.'

Reshma Kurup, an AOL teacher residing in Bengaluru India, works with the underprivileged in slums and has realized that whether it's the poor or the wealthy, people are so involved with making money, that inculcating core values in their children gets neglected. This according to her is the underlying reason strong relationships do not get forged. The major cause of unhappiness in children is competition. They constantly face peer pressure on top of stress from parents, teachers and the educational system. The atmosphere has changed in urban cities. Children have a lot more money, cell phones, and technology rules their lives, but they don't take time for themselves. As Reshma Kurup says:

'In big cities there are more nuclear families and common core values of caring and sharing are reducing. In schools you scarcely see them smiling, they have so much stress. Children think less about the concept of taking care of others, especially of elders, which was part of our culture and is now missing. They benefit so much from yoga and pranayama which is also not part of the school curriculum anymore.'

It becomes hard to remember that your journey is alone and all that walk with you are just incidental passengers, travelling companions who may or might not be seekers on path. If you move away from your center and make your partner the reason to be happy, and then that relationship curdles, it leads to a lot of pain.

Eva Aminoff from Finland is so grateful for being able to pull herself out of depression, negativity and even borderline alcoholism.

'Now I am a really happy person. That's what Guruji wants us to be; centered, spontaneous and enthusiastic. There was a time when I was like that but it got clouded. I really felt I came home after the first

time I met Guruji. His blessing was my most profound experience; it was as if he could look into my heart and take away the pain. He's my savior.'

Eva had been in a relationship for about a year, and thought it was the most important facet of her life. However, things soured; there was a crisis in her relationship and her heart was broken, leading to despondency and depression. Her life crumbled and she did not have the will to carry on. Her mental concept of happiness stemmed from that association and when it ended she was destroyed.

'I was really without hope and I wanted to practically end everything. I couldn't see the light at all and I was scared. I felt alone and sorry for myself. I couldn't see the future.'

Destiny steered her towards taking the course and during her first Sudarshan Kriya, the pain racking her body was leached. She experienced many different sensations and scents and a powerful feeling of being protected by the Divine. Her life was transformed, for in her case, the shift in consciousness was immediate because the pain caused by her suffering had been so acute. She had the experience of bliss all seekers look and long for. In hindsight, Eva laughs and says, *'Perhaps that relationship breaking was the best thing, because it opened up a whole new world. Now life is as simple as noticing the colors of the flowers outside and the birds chirping. I am so grateful just to be here, to be alive. Currently, I'm so happy I can contribute with seva and spread joy.'*

Many relationships fail when one partner becomes demanding and possessive, not allowing space for the other to breathe. For a relationship to be successful it needs to take on a symbiotic flavor where each benefits and grows with the support and care from the other. The following stories shared by Karen and Anand demonstrate the destructive power of control. With control and possession, one partner's personality gets completely crushed. This inevitably leads to a breakup because the affected and controlled party, as in the case of Karen, suffers an identity crisis. However for Anand, although there was a breakup once, this led to an awakening inside him, where he was able to see his earlier errors and rekindle and repair the relationship.

Karen was in a five year long-distance relationship with a boy she met in college. Initially she wanted to get married, but when the engagement became a reality, she panicked. This is her story...

'I began getting panic attacks, hyperventilating and feeling an overwhelming sense of hopelessness. I could not control the thoughts entering my brain and I was not able to work, sleep or eat. At some points I would crouch on my apartment floor, beat my fists against the floor and cry. I couldn't understand what was happening to me. I felt guilt at disappointing my boyfriend, his family. Our parents had met, we even went ring shopping together, but something inside me was resisting. Thoughts flooded my brain and I was suffering mentally. The anxiety was so bad I had to use the emergency mental health services offered at my university. The psychologist helped slightly to make sense of the thoughts inundating my brain, but verbalizing made my problems bigger and I felt like I was developing a dependency for the therapy sessions.

My parents, who were very worried about my condition, informed me that an Art of Silence course was taking place that weekend. I signed up. I was floundering for anything that would help ease my debilitating anxiety.

Attending the course was the best thing that ever happened to me. At first, I was restless during meditations. I would get terrible thoughts and memories that were suppressed from my childhood, things that I never knew were festering. But the combination of wisdom, meditation and the knowledge that deep inside of me is a force, an energy that is innately good, that no amount of psychology can tap into, moved me beyond words. I left the course cleansed, knowing deep down that all things pass and that everything will be

*okay in the end. I realized that I had been defining my identity based
on one relationship. I now know I am so much more. My culture, my
religion or my relationships are mere outward manifestations and do
not define me.'*

Karen had to do a lot of soul-searching to discover who she
was and what she wanted and the process was painful but out
of this pain came wisdom. A year later she had recovered. The
guilt from breaking up left her and she was able to focus on
centering herself to walk confidently down a different path. She
has developed immense faith, is centered and aware that her
happiness exists now, in the present moment.

Anand Kumar was shocked the first time his girlfriend broke
up with him and told him she felt stifled and was not having any
fun. Sometime later, the two of them ended up taking a course
together and something profound happened during Sudarshan
Kriya for Anand. He began immersing himself in Seva and
as he organized courses and worked for others, an internal
transformation took place.

*'The world was the same but the way I started feeling about the
world changed. I felt much more connected, I started feeling things,
where earlier there was a disconnect. I was so happy and all I could
think was that I wanted everyone to do this.'*

He did his daily practice (sadhana) and was so happy, nothing
bothered him. Destiny made his girlfriend move into the same
apartment complex, and the earlier fire was rekindled. He
laughed when she told him he seemed human again and she felt
able to breathe freely. Anand was so blissful, he didn't need the
relationship to define his happiness but they married and now
have a child, a new home and both work for the same company.

*'It's like a fairy tale. Just giving that sense of freedom to yourself
and others makes it work, because you allow them to do whatever they
want. To do that you have to be happy in the first place.'*

His life is now about love, whereas earlier it was a search for happiness in a relationship. The relationship has stopped being about his needs and has converted to one of sharing. Anand puts it very well. *'It is now more about what can I do for you rather than what's in it for me.'*

Relationships and commitment

Many people have commitment issues. They know that the person they are with completes them, yet they are not invested in it totally and at the first sign of trouble opt out. Any relationship has problems of one kind or another. It is rare to meet two people who see eye to eye on everything and are satisfied with everything about one another. Relationships and marriages work because people commit to one another and agree to compromise and support each other no matter what. Looking for love in the relationship may not be the answer because the love is your existence which you recognize as a feeling within you. Technically, love is not an emotion but your very existence. Feelings and emotions keep changing. But love which is unconditional remains the unchanging and that is what you are made up of ... *sat-cit-ananda.*

Love does not reside in your partner. When you recognize qualities you admire or possess in the other person, that moment of surrender makes you aware of your own love which is your core and your essence.

Samir Desai had a French girlfriend with whom he had a turbulent relationship. Samir found that while he loved Julie, he greatly enjoyed being single. Their relationship could not flower because Samir had not yet discovered that relationships are not about love. *You* are about love and your life is about love. Your relationship is more about commitment.

'All men have commitment issues. Growing up I thought I would always be a bachelor. I never saw the need to be married.

*That impression contributed to our problems. Although Guruji says
commitment makes you stronger I never thought that.'*

The process of going through silence and TTC (Teacher
Training Course) made Samir reach his source and almost
seamlessly he was able to take that critical, lifelong decision to
be married. His marriage to Julie took place in the Bangalore
Ashram in a small ceremony with twenty witnesses.

Your first love is always one you will remember, because in
those adolescent years you are searching for true happiness and
it really defines who you are. Your first relationship tends to be
emotionally charged as well, with a deep need to be reassured
that she loves you. Fernando Frassia from Buenos Aires was only
eighteen when his girlfriend broke up with him and he totally
crashed.

*'I cried every day, day and night for two months, didn't know what
to do, and didn't know whom to call. Finally I went to a psychologist.'*

But it didn't help at all. He then remembered the AOL course
and attended for the second time, crying his heart out from the
first day to the last. On the final day, a huge sense of relief came
over him and he almost felt as if he were born again.

*'It wasn't that I gained something during the course, instead I lost
something.'* All the bottled-up pain inside of him came bubbling
up to the surface, and once that was released a sense of calm
enveloped him, bringing with it a new-found awareness. What
hit him during the course was the fact that his heart broke
because he loved someone so much. Realizing this made him
aware of one thing; of all the love that he had inside him for
himself and for others. *'What I was searching for outside, was really
inside me.'*

What makes a relationship unbearable is if you are at the
receiving end of physical or mental abuse. The nature of abuse is
such that the abusers repent and beg forgiveness and in a weak
moment, coming from a space that longs for happiness, their

spouses forgive them and the cycle is repeated. In India, once you are married you are expected to put up with everything for the sake of your children. The woman's role is defined by her suffering and spirit of sacrifice. It is accepted as part of karma and a sense of helplessness ensues. It is only in the last two decades that women are showing the courage to get out of an abusive relationship and that is only because they feel empowered and have some financial independence.

Divya Mehta was in such a relationship for 24 years. Each day was filled with abuse towards her and the children. But she did not have the courage to leave the marriage and waited for a point in her life when her husband divorced her. By this time she was deeply immersed in the Art of Living and a sheath of divinity covered her.

'I am so grateful for the divorce. I have finished that phase and have entered the Golden Phase of my life. I am enjoying every moment of my life and Guruji is right there holding my hand every moment. I have nothing but praise and gratitude for my husband who wiped out all my karma of 24 years. That's why I can celebrate and feel free.'

Sonia Mehra has been through several ups and downs in her marriage and is in the process of getting a divorce. In the last two years she experienced challenges she couldn't bring herself to talk about but there was not one ounce of sadness in her.

'You can give a hundred per cent to make a relationship work. But if two people are moving in different directions, there is no way it can work out and no way can you move forward.'

Both husband and wife were involved in the Art of Living and Sonia feels that without the grace of the Guru she would not have taken this drastic step. The knowledge and the practice brought about a deep awareness of their opposing paths and gave her the strength to take an unconventional step, with no plans for the future.

'I was not helping him grow. We were not serving each other. We brought no joy to each other. I didn't have to ask anybody, it was quite clear for me. With so many years on the path I have made the knowledge my way of life.'

It takes a lot of courage to walk away from a long-standing relationship and from both Divya's and Sonia's experience, it is clear that this came from a space of security and faith that they are taken care of. Some people think that spirituality is acceptance of your fate and the ability to endure. Spirituality does not mean blind acceptance of abuse. It develops in you the wisdom and clarity to take the right decision, make a choice, choose a path and then allow your destiny to unfold. Just being on the spiritual path does not mean you will not face any problems. Problems will arise as they are supposed to. It is your attitude that changes. In fact sometimes in relationships, problems pop up when one partner is on a spiritual path and the other is not.

Maya had a smooth and happy marriage when she became involved in Art of Living (AOL) and that's when her life changed. Her husband was not into AOL and every day became a challenge. He didn't like her chanting, singing or meditating and it took a lot of effort in applying the knowledge to her daily life just to keep the peace. It even annoyed him that she was calm and never argued. As a result, the atmosphere in the house was charged and the aura tense.

'I don't blame him; he just didn't understand any of it. Everything I did he couldn't understand; while chanting Rudram, if I sang and tears rolled down my cheeks, he thought I had gone mad.' He was quite certain that one day she would probably leave the family and go off to the ashram.

Her husband truly believed that spirituality, and Art of Living in particular, took Maya away from the family and it annoyed him when she went into her room to do her daily sadhana. He should have been elated that she didn't argue, didn't cross him even when there was a difference of opinion. Other husbands would have rejoiced if their wife were not into material possessions and not crazy about shopping. Instead it irked him that she was now emotionally independent and didn't need him for support. This transformation was strange and unacceptable to him.

Maya had a hard time trying to meet her family obligations without compromising her spiritual journey. She would wait for her husband to leave the house before doing her sadhana. Sometimes Maya felt her husband was even jealous of her relationship with Guruji. He was annoyed that she adored and respected another man over him, even though he knew this was a spiritual Guru. Maya recognized this and slowly changed her ways.

It took about six months to resolve but Maya initiated all the changes in their life. She had to: she was financially dependent on him and additionally, Guruji had asked her to try and resolve their differences. She stopped talking about AOL and hid this aspect of herself from the world.

Sometimes you have to grin and bear it to maintain the relationships that are important to you and your children.

The awareness to surrender to your situation and take the right decision comes from the space of freedom. When you are not bound by your misery and see that you are the happiness you seek, then you take the right decision. And if it turns out that this path was not the one you should have chosen, you can always elect to walk down another. Either way, your happiness is yours and not dependent on any relationship, choice of a life partner or economic sufficiency. That is just the icing on the cake.

Being Single

All of the above testimonials demonstrate that happiness does not necessarily come from a relationship. While a good relationship with a partner enhances the quality of your life, a bad partner or one whose ideals and values don't coincide with yours, can make life a misery. So is the answer to all this to be single? Can a single person find happiness and not be lonely and searching all the time for an ideal partner?

From the time Lekha was of marriageable age, her parents were looking for a suitable alliance. But each one fizzled out. Either it was his job, his values or his age. Lekha Chari, who holds a very good position in a financial institution in Chennai, wanted to please her parents and find a suitable husband and this became even more difficult as each year passed. The prospective grooms were getting more inappropriate and much older. Slowly the family came to a level of acceptance. They loved their daughter too much to allow her to get into a wrong marriage. There came a point in her life when she took a strong decision to remain single and her parents understood and stopped bothering her. Lekha has a very practical view of her life. She chooses her life as it is without wanting to be somewhere else. All the knowledge and sadhana keep her mental balance and she doesn't hanker after what is not an option.

'It's nice to be married but it's not something I dwell on. I just carry on with my life. If at some time marriage comes around, I'll embrace it, if not, I'm fine with my life as it is.'

Camille Abgrall is single and happy. He is of French origin and lives in Paris. Although he has had relationships in the past, now that he is on the path, he doesn't seek them out. His priority has shifted from relationships.

'I am much more flexible and can take decisions based on the need of the moment and so am available for people and society right here, right now. If I suddenly have to travel around the world even for a year, for Art of Living, I can just do it. I share my love with more than just a single person. My life has become about love of teaching the Art of Living courses and meeting with SriSri Ravi Shankar.'

Familial ties

A happy home with caring parents is ideal but when we look around, we see many instances where the family unit is breaking up and children do not receive the support they deserve from parents. With both parents working, children are put into day care, sometimes even in infancy. When they return from work, parents are exhausted and unable to provide the kind of care they would like to; so they end up punishing the child or being overindulgent. No one has the perfect formula but if you function from a place of love and care and tell the child continually that you are there and will support and love him no matter what, it provides the child a comfortable refuge. You may not agree with every decision he makes but when you correct with love, the result is amazing.

As an elementary school teacher I was instructed not to hug the children, but what was I supposed to do when the first thing on walking into the classroom, was that the children ran up and hugged me? They were hungry for a loving embrace a sense of belonging. Many came from broken homes, single parent homes and even those that had both parents, saw a lot of dysfunction in their environment. For a child, the family is the springboard into adulthood. While we teach them to eat properly, dress properly and do their homework we should also arm them with coping skills; teaching basic human values of caring and sharing, team work and responsibility. Most often children who have harsh childhoods become strict fathers.

Umberto Sartori grew up in a household where his father was very strict and Umberto was afraid of him. It wasn't a very comfortable environment, fraught with fear of reprisal. His basic comforts were taken care of but he had to deal with a very emotionally difficult life. The decisions he made while dealing with these emotions were not very wise, given that he was not comfortable expressing his emotions outwardly. The pain he felt was certainly not physical. Suffering comes in different forms and Umberto's was emotional.

'I would deal with it with anger, heavy drinking and smoking just to release the stress. Nowadays I still enjoy a drink but afterwards I don't think that it does anything special.'

He admits he was a strict parent with consequences for disobedience. This transmitted not only to his children but also to his wife. It was always his way or the highway. But his wife was not ready to be trampled upon, and so, she would fight about everything. It all became about who was in control. Umberto needed to do a lot of soul searching before he let his wife go her separate way. He was terrified to lose the connection but used the knowledge to stay centered, although he was devastated to lose both his wife and daughter at the same time.

'The fear was if I didn't act in a certain way I would lose the connection. It took a lot of deliberation to reach this place. The karma here is the desire to keep the connection with near and dear ones, be it father, daughter or wife.'

After two marriages and two divorces he is a veteran at relationships. After a lot of reflection has been able to let things go.

'They are in my heart. I have recognized that my problems are in me. I don't have my family physically around but I do have the love and awareness that they could not walk away with. When I miss someone, what I am experiencing is my love and awareness for them. It has allowed me to say "I love you" no matter what. Even if we are not together I still love you. And this has become my life; this is a gift I have received from the knowledge: the gift of love.'

Dushyant Savadia, a travelling AOL teacher puts it succinctly. *'Your happiness does not lie in a relationship; it is a spiritual decision. Whether you are married, unmarried, divorced or remarried, that shouldn't determine the quality of your life. Make the relationship with yourself beautiful; be happy from within first; and then you can make any relationship beautiful. Regardless of your marital state, be happy. Life has its own path, circumstances and experiences come and go. What is important is your centeredness through all these events, a smile which never fades and confidence that never breaks; then nothing bothers you. Art of Living gives you this power.'*

Dr. Neelam Raval says that in India, basic family values exist but today, both parents work and nuclear families are common. The stress between parents gets reflected on the children. Where earlier, grandparents provided the emotional support in the home for growing kids, today we see many elderly couples living alone. *'Children don't get the support and love of grandparents. Most families today want one progeny and work to give that child the best. Both parents working and lots of money coming in without inculcation of proper moral values, especially according to Indian Vedic Culture are not conducive to healthy child psychology.'*

The underlying foundation according to Dr. Raval has cracked. This is the reason that divorce is on the increase and young married couples have no one to turn to for the support they need. Economic stress in an increasingly competitive world has taken root in frayed relationships and this has affected people across the board, from youngsters to the elderly.

Relationships involve skill. There are those relationships we choose and others that are foisted on us by fate. No matter why we are involved with people, a relationship is one that places demands on your time and involves giving a lot of yourself. As I was writing this, I read a joke on Facebook that lightened the mood and somehow placed everything in perspective.

An Indian and an American were having drinks at a bar. The Indian explaining arranged marriages said, "My parents want me to marry some homely girl from back home and I have absolutely refused and now I have a heck of lot of family problems." The American explaining love marriages looked at him quizzically. "Let me tell you my story. I married a widow whom I deeply loved and dated for three years. After a couple of years my father, fell in love with my step-daughter, and married her, so my father became my son-in-law and I became my father's father-in-law.

Legally, now my daughter is my mother and my wife, my grandmother. More problems occurred when I had a son. My son is my father's brother and so he is my uncle. The situation turned worse when my father had a son. Now my father's son, my brother, is my grandson. Ultimately, I have become my own grandfather and I am my own grandson and you say you have family problems?"

We are born alone and die alone. In the interim we play on the stage of life where we need to interact with others. The trick is in finding the right rhythm between the silence and company. While walking this fine line, just stop every now and then and accept that you alone are the reality and everything else is transient. What reality is in the present is what you feel right now, so why not make that choice to be happy?

If I leave you with one thought in this section it would be to use knowledge, breath and meditation to realize that you are the source of the love you seek. You are a fountain of bliss. Don't look for the happiness outside of yourself. Love is a feeling that exists deep within you and it is possible to dissociate from the pain of broken relationships and lead a contented, happy life. In the present moment all that matters is that nothing has the power to rob you of happiness and love.

11

#5 Environmental Issues

Events come and go. They perish like flowers. But every event and every person contains some honey. Like a bee, just take the honey out of every event and every moment, and move on. Be like a busy bee and be in the Being.

—H.H. SriSri Ravi Shankar

The environment plays a key role in keeping the body healthy and the mind alert. Issues like pollution, gas leaks, nuclear mishaps, deforestation and global warming are a result of man's economic quest with disregard for long-term consequences. Man and nature are closely connected and the happiness index is deeply affected when nature exhibits its full force and fury. The memory of widespread destruction of habitat and property though temporary, can have traumatizing and lasting effects on the state of mind.

Hurricane Katrina was the storm of the decade in the United States. We watched the news in dread as it developed into a Category 5 hurricane, knowing the desolation was going to be catastrophic. I still recall in horror as we observed the hurricane almost engulfing the Gulf of Mexico, barreling down until it made landfall in Louisiana and Mississippi.

Allen and Becky Freedman live in New Orleans. This was where they married and had children and grandkids.

'We love our city...the grand oak trees in Audubon Park...the sound of the streetcars going down St. Charles Avenue...red beans and rice with French bread...Mardi Gras...Jazz Fest...and the friendliest people in the world.'

On August 29, 2005, Hurricane Katrina flooded the city under eight feet of sea water for several weeks. Over 140,000 homes, the streetcars, and thousands of trees were destroyed. Over 500,000 citizens evacuated; some never to return. Like many others, they lost almost everything: their house and all of their material possessions.

Allen's business was ruined, the building so badly damaged that it was virtually inaccessible. Finances were foremost in his mind and he was preoccupied with thoughts of making payments and recovering. As a result, he couldn't concentrate on work. The aftermath of the hurricane sank both Allen and Becky into depression for which they sought professional help.

'Using food as a way to cope with stress, we put on weight. In fact, just about everyone in New Orleans gained weight. It was commonly referred to as "Katrina pounds".'

Unable to sleep or work, the effort of trying to get back on their feet was overwhelming. In the interim Allen was forced to sell his business. The stress was crushing and the smiles were wiped off their faces.

One Saturday morning in March 2007, while driving through Tulane University, he saw a banner announcing SriSri Ravi Shankar was coming to New Orleans the following month to talk about inner peace, breathing techniques and meditation. He had never heard of SriSri before, but thought he would attend.

The talk was about the power of the breath and the relationship between thoughts, emotions and breath. After teaching a breathing technique called alternate nostril breathing, SriSri explained that a little attention to the breath calms the mind and brings it to the present moment. He described the usual activity of the mind going from the past, with thoughts of resentment or regret, to the future, with thoughts of worry, and said this vacillation causes stress. *'Wow,'* Allen mused. *'This is exactly my experience.'*

Both Allen and Becky had tried meditation before briefly. *'We didn't know that meditation is more than sitting with the eyes closed.'* SriSri then led a guided meditation for twenty minutes which to them seemed like only five. They were relaxed and actually smiling. Both of them knew what they had to do next. In the midst of tax season Allen took time off from work to attend the course.

After the first Sudarshan Kriya, he felt lighter and more energetic like he had dumped years of emotional baggage he had been carrying around. The change was visible to their friends and when they inquired what happened, he replied, 'The *Art of Living.'* They doctor noticed the change also and weaned him off all medications.

'Becky and I still live in New Orleans. Much of the city has been restored. Houses have been repaired or rebuilt, the streetcars are rolling again and thousands of new trees have been planted. Mardi Gras and Jazz Fest are better than ever. Plus, we've lost our Katrina pounds. But all of this would not have mattered if we had not learned how to release the trauma we were carrying with us and manage the stressful situations we still encounter in our regular, everyday life.

I feel as though I was given a gift. It is the gift of a healthy mind and body. It is the gift of happiness. It is the gift of relaxation. It is the gift of belongingness. I wanted my family and friends to experience this gift as well, so I became an Art of Living teacher this summer. I will teach my first course next month. What a journey! From being "stressed-out" to helping others out of stress, I can now see a blessing

in Hurricane Katrina. It brought me to the Art of Living. Now I am
smiling and laughing and loving life again!'

Allen was fortunate to have received the help he so needed at
the right time. The opportune assistance inspired him to become
a teacher and spread the happiness. Unlike others he was able
to look back and see the natural disaster and its effect on him
as a blessing instead of a problem. Art of Living has dedicated
teachers who are the first to arrive at the scene of disaster and
offer help in terms of clothing and other necessities but more
importantly, offer a gift of healing and recovery.

Haiti: An environmental crisis

The problems in Haiti are very complex. 98 per cent of Haiti
is deforested, leading to massive soil erosion and flooding. The
population is dependent on wood-based charcoal for energy.
Lack of clean water and sanitation systems contribute to very
high public health risks, including the cholera outbreak of 2010.
While Haiti is an agricultural economy with ample sunlight
and rain, its rapidly growing urban populations have lost their
connection with the earth and their ability to grow their own
food. With staggering unemployment rates, families are left with
few means to avoid starvation.

Many Haitians are disconnected from how their actions
impact the environment, and are unaware of the alternatives
available. There is a general sense of hopelessness and an urgency
to survive.

Uma Berlin first visited Haiti in 2008, to observe the Youth
Leadership Training Program, (YLTP) a program of Art of
Living's partner organization, the International Association for
Human Values (IAHV). Having graduated from Harvard and
leaving a PhD program in Clinical Psychology, Uma had been
teaching Art of Living and IAHV programs to youth and adults
for several years. She feels a sense of fulfillment and meaning

in bringing peace of mind not just to everyday American communities, but also to communities in need; college students traumatized by school shootings, Bronx gang members, and prisoners.

Uma went to Haiti looking for her next challenge, to test her ability to live the knowledge in experiences well beyond her comfort zone, to draw out new skills and dimensions to her personality. The YLTP was being offered to 154 Haitian youth by Bill Herman, a seasoned Art of Living teacher who brought the YLTP out of India to the Western Hemisphere. Uma felt something click within her, just by being in Haiti. Haiti is full of life, intense and mystical, contradictory and difficult. She found the Haitian students blamed the world, the government, and each other for their lot in life, yet were fierce and proud to be Haitian. They were promiscuous and irreverent, yet were deeply spiritual and prayed fervently. They were waiting for someone to solve their problems for them, yet were too jaded to believe that would ever happen. They were survivors lost in the odds that were stacked against them.

Without access to educational or professional opportunities, Haiti's youth will soon be handed over responsibility to lead the country. Uma was struck by how critical Guruji's knowledge was to mobilize these youth into dynamic action and responsibility. Meditation and Sudarshan Kriya heal their minds from trauma. Knowledge rebuilds their frame of mind, allowing Haitians to move beyond survival and dependence on foreign intervention towards sustainably rebuilding their country.

Over four years, Uma developed IAHV's Nouvelle Vie Haiti program, which has now impacted about 10,000 Haitians, its approach and leaders receiving praise and funding from the World Bank, UNICEF, USAID, and the UN-FAO. With 350 Haitian youth having undergone the YLTP, about 100 implemented service initiatives in their communities, addressing issues around trauma, the environment, food security, vulnerable children, and sexuality. Nineteen of Nouvelle Vie's strongest leaders have now been trained as trainers, and leadership of Nouvelle Vie has now been transferred over entirely into their hands.

Uma has found that the knowledge and practices Guruji has brought, not only transformed her students into leaders of change, but have allowed her to persevere through the physical, psychological, and emotional challenges of working in a country as devastated as Haiti. Uma found many humanitarian aid workers face burn out, becoming bitter and cynical. Without tools to release the intense frustration, sorrow, guilt, anger, and disgust that can arise through their service, many would abuse drugs, alcohol, and sex to cope.

'This knowledge has literally saved my mind. Just when it seems like too much to bear, too much to witness, I can tap into that part of myself that is beyond the world I see around me. On the level of experience, I know that underneath all the misery, there is love that is untouched, pure, and perfect.'

Misery resulting from environmental issues may be permanent, as in the case of nuclear disasters or temporary as in the cases cited above. Whether you are a victim or an aid worker, the pain you feel can get embedded in your psyche and have long term consequences. No matter what you have endured, no matter what your circumstance, it is important to know that there is always a solution in sight. Guruji always says that the Divine never presents a problem without offering a solution. It does not help to wallow in self-pity and bemoan your circumstances because, most often, help is just around the corner. The process is long-term but it requires effort on your part to want a solution, recognize the helping hand and respond to assistance. Healing is a gentle process which requires time but you can feel in a single moment that through this healing process you are centered and filled with hope and enthusiasm, understanding that tomorrow is another day.

The happiness decision is a spiritual one, which brings you into the present moment, free from the burden of the past and the worries of the future. If in that moment there is intense anger, pain or disappointment then feel that emotion fully. Immerse yourself in it completely without any denial. This will allow the emotion to move through you and when it passes, once again bring yourself into the moment and feel that sense of calm and peace and bask in your true nature. That is how you navigate challenges, by recognizing that emotions always change and whatever you are going through will also pass.

Our lives are inextricably connected to the world around us. Situations arise which are out of our immediate control and throw us off balance. While affected by the wrath of nature, it is important to recognize that this loss of happiness is temporary and will pass. A good way of mitigating your personal misery is to reach out to others in their time of need. This moves you out of the space of *'Why me?'* into *'What can I do for you?'* Seva is the best salve to heal the wounds of trauma. Just by lending a helping hand it is possible in the midst of chaos and misery to slip into the present moment and enjoy the grace and gratitude that comes from helping someone in distress. As for your own misery, have faith that someone is out there who cares very deeply for you. As you grow on the spiritual path you will come to realize that pain is inevitable but misery is optional. Having faith that someone cares for you, empowers you to transform your mindset from being a victim or culprit, to courageously taking responsibility for your feelings and emotions, stopping the blame and feelings of helplessness.

12

#6 Political Climate

We need to spiritualize politics, socialize business and secularize religion. Devoid of spirituality, politics breeds corruption.
— H.H SriSri Ravi Shankar

Living in a democratic country like the United States, we go about our daily lives without feeling there are any serious problems imposed on us by the State. We are fortunate to be able to voice our opinions and affect change that maintains our life, liberty and pursuit of happiness. This is a constitutional right and there are channels to enforce and maintain our freedom. While many living here in the United States find fault with aspects of the Government, they have no idea how fortunate they are to live in freedom. This is regrettably not true of many who by a quirk of destiny are born and live in certain developing countries with tyrannical regimes, especially in Asia and Africa.

Imagine being forced to control your thoughts, speech and dress and being denied access to basic amenities because of autocratic government dictates. Living in a free country, I cannot even envision a life like that, one that stifles your individuality and at times dehumanizes you. I spoke to two ladies from the Middle East who were so terrified to even speak of their pain and certainly did not want their names disclosed for fear of reprisal. When I assured them that they were safe and as US citizens they had no cause for worry, they laughed in disbelief. Ultimately their fears won and they recanted their stories leaving me aghast that they did not feel safe or free living thousands of miles away from their homeland in a country where they reside as free citizens.

Togo is a small country in West Africa with a population of approximately 6.7 million. From the 16th to the 18th century, Europeans in search of slaves converted the area into a major hunting ground and the surrounding area was popularly called 'The Slave Coast.' The country gained independence from France in 1960 and soon after, there was a dictatorship for almost forty years. For the 40 different ethnic groups, the hardship has been continuous, beginning with the loss of family during the slave trade, to poverty and unemployment in modern times, a corrupt, leaching and uncaring government and poor access to healthcare and basic education. There were only four or five physicians per 100,000 people in the early 2000s and approximately one half of the population lived below the international poverty line earning less than US$1.25 a day.

Nirmal Matella was chosen by SriSri to go and start the Art of Living program in Togo. When he reached West Africa, he was dumbfounded at the hopelessness and inertia he saw in people.

'People are very poor and have lost hope in everything; in people and in life. After so much suffering, they have lost the will to live. It's been forty years since independence but there is a spiritual vacuum.'

Nirmal joined the Art of Living only in 2005 but was so taken up with the change it affected in him, he became a travelling teacher and the desire to transform people's lives became foremost in his list of priorities.

His job in Togo defies description and his first target group was the youth, who had lost confidence in the system, had no spiritual guidance and no hope of envisioning a future, let alone a bright future.

'*We have a bigger responsibility while bringing the change; to break the misconceptions and then bring the change.*'

His first group, after undergoing a six-day workshop, saw a tremendous shift in their energy level and confidence. Seeing the effectiveness of the course he has enlisted local help to promote the cause. The vision is altruistic yet Nirmal is the lone soldier battling, but he is armed with the confidence the Master has in him and he carries this energy in spite of seeing pain and suffering around him. His personal sadhana is what grounds him and he is very disciplined about it. I asked what motivated him and he related this story.

'*Initially it was a little tough for me. However, the "BATA" story has inspired me a lot. The managing director of a shoe company sends two employees to Africa to set up their shoe business. After a week the first employee calls the boss and says, "Boss, what's this? It's a total waste of time, effort, money and manpower. No one in Africa wear shoes, I am coming back, so please be ready with my next assignment." And he disconnects.*

The second one calls and says, "Boss, it's amazing, it's wonderful. You know, no one wears shoes in Africa, and it's a huge market for shoes. Please send some more people; I will need more time here".'

Cocooned in our little world of air-conditioned homes, reality TV, shopping malls and free air, we are completely oblivious to the pain and suffering of others like ourselves half-way across the globe. We don't hear about it often and when we do, we spend all of thirty seconds lamenting their lot before moving onto our next task. Our sense of belonging doesn't extend beyond the living room and we really don't care too much about what takes place outside our shores.

Some pearls like Nirmal emerge in a sea of disconnect, who devote their lives to transforming that of the underprivileged and alleviate suffering, one individual at a time. Very few are given the opportunity and even fewer rise up to the challenge. It is his karma and the will of the Guru that has brought him here. His job is not easy but he takes courage in the confidence his Master has in him and he lives totally in the present moment comforted in the knowledge that his seva brings meaning and purpose in his life.

13

Die to the Past

You die for the past, but when you let the past die, then you are living for the present. The Art of Living and Art of Dying are two sides of the same coin. You should die for everything that has happened in the past. Live in the Present! If you live in the present you have to discard the past. If you know the Art of Dying, every second of life blossoms in its highest state.

—H.H. SriSri Ravishankar

Every moment is an opportunity to let go of the past. Have physical, not psychological memories of past events. Samir Desai lives in San Francisco and his last few years on the path has been devoted to using this insight to improve his awareness and sink into the present moment.

'Before AOL I was regretful of the past and that has disappeared. There was a volleyball game between two rival classes in our high school. Our team was up 2-0 and our main player was sick, so we took a break to let him rest. Then we lost the next three sets and the championship. For years after that I could relive the pain of defeat and the emotions I felt, and this would especially get ignited if I met someone from school. Today I see them reliving each moment but for me there are just physical memories with no emotional baggage.'

Once you bury the past and slip into the present moment your true purpose becomes crystal clear and you move through life with the skill of a sailor navigating a storm, maintaining your composure and centeredness and surging ahead, taking comfort in the knowledge that right action in the present moment will lead to clear skies ahead. For many the answer lies in seva. Samir Desai truly believes in the power of service undertaken with no expectation.

'The biggest impact of AOL is moving out of myself and doing Seva, because I know it's what he would want me to do. He is my guide. Reading his knowledge, basing my next step on what he has indicated gives me strength, because the spiritual path is tough.'

Destiny vs. Free will

Guruji has said that it is better to look at the past as your destiny and the future as free will and enjoy the present moment. The nature of the mind is to hold onto negative events that have taken place and brood about it. *'I should have said this or could have done that.'* The reality is that what happened is over and now is the time to move on. Guruji refers to past memories as *'double exposure films'*. Those of us who belong to the generation of actual film and hard copy prints understand the frustration when an entire reel has been exposed twice. Images get superimposed on others and the end result is a mishmash in which the story is lost.

Most often it's only minor things that nag the brain. No one has sleepless nights over global warming and the poverty line. Camille Abgrall from Paris, France is firm about his views on this. *'Bury the past and move on. Things stick to the memory and the mind and need to be released. Most often it's the small stuff which needs to be dropped and this is done through practice: it's a continuous process. Now I can move through the small mind and not live with my memories.'*

Camille and Dushyant have this awareness after being on the path for several years. Knowing that you are in the past requires awareness and practice. Over time, it becomes a habit to momentarily let it flash through your mind before you let go and return to the present moment. As Dushyant says:

'I have no regrets. I have made mistakes but don't have time to brood about what I did. I have 30-40 years to contribute to the world. I have to make a conscious choice. Shall I spend the rest of my life regretting my past and grumble and complain, be angry and brood? Or shall I take responsibility for my present? As Guruji says, "Walk with confidence in this life and know that everything will be taken care of by the one who created you and brought you here".'

Dushyant is far too busy to ponder about the past. He has had a colorful past and you will hear his story, but that happened a long time ago. Now, as a traveling AOL teacher, his time is at a premium and that helps him to simply move forward.

Life is a Happening

My dear friend Pawan Mulukutla, who lives in Bengaluru, India, is the one I call when I have no answers. His advice is almost as if Guruji were talking to me. He is so steeped in the knowledge that every word is heartfelt and experiential. Pawan has an uncanny knack of putting things succinctly. He fully understands the futility of regretting the past and knows that one who is not on a spiritual path is completely unaware of where the mind is.

'Till you come into spirituality and are in touch with yourself, you will feel regret. Once you are on the path there is no room for regret. Life becomes a celebration when you know that everything is just "a happening" and you are here for a while to stay and go. It's like holding onto a flowing river and arguing that this is life. Every moment there are new drops of water. You try to hold onto a part of the flowing river and that is not even feasible. It is your own delusion. Regret is just holding on to some portion of life that has

already happened. Life is so huge and so big and every moment is a possibility.'

Step out of yourself

The reason to constantly regret the past is an overwhelming importance given to oneself. *My problems, my children, my success and my job,* become the most important items on your day's agenda. Once you look beyond your immediate concerns and begin to ponder whom you can help, your own past fades away. As Kiki from Chicago says: *'If I worry too much, that is an indication that I have got caught up in myself; everything is me, me, me, me… When I step out of that then there is no room for regret.'*

Kiki took a moment to recollect her story. She had some medical and marital problems and she had to think before recalling that time in her life. Before taking the Art of Living course she was at a low point. Her marriage was ending because her husband of 13 years was in and out of hospitals, detox units and rehab, the result of a problem caused by prescription medicine overuse after several back surgeries and continual pain. This resulted in extreme financial pressures and great emotional upheaval in their lives. In addition, her body grew something called jumbo intra-muscular lymphomas, fatty tissue in between the muscles that required invasive surgery with no guarantees. It could and did grow back many times. She was due for a second surgery and the doctors and specialists were not offering many choices. There was the fear it might render her disabled for life. She was seeking support everywhere—church groups, support groups, and therapists and felt she was really at the end of her rope.

When she found the Art of Living the shift in her mental state began. Slowly she felt the onset of change in her mind set.

'The first thing I noticed was that I stopped blaming my husband and realized I wanted the best for him. However, I felt dead inside.

I was 40, divorced, had no children and had health problems. The future didn't seem very bright.'

Over time, she was more and more in the present meditative state and something strange happened: she forgot the pain of her past.

'I don't exactly remember the pain. I remember the good parts but don't remember the bad ones, and I don't really try to recall. I recollect waking up one day and realizing the chatter in my mind was gone. I still have health concerns but I don't worry. I feel free. Life isn't perfect; I still have times of anger and sadness but the past is really dead. With continued practice I notice it doesn't grip my mind whatsoever. I live more from my heart.'

At a silence course in the Boone Ashram, Guruji was asked a question by a person who could not forget an incident in her past. He smiled and said, *'In a car, just imagine if the rear view mirror was as big as the windshield and the windshield as small as the rear view mirror. Would you be able to drive at all? You cannot keep looking back. Just a glance in the rear view mirror is enough. Look back for a moment and forget it. Your future lies ahead.'*

The movement from the mind to the heart creates magic in that you are so happy to be in the bliss of the big mind that the nonsensical, futile chatter of the small mind stops. It does keep rearing its ugly head every now and again and that's when the Art of Dying, the dying to the past, becomes crucial. You stop and examine your thoughts and in that moment drag it back into the present. Realize that in this moment the thought of a past reality is a lie. It doesn't exist, perhaps it never did.

The present is the only reality between past and future

Without ever sitting down to reflect on what constitutes happiness, we are buffeted by the senses, moving from shadowy images from the past to blurry mirages in the future. All we have is the present moment and it is only in the 'now' that we can be happy or miserable. This is the only reality and living in the past and future just robs you of the enjoyment of the present.

I am reminded of my daughter's childhood when they were preparing for a play at nursery school called *The Little Red Hen*—a story about a fowl that planned and saved and cooked food tirelessly for the harsh winter, while her friends played and fooled around all summer, only to starve when winter arrived. I can't recall what her role in the play was, but she memorized everyone's lines including the narrator's, and then performed the play for us on demand. She even included the moral of the story— *'Don't waste time today, plan your tomorrow,'* though she may not have realized its implications. Many stories, parables and fables warn about the dangers of whiling away the present only to suffer in the future. While the future is important, Guruji also reminds us constantly about the present. *'The present moment is a gift from God,'* he says. *'That is why it is called the present.'*

Postponing Happiness

Just like in the story of the Little Red Hen, people fall into different behavior patterns based on their philosophy on life and their social perception of happiness. There are those who can only be happy given a condition in the future. A close friend of mine was terribly depressed, unable to find a job after being unemployed for several months. Her earlier job had given her a lot of flexibility and she had leeway to deal with family problems as well as socialize, plus there was the fat paycheck at the end of the month. When she got laid off she was fine initially, enjoying the paid vacation, not really worried. Then suddenly, uncertainty and fear for the future gripped her. She would not go out with us to eat at restaurants and felt guilty shopping for herself. The months wore on and she was still not able to find the right job. I could see how her worries weighed her down. I persistently told her to enjoy these months of freedom where she could spend quality time with her children, cooking special dinners and snacks for them, or just spending lazy afternoons absorbed in the thrills of a murder mystery novel. But she did not hear me. She could not. How could she indulge in such luxuries when she was not contributing to the family income? No. She would only be happy when gainfully employed. Her mind only saw happiness in that future in which she would have a job.

Well, the job came along a few months later and it was an exacting one. She had no time to do all the things she had got accustomed to all those languorous months at home. When she came home, she was too exhausted to do anything. Now that she had the job I expected to see her upbeat and happy. But no. It has been three months and I am still waiting for that brilliant smile to light up her face. Now she is overwhelmed and has no time. She is tired and overworked and still not happy.

Postponing happiness after some event in the future robs you of happiness today and all we have is today. The future has possibilities but if you are not happy today you cannot be happy tomorrow because you are linking your happiness to an event—a job promotion, a new baby, a new car, or a new designer outfit. All of these have the exciting promise of joy and happiness, but that happiness wanes when the job responsibilities keep you at work 50 hours a week, or the baby cries all night, and the car is now five years old and outdated and the outfit has already been seen by everyone at some event and cannot be reused. Then you make a new list of things that will make you happy. A holiday, your son graduating and moving away, retiring…the list just goes on.

There is a pattern here which has to be recognized if you want to be happy. Make that choice to be happy now, and then if the job comes, if you get a new car, or are blessed with a baby, consider it a bonus. It's like frosting on a cake. It makes life sweeter but your cake is already sweet enough. Being satisfied in the present moment gives you the feeling that your cup of happiness is full. You don't have much, but then you don't need much. Conversely, you have everything and need nothing more.

Ronnie Newman, a Harvard University-trained researcher scholar, spoke about this very point when she explained her views on happiness. *'Many people don't know what they are looking for, so they look on the surface because it is painful to look inside. You need to have a skillful teacher to guide you and tell you it's safe to look inside and not many people have that.'*

Honestly, my only regret in life is that I didn't come to this Path sooner. If I had the benefit of these ancient breathing and relaxation techniques in adolescence, my life might have taken a different course. I am filled with gratitude each day for being able to create this shift in consciousness and getting a glimpse of the one indivisible Brahman. It has permitted me to escape from the chatter of the *'small mind'* into the bliss of the *'big mind'*. To understand the difference between the two, imagine you have a camera with a telephoto lens and have zoomed in. Now all you can see is only part of the landscape. You are perhaps focused on a tree, a flower and can clearly discern a bee buzzing around a bloom. That encapsulates the character of the small mind. When you are caught up in the dynamics of the small mind, you obsess with small, nagging details, which at the time seem overwhelmingly important. Whether it's an event from your past or a desire for the future the mind gets so consumed with the cycle of thoughts it does not permit you function normally. You now believe that your happiness lies only when that problem is fixed.

Now let's return to the analogy of the camera and imagine you zoom out and capture the entire panorama of the surrounding landscape. You see the vast expanse of sky, the lush greenery around, including several trees and shrubs. However, you cannot see the bee buzzing around the flower. It has not disappeared. It still hovers around the bush but you don't notice it as you are now focused on the expanded vision captured on your lens. That is the beauty of the big mind. It allows you to expand your vision so that the small stuff moves out of focus and just falls by the wayside. The problems from the past and desires for the future still exist but you cease to give importance to them. Instead you focus on the bigger picture and enjoy the present moment.

Each day opens up new possibilities and every failure is a stepping stone to innovation. Life has become interesting and while I recognize that I am new to the Path and have a lot to learn, a lot to fix, a lot to change, I am grateful that at least it happened now. I have a fulfilling journey to travel further down the Path; one that is blessed by the Guru and the Divine. As for the events in my past... well... that was my Karma.

14

Understanding Karma…Somewhat

*Karma is the strongest impression in the mind, the action it propels
and the resultant impression it provides for the future.*
                                                    —H.H. SriSri Ravishankar

When I grew up in India the word Karma was used loosely.
Every time something untoward occurred, a death or an illness,
it was assigned to Karma. I came to believe that Karma, your
destiny, was unshakable and no matter what you did, your future
would unfold in the manner fated. Your control was minimal. You
didn't choose the body at birth, and you had no inkling about the
time and manner of your death. Both were preordained and we
were mere actors playing out Krishna's *Leela:* his cosmic game.

Karma in my mind was also inextricably connected with
reincarnation. In this assumption I was partially correct. Your
actions in previous births gave you the esteemed opportunity
of being born a human in the present life, and if you continued
to evolve over successive lifetimes, you would reach the feet
of *Narayana* and never be born again. At least that's what my
grandma said. Every time I did something bad, she threatened me
with certain doom, saying I would be born again as a cockroach,
or some other lowly creature in my next life. Karma seemed to
be unconnected with the present, it was rooted in past lives and

determined your future lives. In the present, Karma reared its ugly head only to mete out punishment, illness, poverty and misery.

As I was growing up, I always told my grandma Karma was a convenient copout for lazy people. It was easy to blame Karma for everything that went wrong, especially when waking up and changing things involved effort, intention and action. I understood death was sometimes out of one's control, but what about poverty? Streets of every big city crawled with beggars who I believed were lazy and didn't want to find legitimate work. Begging on the streets allowed them to make money in the easiest conceivable way with the least possible effort. The sheer number of homeless in the streets made me insensitive to their plight and I refused to believe the Karma excuse. And as far as illness was concerned, modern medicine had answers for so many maladies. Diabetes and epilepsy were no longer illnesses to be feared. Sickness was preventable, it wasn't your Karma. If you were diagnosed early enough, that Karma was alterable. In India to this date, some people, especially those that live in rural areas, do not go to doctors because of their belief that their illness is punishment for bad sins by a cruel and vengeful God. As a result they are stuck in inertia, accepting inevitable death as their merited path. In my mind, this life presented the only opportunity, at least the only one that I was aware of, and it seemed a waste of precious time to worry about future lives. Karma seemed to be an impediment to exercising free will, an easy excuse for doing nothing.

In my early twenties I picked up the Bhagavat-Gita[1] in an attempt to read and understand what the great Masters said about life and living. Not knowing Sanskrit well, I did not even begin to understand the depth and magnitude of the scriptures. I read the verses anyway and even though I didn't understand

---

1   The Bhagavat-Gita is a dialogue between Arjuna and Krishna in which the philosophy of the Vedanta is revealed to the devotee by the Lord. It is part of the great Indian epic "The Mahabharata."

much, some stanzas stayed in my mind, '*Karmanye Vadhika Rasthe Maa Phaleshu Kadaachana...*' Krishna advising humanity, Arjuna in particular, to perform action without expectation and attachment to reward. The concept didn't appeal to me at the time because I didn't believe I performed random, selfless acts. I respected my elders and I cared for my family because it made me happy. When you gave, you received. The whole scientific world was rooted in cause and effect and I didn't understand its intrinsic connection to Karma.

Through most of my youth misconceptions about Karma prevailed in my mind. It was only after marriage and my encounters with emotional turmoil, with marital problems and dealing with a challenging mother-in-law that I turned to spiritualism. I attended lectures and read anything I could lay my hands on. It was a good beginning but reading the scriptures is far removed from the actual experience of spirituality which began after I joined the Art of Living. It was then that I got a glimpse of the intricacies of Karma. In my mind, instead of focusing on bad Karma and its impact on my life, I decided to explore ways of increasing my benefits and accumulating good Karma. My thought patterns and consequent actions began to change. Over the next few years my whole attitude to life metamorphosed. Once I understood that through spiritual practices like meditation, pranayama and yogasanas it was possible to defuse the effects of my previous karmic history, my focus changed.

My mind was filled with questions. '*Why do I meditate? What am I seeing when I meditate? What is this nothingness? Why am I in this world? Do I have any purpose for existing? How do I discover the purpose of this birth? Is this world everything? Does reality stretch beyond this mundane existence?*' These thoughts swirled in my brain and I looked everywhere for answers. I read voraciously, trying to make sense of my mental turmoil. From my quest three books stood out. These books not only explained existence but led me into the esoteric world of reincarnation, rebirth, the Universe and the Brahman. The first book was *Many Lives Many Masters* by Brian Weiss. The second was *Yoga Vasishta*, a masterpiece of commentary by Swami Venkatesananda, and finally *The Mystery of Reincarnation*, by J. Allen Danelek. All three books opened my mind up to a world of possibilities, replacing the skeptic in me with a believer.

Before we examine the dynamics of Karma it is necessary to look at reincarnation and rebirth.

Reincarnation and Rebirth

Although I get nervous at the thought of ghosts, I have always been intrigued by the concept of reincarnation. The idea of bad spirits looming around always terrified me, until my mother taught me a chant which reassured me with the thought that if God was with you, no spirits could ever approach. Still, even until recently, I never believed in psychics and séances and thought of them as fraudulent, cheating people into believing they communicated with spirits. Recently however, the idea and concept of spirit has taken on new meaning.

Spirit and Space

The practice of meditation created that shift where I began to view myself as the Self and not just the body. With a switch in perspective, the image of the self became spirit and space and surprisingly in that space there was only the Divine. There was no room for fear. Having experienced an unbounded state of consciousness that is not wakefulness, not sleep and not a dream state, I believe I may have had a glimpse of what the Brahman could possibly be.[2] For the first time, the certainty

---

2   The Brahman is the first cause and last refuge. SriSri says the truth is contradictory. While the journey is to know the Brahman, yet its essence is unknowable.

of a state beyond living became more believable. Having experienced the futility of desires and material possessions, I knew that this world was not about to give me the answers I was looking for. There had to be something more than this mirage of existence. My mind wanted proof and as I read more on reincarnation and watched videos of those who had crossed over with near death experiences, I understood that reality exists between lifetimes.

Rebirth

Reality exists in that resting period between lives for the soul before entering another body for rebirth. This is done in order to learn something new or repeat past lessons that allow for further progress, the end desire being *Samadhi*, or union with the absolute. This process of returning to the world in a human body is called rebirth and this is our journey; yours and mine. We are reborn in certain circumstances based on what we need to accomplish to fulfill our destiny. The fallacy that you don't choose your parents is therefore negated completely because the circumstances from previous impressions will make it so. You will choose which family you need to be born into for your purpose to be served. In fact, Guruji says that, often, two people come together against all odds and once the child is born, they sometimes go their separate ways. In past life recollections it has been noted that what you despised in one lifetime determines your next birth. Furthermore, people around you tend to coexist with you through different lifetimes. These need not necessarily be your blood family but are more likely your spiritual family. Often the soul closest to you is the one who teaches you the toughest life lessons. He or she could be the overpowering boss, the punishing teacher, the controlling husband or the domineering mother-in-law. One could argue that such recollections are a figment of the imagination. However, it does happen that people are guided by ideas that appear in dreams and it is possible to recollect a previous life.

According to the scriptures in the Hindu tradition, such impressions and memories are buried in the deepest recesses of our consciousness and the ones that readily come to the surface during regression and deep meditation are the traumatic events. Often these impressions are so strong that they leave a deep imprint in the present life, in the form of physical scars, phobias, fears and anxieties. Sometimes glimpses of past life connections come up in food, clothing and career preferences. This is probably the reason, for example, you love Mexican food, listen to flamenco music and watch crime thrillers.

The Eternity Process

The Art of Living has teachers who conduct a process called the Eternity Process that is open to those who have attended several Art of Silence programs. Very often, after undergoing this process, strong patterns, habits and addictions can be released. Fears and anxieties lessen and there is experiential knowledge that the self is, has been and will continue to be.

After undergoing the process three times Madhu Bhardwaj from Mumbai explains its importance: '*The eternity process connects you to the people close to you. It helps to remove deep impressions from lifetimes where issues were not resolved. You surrender your past.*'

Marita Andreassen,the National coordinator for AOL Norway, is an Eternity Process teacher who believes the process helps people leave old patterns. People come with so much tension which translates into physical symptoms, with pain in the body and they don't know how to release it. They don't know what it is and why it's there. Through the process, the teacher helps you to go back in time and discover patterns embedded in the subconscious and then release it. People also come with unnatural fears and trauma, most fear the future and sometimes suffer from repressed trauma from childhood or previous lives.

This often doesn't come to the surface during Sudarshan Kriya which only reaches the conscious mind. They need the personal guidance of the teacher to facilitate deep relaxation that accesses the unconscious and the super-conscious mind where these problems originate and this helps them face and eradicate their problems.

When they realize that their fears are based on events which occurred in their past, either in this life or a previous birth, they are more able to face their terrors as threats which do not exist in the present moment. They can therefore release their fears. As Marita shares:

'One person had nightmares for a long time. During the process he experienced being drowned and suffocated, and as part of the process he was able to release old impressions. After the process, the nightmares were gone.'

The beauty of this process is that it provides access and release to deep-seated impressions resulting in relaxation at a profound level, which releases tension in the body.

Dushyant Savadia, a traveling AOL teacher, was instantly recognized by Guruji, and, in that first meeting, he knew he was born to do the master's work. From that time on, Dushyant has been deeply connected to the Guru and when he regressed during the Eternity Process, he was surprised to see that in each lifetime he was with Guruji. For Dushyant, his past unfolded like a 3D movie and the release and sense of fulfillment afterwards left him in bliss.

Although I was a nonbeliever in reincarnation and past lives, during the course of my interviews I heard so many convincing stories that have made me ponder. I can't wait to take the process. I know it will answer many of my queries and perhaps change some habits and patterns I long to break.

Reincarnation

There are those who have lived millions of lifetimes, learned and evolved to such an extent that rebirth is not necessary. Such evolved souls who are one with the Brahman are called *Siddhas* or Masters. Every now and again, such Masters choose to bless us by descending to the level of humanity and share the benefit of their knowledge and grace. These rebirths are referred to as reincarnation, where the Master descends as an *avatar*— incarnation of the absolute. Through history we have seen many Masters, from Buddha to Muhammad, Jesus and Sai Baba and their legacy lives on. To have a living Master is a privilege that few people in history have experienced. SriSri Ravishankar is an example of a Living Master—an avatar who has chosen to descend and guide us in our spiritual journey, allowing us to progress towards achieving the ultimate goal, which is to discover the source of love which exists within us.

Anand Kumar from Bloomington Indiana, believes in Karma, especially when it comes to finding a Guru: '*Your Karma dictates whether your reach the feet of a Guru; whether you think you choose him or he picks you is immaterial.*' If it is in your fate to tire of the material world, then you will seek out a Master, a Guru, to be your guiding light. Until such time no matter what you read, what you endure and what you hear, the need to descend from head to heart will not happen, perhaps for several lifetimes.

Karma is often misrepresented as rebirth, or the law governing rebirth. While it is based on the premise of rebirth, Karma encompasses much more, offering valid explanations for your life situation, the problems you encounter, the place you live in, your fortune or misfortune.

SriSri explains the dynamics of Karma in a succinct 20-minute talk that somehow encapsulates everything for me. His ability to simplify the complexity of Karma makes the highest knowledge accessible to the lay person. His explanation of Karma is the essence of what you need to know in order to live in this world and reap the benefits of life. This knowledge is a small island in the ocean of what Karma signifies, yet for an ordinary mortal, living on this island is enough for survival, to successfully navigate through life.

15

Stages, Types and Modalities of Karma

Only human life has the ability to free you from Karma. And only a few thousand aim to be free from it. Performing actions alone cannot eliminate Karma. Only through grace can the bondage of Karma be burnt.

—H.H. SriSri Ravishankar

The word 'Karma' means action. There are three stages of Karma. The first stage is latent action, in which the seed for action is planted. It is the thought which germinates in the mind before it crystallizes and finds meaning in action. The second stage of Karma is the action itself, and the third stage is the impression that is left after the act is committed: it adds to future Karma. Karma in other words is a *strong impression* which fuels action. It exists like a bank account accumulating and depleting through lifetimes based on the quality of your actions.

Good actions or good Karma bring positive feelings of happiness and joy, whereas bad actions result in pain and suffering. Good action or good Karma is needed to eliminate bad Karma. It leaves the benefits of good Karma untouched because goodness is your true nature, which you only become aware of when the body is relaxed and at peace. Then only positive Karma is experienced and that is because at your core is joy, beauty and happiness. However, in order to remove the effects of bad Karma, good Karma gets used up and needs to be replenished. Using a bank account analogy, debts need to be paid with your current salary and though your credit rating becomes better, the reality is that your money is spent. Guruji uses the analogy of utilizing soap to wash a dirty body. Once the soap is used, it is gone and you need new soap to cleanse the body the next time. In the same way, good thoughts, good actions and good speech can be used to erase some of your Karmic debt.

Three Types of Karma

Karma itself is of three types. The first is called *Sanchitha Karma* or accumulated Karma. This is your karmic debt through lifetimes which can be reduced or increased depending on your actions. Many aspects of your life are controlled by Sanchitha Karma; where you are born, who your parents are, how long you live, how rich or poor you are, and whom you meet. While some of this karmic debt can be reduced or modified, once it begins to play out in your life, it has already become *Prarabdha Karma*, the second type of Karma, over which you have no control. So what past actions will be Sanchitha, over which you have some control and which will be Prarabdha, over which you have no control?

Guruji says it's like flinging a bunch of seeds, chikoo, mango, papaya or apple seeds into farmland. Each will sprout at a different time. Some take days while others take years. How and when your Karma manifests is not predictable. One morning you could be happy dressing up to go to work, only to discover that the job no longer exists. Recently I witnessed the following situation. We were in New Jersey to attend my niece's engagement. My brother-in-law spoke to his aged father, who lived in India, before taking off from Fort Lauderdale, Florida. When he

landed in New Jersey he received a call from his brother saying
their father had passed away. The family was overwrought. What
were they to do? 200 guests were invited. Should they cancel
an event that symbolized a young couple embarking on a new
journey or should they show due respect to their fathers passing?
The whole family congregated and everyone had different things
to say. Some advised against it, saying bad Karma would follow
the couple. Others said the old man had lived a full life and his
last words were blessings for his granddaughter, so the ceremony
should go on. What was the correct thing to do? Here was a
classic example of Sanchitha Karma and Prarabdha Karma at
play simultaneously. Ultimately the family made the tortuous
decision to go ahead with the engagement. We all knew that the
old man would only have blessings and good intentions towards
his granddaughter and while death was inevitable, life had to go
on. The engagement took place as planned.

The third kind of Karma is *Agama Karma* which is debt
accumulated in the present life and which will manifest as
Sanchitha Karma either in the distant future or in successive
births. This is why it becomes important to be mindful of all
your thoughts, speech and actions, for impressions left by them
will have the necessary effect. That mindfulness only exists in the
present moment, when you are aware of all your emotions and
senses and can wait to respond after weighing the options.

Modalities of Karma

The modalities of Karma are through thoughts, speech and
actions. When someone insults you and you remain silent, they
take on your bad Karma. If instead you yell back, you take on
theirs. While bad karmic action can be seen, experienced and
easily understood, it takes years of repair to nullify its effects on
the ambience and immediate environment. The 30th Anniversary
celebration of the Art of Living took place in Berlin, in July

2011, with the sole purpose of group meditation in the Olympic Stadium, to change the negative energy in the area. 50,000 people from 151 countries congregated and sat in meditation, praying for the healing of souls, for forgiveness and good intention. This scene was the antithesis of the very purpose of the stadium, built by Adolf Hitler in 1936 to further his plans for an Aryan fascist supremacy.

The harmful effects of malevolent thought increase your Karmic debt twice over. In order to reduce your Karma you need pure thoughts, gentle speech and caring actions. Neither your thoughts nor actions or speech should be designed to hurt someone else. The next time you get the last vicious word in a heated argument, think that while you feel like the winner, you are actually the one who has accumulated bad Karma and now you will need to work twice as hard to remove your debt.

All addictions are a result of Karma. Whether it is to coffee, nicotine, alcohol or drugs, addicts feel they have no control whatsoever over their habit. It is deeply entrenched into their psyche, almost as if they were being controlled by an outside force. That outside force is your Karma. But one day the addict wakes up and realizes that the present moment holds the key to changing Karma and he makes a deliberate choice and says, *'Enough. No more. I will not allow this to control me anymore.'* And with every day that he resists temptation, the Karmic hold weakens and eventually falls away.

16

Spiritual Practices and Karma

A master is like an ocean. The Ocean is there, readily available. It does not reject anybody.

—H.H. SriSri Ravishankar

Sudarshan Kriya, meditation and other spiritual practices help to release the burden of Sanchitha Karma. Jakob Lund is an AOL teacher who works in the Prison Smart program (See chapter-38) conducting Art of Living courses with prisoners in Denmark. He helps criminals of all kinds discover their inner tuning and face the repercussions of Karma. The course for the first time allows such people to get in touch with their inner voice which so far was silent, thus giving them the opportunity to move forward without their baggage of guilt and remorse. As he puts it: *'I see Karma as past impressions. There is darkness in some people and if that person allows light to enter, you can make the Karma disappear. When light enters the room there is a lot of change. But this takes time and the person needs to be ready to prepare themselves and that's what AOL does.'*

Ask anyone who practices pranayama and meditation regularly and they will tell you that life is beautiful. Things are happening the way they should be. I am not saying that if you meditate nothing bad will ever happen to you or that the body can be completely free of illness and that you will live forever. No. Life happens. Every day there are new challenges. Each person's Karma is different, each person has a diverse basket of problems.

Ronnie Newman has been conducting research for the Art of Living for over two decades. In spite of being a meditator, she had to suffer the effects of painful Karma. From 1980-1983, when she was in the Middle East, she was forced to face a horrible experience. It sounded like a scene from an action movie when she told me of her experiences of betrayal and disillusionment working as project director for a humanitarian research project in the Middle East. As a result of all the stress from this situation and contracting parasites, her immune system got compromised and she became very ill. She broke out in constantly itching rashes on her face, neck and other parts of the body, and was sleeping twelve hours a night. She had to take medical leave from the doctoral program at Harvard in which she was enrolled at the time. This condition persisted for several years.

She was at one particular point feeling unusually intense physical discomfort in spite of having been on the path for so long and still suffering. On that occasion, she asked Guruji if she deserved to be healthy.

Guruji looked at her sternly and replied, '*You need to be more grateful. If you hadn't clung so tightly to your sadhana all of these years, you would have been bed ridden for the past thirteen years. You need to be grateful you can even move your arms and legs.*'

It was the combination of Sudarshan Kriya, asanas, pranayama and meditation done in a spirit of surrender that pulled the Sanchitha Karma out of her and reduced the severity of her Prarabdha Karma. The Grace of the Guru was what allowed her to keep going.

Karma can be observed when problems arise relating to health, wealth, relationships or peace of mind. None are pleasant, but having the correct attitude helps to place these problems in the right perspective and realize which can be overcome and which have to be experienced.

I want to share two stories with you, both of which left me puzzled, both of which are about being in a dark, miserable place, have no logical reason for happening, and have found resolution and release in meditative practices.

Maria, from a local satsang group, volunteered for an interview. As she spoke, I saw that embarking on a spiritual journey at a young age had great benefits. She was happy, centered and seemed free of any obstacles in her life. But that was not always so. She began talking about her childhood and the pain was so intense, the story just gushed out.

Her father, Juan, was very sick before he did the course. He was going through problems with his wife and they were separated for some time. That period was very hard on the family. She described Juan as very chauvinistic, expecting the woman to do everything in the home and care for the kids.

'He didn't really care for anyone, he was really selfish. He left the family and went back to the Caribbean to have fun, without thinking of anyone.'

Maria, a ten year old child, suffered emotionally. She was old enough to realize her Dad was having an affair but unable to do anything to prevent it.

'It was part of our culture and it was okay for the father to play around and the mother to accept it, but I was not okay with it. I knew what he was doing and I was very angry with him. I remember, one time, meeting his girlfriend and he wanted me to go up and hug her and I refused. I gave her the look and she started crying. Seeing that made me happy. How could I be nice to her when all she did was cause misery to my family? I couldn't understand why my Dad expected me to be nice to her.'

Parents think their kids don't know but Maria was quite aware and realized her mother turned a blind eye, pretending like nothing happened. It was terrible, because Maria loved her Dad so much and couldn't bear to be away from him. As a kid she always asked whom he loved more; her or Mummy. And he would whisper, '*You, but don't tell your mum.*' What he did affected her all the more because she thought he had to get love from someone else and didn't love her.

Once I heard Maria's story I knew I had to speak to her father Juan, whom I knew for the last five years as someone centered and loving, always with a smile and words of encouragement for everyone. His home was so welcoming and the family appeared so close. I would never have guessed what Juan had to endure to reach this beautiful place.

Since Juan was young, he was exposed to spirituality because of his sister, with whom he was very close. It was because of her that he decided to move to the United States, although back home he had a lucrative job as a University Professor teaching architecture. He was married with three children and life was smooth sailing until one person entered his life, heralding his darkest period. He got involved in a relationship and was so obsessed with her he didn't realize the hurt he caused his family. But somewhere in his mind, the guilt of wrongdoing began festering and this grew in him like an internal tornado until he was so sick, he couldn't think.

'*I got so ill; I was suffering so much. I asked God to release me. I was so sick I could not even hear the voice of my children.*' The family moved to New York City and Juan went back to the Caribbean. He had to be with his lover, yet this was exactly the reason for his mental debilitation. Everything was dark in his life and he began to feel that someone had put a hex on him. His nervous system was in a state of collapse, he slept fitfully, two or three hours a day, often awakened by nightmares and visions; his

blood sugar and blood pressure were sky high. On his back he
felt as if a thousand nails were piercing him. The feeling was so
unbearable that one time he rolled on the ground of a parking lot
to try and rid himself of the sensation. He felt ashamed that, as
an academic and educated man who had been born to do great
things, he was reduced to this state. The emotion and guilt were
manifesting as physical pain, and his mind could not fathom
anything nor hold a single thought. He did not understand what
was happening to him. Two years passed and he didn't know
where he was.

*'I was in a dark hole but I knew God would take me out of this.
My wife was upset and she fought with me all the time but I felt as
though I had a rope around my neck. I never abandoned her. I kept
in touch, trying to explain, asking her to be patient.'*

His family met Reiki specialists and psychics and, based on
their evaluation, were convinced he was a victim of witchcraft.
One psychic went as far as to say his lover was mixing something
in his coffee and another said this lady had been with him and
tried to possess him during many lifetimes. Then on one visit, a
psychic told him he would meet his Master and the lifetimes of
pain would end; the cycle would be broken.

*'Meeting Guruji was meant to be. I didn't do anything; everything
fell into place. I recognized him and I took several courses, but he made
me wait 15 years before I could teach meditation. One day while
meditating I surrendered and said, "Jesus, you are my master, guide
me; and if there is another Master, tell me"; and the pain within me
moved like wings out of my body.'*

Juan now recognizes that the pain was necessary for him to
find the path. He knew he hurt his family but he was not in
control at the time. Juan doesn't blame himself and his daughter
doesn't denounce him either. He claims to have been in a state
of ignorance with no awareness. Maria recognizes now he is in
another space, one filled with love and care. Though Juan has

apologized profusely to his family for all the agony he caused them, Maria has never felt a need to forgive him. The love that binds this family together is in itself a visual demonstration of forgiveness.

Juan realizes the powerful play of Prarabdha Karma he had to go through. He is filled with gratitude and holds the power of the Sudarshan Kriya and meditation, practiced in a spirit of healing, coupled with the grace of the Guru, as keys to his present state of bliss. These created the miracle in his life and brought the sunshine pouring in. He smiles and declares, '*Everything happens for a reason. No point saying to people don't do this or that, because they won't hear you. Things happen. Life happens. Maybe that's what they need at the moment, even if it makes no sense to feel guilty. Accept things and move on. A child who falls, gets up and starts walking, and they do this over and over. All of this is the process and learning how to walk is the Art of Living. Have faith and trust that in that dark moment there is someone watching over you and that person will help you out.*'

What is truly amazing is how the family has put all of this behind and support and love each other. Juan's wife is the epitome of grace and the backbone of the family keeping everyone together with a smile and a lot of love.

When I interviewed Divya Mehta from California, she mentioned a Japanese girl who came to Satsang but never smiled; a girl with the saddest eyes ever.

Divya recalled: '*Cici would come for Kriya. She looked so sad. I thought to myself, what is so bad that she is like that, with a face of stone? She is now a teacher and she doesn't stop smiling. You look at her and the smile just comes up on her face.*'

I called Cici and we spoke for an hour. After listening to her story I swore I would never complain again about my life. Cici was in such a dark place for so long, it was nothing short of a miracle that she was able to break out and see the light again.

Every lifetime is an opportunity for you to wipe out past Karma. However the material world and resultant delusion does not permit you to give yourself that chance for redemption. When you go through successive lifetimes and build bad Karma upon bad Karma it gets compounded, and then you find yourself in a situation that is evil and oppressive, no matter where you turn; that is Cici's story

Cici was born in Japan and came to the US at the age of 16, as a student. She was married very young to a man from Fiji and had a son by the time she was 20. The relationship was terribly abusive and she tried leaving him three times in twelve years. There was a lot of physical as well as psychological abuse. He was an alcoholic and was doing drugs and this made him unbearable to be around. She told me that because of her Christian background she thought she should be subservient and accept everything. She recalled how her Sunday School teacher had told her that when one married someone, one had to stay with him for the rest of one's life. That thought remained with her and she believed if she prayed to God, then somehow her husband would become a nice person and the marriage would work out. She had no family and no one to ask for help. The more she was abused the more she withdrew from the world, and the more subservient she became the more he abused her... and the cycle continued. She always had bruises and hid it from others.

He would get drunk, be abusive, then there would be a sweet period and she would forgive him. She was abused and then forgave him about a 'million' times. One time, she ran away from him and actually went back to her mother in Japan. Two years later, after leaving him twice before, she finally decided to take legal action and get a divorce. She had started Martial arts classes a few years previously and after winning the US Martial Arts championship, she was going to China for further training. And that's when she met her second husband, who was on the

National Chinese team. On her return, the divorce was final but she lost everything. She had no house, no car and no job.

She and her second husband taught Martial arts in a studio. She was still reticent but happy. She noticed her son was becoming more withdrawn. Having seen his mother's abuse and himself been bullied by his father had affected him as well. Overall, in spite of these difficulties, her life was much better than before.

But abuse followed her like a moth to a flame. Once, when she was in the studio, her second husband attacked her. His temper flared over an argument and the next thing she knew, he held her neck with one hand, hand and pushed her so that her back was against the wall with her feet up in the air. She tried to struggle but everything turned white and she lost consciousness. When she awoke she was on the ground. Perhaps it was the stress of living in a new country, where things were beyond his control, which triggered this outburst. He felt the need to control his wife. The police arrived and she filed charges for domestic violence.

The fears from the past now ballooned in her head. She was terrified. Since they worked at the same place and the owner was her husband's friend, she stopped going to work. That whole summer she was so scared, she pretty much locked herself in her room and didn't go out of the house, didn't talk to anyone, didn't see anyone. In the dark confines of her room she became paranoid. She felt anyone who came around her was going to hurt her or take advantage.

She had court-mandated counseling but it wasn't working for her. The counselor wanted to put her on medications, but she didn't want to take any.

'Many times I contemplated suicide. I couldn't sleep… I was scared if I heard any noise outside. I thought people were trying to kill me. I felt it was better to die than live like this.'

By this time her son couldn't take it anymore and ran away. She was devastated! The single ray of happiness in her life was extinguished, plunging her into an abyss of darkness.

Cici took the AOL course that October and then in December during a follow-up session, she met Divya, who invited her for Seva. She started immersing herself in Seva and attended knowledge sessions and finally, one day, she broke down and cried in front of the group.

'I had such a deep experience during the course. The earlier sleepiness was alleviated by the Kriya, and I thought to myself that whatever it was, I wanted it to go on.'

She started talking to people around her while earlier she was too scared. For months she never went to work because she feared she wasn't ready and might freak out in class or harm her students. A few months later she found a new job as a schoolteacher. Her son chose to stay in his father's garage. When she saw her son some time later, she was shocked to see how he lived in a dark garage. He wouldn't talk to her or come home. He had repressed anger and his father got him into trouble all the time and even took money from him for drinking or gambling. Yet, emotionally, he wanted to be near his father. He had taken the AOL Yesplus course for youth but didn't do the practice. Cici surrendered to the situation.

'I didn't exist and wouldn't exist without AOL. It's only because of Guruji's grace, the kriya and knowledge that I am here today. Everything is happening now because it was preparing me for this. I was on a path for a long time without knowing it. I am so grateful. I read Celebrating Silence (A book of Srisri's knowledge sheets) and every time I read there's always something new. Being in the present moment leaves me untouched no matter what. Guruji said I'm always with you and that really did it for me. I feel that he is always with me.'

Cici is now a traveling teacher. She has become strong and can now take care of others. She is full of enthusiasm and is excitedly making plans for the future. It took her fifteen years to burn her Karma but today she is resilient and centered, and her face always sports a smile. We corresponded recently and I was thrilled to hear that Cici's son returned home out of the blue. He met Guruji at the LA Center this April and then decided to take the Part-1 course with his grandma (Cici's mother) in summer when she visited. Cici believes her son still needs to do a lot, like finding a job and going back to school, but he is feeling better and lives in her home. In between assignments Cici was able to spend three months with him at home before Guruji sent her to Japan.

Her story is a source of inspiration for me and I hope that after reading it you will help someone escape the cruel clutches of Karma and discover their true self, the happiness and joy that are gifts of the present moment.

While facing tough situations it becomes hard to stay focused and be happy. Once you recognize that it is Prarabdha Karma at play, over which you have no control, the mind withdraws and becomes calm. It identifies the inevitable and stops asking why. *Why me? Why now?* These questions have no answer and they only create mental turmoil.

Sudarshan Kriya and meditation allow you to be in the present moment and give you the realization that while the body is mortal the soul is not; *you* are not. And it is *you* who gets liberated and soars to freedom, all because you were able to search within for happiness, not permitting your Karma to interfere in any way with your blissful state of mind. When you delve into yourself, into the unshakeable stillness, you are able to see action in inaction and inaction in action. In the quiet comfort of meditation you can observe dynamic movement and then can find that still oasis even when surrounded by cacophony and chaos. That is the Art of Living.

The three S's—Satsang, Sadhana and Seva can help reduce your Karmic debt and bring you closer to your true self. Satsang is the celebration of divinity in a group setting through music and rhythm. Sadhana is the daily practice of pranayama and meditation and Seva is selfless service.

Ten years ago, I recall how I was in a constant state of agitation. I lived in the small mind, never at peace, always questioning my destiny. I was resentful towards my husband because I was a stay-at-home mom, yet I didn't know what I wanted to do. Be a teacher, pursue a doctorate in criminology or take a course in linguistics? Every day I thought of new possibilities. I felt fate was against me. I was born under an unfortunate star and would struggle to achieve anything. Nothing made me happy and I was always gloomy, with a permanent scowl on my face. Eight years ago I learned Sudarshan Kriya and a couple of years later began practicing two or three times a week. My faith completely changed, my practice became more regular and I attended weekly Satsangs. A very subtle revolution took place. It was as if an invisible force had lifted me out of my cesspool swirling with bad energy, irritations and botherations. I was suddenly amazed with the gift of life. This sounds like a fairy tale, but many others can also vouch for the truth of this statement.

At the age of 48, I discovered a talent for writing. If I had not been on the path, I would never have realized this latent talent and discovered a career. I published my first book at the age of 50, and began a brand new career. In many ways I made choices to change my Karma; viewed another way, my destiny was revealed to me through meditation.

While Karma is understood in some form by the fallible mortal mind it offers a plausible explanation for many things. Why you were on a beach in Indonesia when the Tsunami hit or why you escaped from the burning twin towers or why a baby fell from the second floor and was unharmed. It offers solace for the survivor and compassion for the sufferer.

Quite plainly, while going through your Karma you have two choices. Let's imagine there is a forecast of rain and you have to complete a chore. You then leave the house wearing boots and carrying an umbrella or rain jacket. Then, no matter how hard it pours, you don't really mind because you are prepared. The weather might lead to some fever or a cold but you know it is temporary and you can take care of yourself. That is the shield that sadhana provides. It prepares you for any outcome so that you deal with it in a calm, responsible manner with least harm to the Self.

The other scenario is that you don't read the weather forecast and are caught in a storm with no umbrella. Drenched completely, you sit and lament and wonder why the weather chose you. Why you have to be the one suffering. You don't act; instead take comfort in your mournful moan. Remaining in wet clothing leads to weeks of fever and pneumonia and all the time you have no ability to see that there is always a way out of a predicament. You can either make the choice to prepare mind and body for any eventuality or lament when that situation plays out in your life. Either way Karma will play out. How Karma impacts your life, depends entirely on your attitude and centeredness.

Group Karma

In addition to individual Karma there is also Group Karma. This is the effect of Karma based on where you live. The local economy can affect your job situation and terrorist threats can affect safe travel. Group Karma can be seen very clearly when catastrophe and natural calamities affect a location. If you live in Florida, your house may be wrecked by a hurricane. If you hail from Puebla in Mexico, then the volcano Popocatepetl can erupt at any time. If you are on a subway in a metropolis at night, you could be mugged, and if you live in New Orleans, then you may have been a victim of Hurricane Katrina.

The effects of Group Karma were seen during the Holocaust, where thousands of people were drawn into the evil propaganda cast by the Nazi party, just by virtue of their location. They were affected by the politics of the time. This is true of genocidal acts the world over, where one party or group goes on a rampage and people fall victim to their actions. In recent years we have seen this play out time and again from the September, 11 attacks to college shootings. In such cases it is the aura created by the people surrounding you which becomes overpowering and overrides your personal Karma. Even in such situations your personal Karma sometimes supersedes the effect of evil and you become a survivor of the Holocaust, or, say of the shooting rampage at Virginia Tech. Swami Pragyapad, a senior teacher, while explaining Karma and Group Karma in particular, presented a beautiful analogy.

'Imagine you plant an apple tree. After some years you get delicious, rosy apples and that is the effect of good Karma. Sometimes rotten apples fall from the tree and that is your Prarabdha Karma. If the tree is tall, some fruit, good or rotten, may fall in your neighbor's yard and that is Group Karma.' He smiled and said: *'Understand? Either way Karma is inevitable.'*

17

Distortions of Love

Anger: The first Distortion

Rage has no ears, nor does it have a vision. It only leads to reaction.
And reaction leads to regret. Regret causes frustration. Frustration
clouds reason. Unreasonable acts provoke rage, starting a vicious
circle.

—H.H. SriSri Ravishankar

We all seek perfection in our lives, some deliberately, others not
so aware of this motivation. All that we do is undertaken to
achieve happiness in some form; the desire is to reach a place
lying anywhere between satisfaction, delight, happiness all the
way to bliss. Even as we immerse ourselves in our daily activities,
whether it is working in the yard, listening to music, watching a
movie, or playing a game, we are not overtly aware of a natural
impulse to get back to the source, to seek joy that is at our core.
No one willingly involves themselves in any activity that makes
them unhappy. We all want to be happy no matter what we
do. What leads to unhappiness is when the outcome of such
endeavors falls below expectation. Every action seeks flawlessness
and when the result falls short of our anticipation of perfection,
it leads to frustration, which vents in anger. Anger is the first
distortion of love.

Anger from expectation

Idayo Sabo from New York had a strained relationship with her parents. Her mother was West African and her parents divorced when she was two years old. Born in Dakar, Senegal, she moved to the United States with her mother, when her father left the marriage for another woman. Her mother was not educated past high school and raised Idayo alone as a single parent. She had to do several jobs and by the time Idayo was five, she was staying home alone. During this period her mother got really depressed and decided to move back with Idayo to Senegal for a few years. When she returned to the United States, life became really difficult for her daughter. By then, Idayo was fifteen years old. She had to grow up and be the adult in the home much before her time. She did her mother's taxes, facilitated at parent-teacher meetings, and attended to household chores. This forced entry into adulthood built a lot of resentment within her. She began to dislike her mother and vented her anger at every opportunity. She blamed her mother for all the problems she was facing as a teenager of mixed ethnicity, trying to fit in and find meaning. Her mother seemed to be an unnecessary impediment in her life and every encounter with her was an opportunity to spew anger. Her mother could never live up to her expectations of what a caregiver ought to be and this shortcoming built waves of anger within Idayo. At the core of her anger was a deep desire for acceptance and love.

'I would just look at her and be angry. There was so much blame. If I felt miserable I thought it was her fault. I felt neglected and not given my due, not given interest or attention. I blamed my dad as well but as he wasn't there, my mom took the brunt. Sometimes she fought back but most often I just stormed off. In some ways she understood and felt she deserved it.'

Idayo took the course in 2004, during which there were some vivid moments when one shared personal experiences with the group. She expressed love and gratitude for her family, and that surprised her, because her typical feeling was anger and resentment. After the course she found herself able to accept the past, feel blessed and move forward instead of looking back.

'That ability to accept people as they are has been more significant. The whole experience has been a blessing because it has made me stronger. It is what is and I have become more detached from that experience. I also have fewer expectations now. Part of the anger was that I expected my mother to behave and act in a way she was not capable of. There's a lot more acceptance for who she is, what she is and what life meant.'

Indian Mythological references to Anger

Historically, anger has been the downfall of many great people. For ancient seers in India, anger wiped out merit gained from years of penance and meditation. Sage Durvasa was notorious for his angry curses. Once, Shiva the Destroyer went on an angry rampage, causing havoc and destruction around him. His wife Parvati was unhappy with his anger so Shiva deposited his anger in Anusuya, wife of Sage Atri (Shiva could do that, he was God). The result was the birth of Durvasa. It was hardly a wonder Durvasa was always angry. Ancient mythology is filled with stories of the *Devas* (gods) placating Sage Durvasa's anger and averting his curses. There are several stories about Shiva who was notorious for opening his third eye when in a rage, so burning everything that presented itself before him, reducing people and things to mere ashes (hence the nickname *the Destroyer*).

Anger is a temporary emotion

There is no doubt anger is detrimental to physical and spiritual health. When anger rises, rational thought is impossible, resulting in irrevocable action and irreversible expression. At those times, hurtful and sarcastic words spill out of the mouth; one says things otherwise inconceivable.

A friend of mine walked out on a lucrative job some years ago when his boss insulted him by yelling at him in front of others. Of course, this led to further problems for my friend, for new and equally lucrative jobs were hard to come by. If he had realized at the time, that all he had suffered from was a bruised ego, the moment might have blown over and he might have held onto that job. The boss yelled because of a job done imperfectly: he was perhaps beset with other pressures, making him momentarily lose reason. Naturally, wisdom comes with hindsight and my friend was scarcely able to think, let alone commiserate with his berating boss. Understandably so. Nevertheless, the harm was done and it was irrevocable.

Anger is temporary insanity

In judicial courts, there are many crimes upheld and condoned with a lesser sentence for being committed in a moment of *temporary insanity*. Prisons all over the world are filled with inmates who have committed crimes of passion: murder, rape, assault—acts of lunacy committed without any thought of repercussions. Many prisoners in Art of Living's Prisonsmart Program, after taking the course, regretted they had not been able to reign in their temper, resulting in impetuous actions which led to their incarceration.

I have known and lived with anger for several years. Ask anyone in my family. I was always yelling and screaming. Either my daughter spilt coffee, or my husband forgot my birthday, or my sister expected too much from me or a friend took me for granted. In a single day, I lost my temper at least a dozen times. Maybe more. Perhaps the best outcome of joining AOL is that I have let go of anger and my family is very thankful for that.

Anger made me exalt small things, minute incidents, making me lose touch with myself and others. One of the best phrases I learned in this journey is: *So what? So what* if the juice spilt? *So what* if my sister wanted too much? *So what* if my husband forgot my birthday? I was just festering in the small mind, making a big deal of things that didn't really matter in the long run. They were minor frustrations that didn't deserve the attention I was giving them. The sun would not stop shining if my daughter didn't put her shoes back on the shoe rack. Despite several angry outbursts and then, over time, relatively calm requests, she still doesn't do it. But now I smile and say, *so what?* And I do one of two things; either I put the shoes back on the rack myself, or make the umpteenth request in as pleasant a tone as possible. As a result, the ambience in the house has changed. Everyone is more upbeat and, I see now, how my mood affected the entire household. My children are less rebellious and more communicative. I feel much better, calm and quiet, and for a change and my blood pressure is under control.

Timothy Wong from Hong Kong cautions: *'"So what?" needs to be used with awareness and a sense of responsibility together with the course points, otherwise it can lead to irresponsibility and carelessness. It is really a conscious decision of letting-go of a situation by recognizing that it has moved you away from your center. One also needs to be careful in using it to justify/rationalize one's action which can lead to spiritual stubbornness/blindsiding.'*

Veronika Niyazova is an Art Excel teacher in Florida. She is deeply attached to the Guru and uses the knowledge consistently. *'One thing I use a lot in my daily life is "So hum So what". A lot of times I feel people judge me or I have health issues and am told not to teach and though I feel disappointed at the time and even get angry, I just say "So hum So what," and let it all go.'*

Anger leads to regret

Once you lose your temper you are irrevocably drawn into a chain of events. If you are a mother who has just spanked her young child, the remorse is almost immediate and then you are filled with regret, offering candy to placate the screaming child. Sometimes you feel justified about an angry outburst and that leads to more negative feelings of hatred and revenge, even more damaging to your peace of mind. This makes you so bitter that eventually you repent being caught in this quicksand of emotions. Whichever way you look at it, no one likes angry people. Look around and you will see that people naturally gravitate towards those with a balanced outlook in life. Your mood defines who you are, who surrounds you and how everyone in your immediate environment feels. You have a huge responsibility towards everyone near you, and their needs would be best served if you dropped your anger right now.

Amit Kumar Vyaghambare from India confesses to being very short-tempered before he joined AOL but condones that anger by saying this was common behavior for Indian males. Naturally, it was his wife at the receiving end. Small things would set him off and he would scream at her, only to feel terrible a moment later when the anger passed.

'If I put something on the table and someone touched it, I would get mad. I couldn't control my temper and I would regret it later. If someone questioned me about anything or even if they made any suggestions, I would get crazy. I didn't want any interference.'

Only his two-year-old son was spared. His wife was unhappy but learned to live with it. Even so, one incident made him sharply aware of his actions. His wife was pregnant and he shook her violently. Luckily, nothing happened but it made him acutely aware of his loss of control. The practice of Sudarshan Kriya has allowed Amit to release his anger.

'I don't know where my anger has disappeared. Now if I get angry it's on the surface. I realize whatever has happened will pass and somehow things just pass and I don't give in to anger.'

The Dynamics of Anger

The first step towards defusing anger is to observe its dynamics. Because anger is an emotion, the best way to defuse it is through awareness, by understanding what the common triggers are. At what time and in what circumstances is it most likely to occur? Does it arise when you are in a hurry? When you are tired? Is it a situation that occurs repeatedly? Is it a person who irritates you? Identifying your triggers brings you one step closer to understanding anger through acceptance.

The next step is of present moment awareness. Let's say someone deliberately took the parking spot you were pulling into. Why not pause and examine your choices? You can lose it and yell, bang on his car, maybe even punch his face. But is it worth it? Not only will the emotional roller coaster exhaust you, but you may also end up in jail for aggravated assault. Just find another parking spot. It's just the easier and more sensible route.

What if the reverse situation occurs? You pull in into a parking spot and an angry driver comes up to you, ready to punch you. Two things can happen. You react to his potent anger and both end up in fisticuffs. Or, you combat his anger with your calm. If your serenity is more pervading, complete and supreme, it is bound to reduce, even eliminate his anger.

Guruji and Anger

SriSri always reacts to everything with his charming smile. Whether he is greeting an angry mob, or gets insulted by someone, or is accused of being a fraud, he reacts with a smile. While Guruji describes anger as a distortion, he merits its use in some circumstances. People close to him say that at times he does raise his voice.

Madhu Bhardwaj, an AOL teacher from Mumbai, is only focused on the Master. She doesn't worry about anything people say or do and realizes she is really blessed to be so close to him: '*He walks the talk. When you see how he conducts himself even in the way he looks at people; it's almost as if he tells you, "this is how it is done". I have seen him yelling at someone and then he turns to look at me and in that split second there is a smile on his face, as if he never got angry. It's as if he were saying, "Show you're angry but don't let it descend below your throat".*'

Don't Hold on to Anger

The next step is in 'anger defusing'. Do not hold on to your anger. Look at the big picture. You are merely reacting to a situation and not accepting it in totality. Don't identify with the emotion and it will pass. Frustration, regret and disillusion come from holding on to a situation and churning it within, examining and analyzing it to death. The result is more anger and disillusionment. Holding onto the situation makes the event bigger than it is. Let it go. Let it pass. It is not that important. What is more important is your peace of mind. Don't give the power to others to push your buttons. The buttons are yours and you should push them wisely.

Dr. George Lavrelashvili lives in Tbilisi, Georgia. He recalls with regret a turbulent past when he gave vent to anger frequently, but coming to the path has made him realize the futility of his earlier ways: '*I like myself much better and people around like me better. Everything pushed my buttons. There were things about me that I never wanted to face and accept. I was very abusive and I have been known to hit people if I got angry. What I have learned now is that it's possible to smile back.*'

Anger: A safety valve

Anger outbursts are safety valves; sometimes, these are necessary in order to maintain mental sanity. Many times a situation bothers you, overwhelming your thoughts. At such times it might be better to yell and scream for a moment and then let it go. Forget about it. Your display of anger is over, an event that took place in the past, not in the present moment. Don't attach any importance to it. It was needed to get the job done and that was its sole purpose. Life is much more peaceful once you defuse your anger. When you are not aware or do not understand the causes of your stress it gets released as anger outbursts.

Anger: A release of repressed stress

After the Part-1 course, instead of being calm, Sridhar began erupting in anger. He needed no reason and his wife was annoyed that instead of becoming better he had become terrible. Sridhar spoke to some AOL senior teachers, and they said that perhaps a lot of repressed stress was being released as anger. *'Over time I continued the practice and with the focus on the breath it has disappeared. Now I have the tool of awareness. I am more aware of what is happening even when I get angry.'*

Like all other practices, anger defusing, too, requires practice. You have to reflect, recognizer the triggers, examine the outcome and get out of the small mind. Then your true nature will shine through. You will become such a fountain of joy that people around you will not be able to stay angry for long. By defusing your anger you would help yourself and those around you. Is that not something worth doing?

SriSri says that if you have to be angry, direct your anger at divinity. Unfortunately most of us love God, and get angry with humans. Realize that turning your anger towards humans backfires and has many repercussions. Instead, be angry with the sun and the moon and the ocean. That cannot harm you.

The Infinite is gigantic enough to absorb your anger without a response. Get angry with the Divine for all the injustice and corruption in the world and then channelize your energy towards eliminating them.

The world around us is perfect. The imperfection lies within us and we have the power to eliminate it. Imperfection is non-acceptance of the present moment or situation. We need to recognize that the present moment is inevitable and not in our control. So the whole context of perfection and/or imperfection is only contained in our perception and not in reality. In reality every moment is perfect and complete.

Harry Kahn is part of our local Satsang group. In Coral Springs, I have never attended a Satsang with Harry not present. He is so devoted to Guruji and so committed to the Path, he never misses the recommended weekly satsangs. He always greets you with a welcoming hug and his face is all smiles, so naturally I was surprised to hear that Harry or Hari, as he calls himself, gets angry very easily.

'My most common trigger is usually from frustration, which shows up when I cannot find something like my keys or wallet. I like and appreciate efficiency and order,' he states. Small things would cause Harry to lose his temper frequently, sometimes in inappropriate situations, leading to plenty of regret. A lot of his anger rose from expectation of a certain behavior or a certain response. All of these are relatively small matters and really don't matter when you consider at the big picture.

Hari has taken the steps to increase self-awareness and steady behavior modification has given him the desired results. The keys, he explains, lie in pranayama and meditation.

'I have become more self-aware and I have realized that my frustrations and anger are from expectations of perfection, from myself and others. Since I have become more conscious, with the help of Art of Living practices, I have greatly improved, and I let go more

quickly and easily when I am upset and irritated. My entire life is much less stressful and more peaceful because of the benefits I have received from pranayama and meditation as taught in the Art of Living courses.'

I will always remember what he told me next. *'Guruji told me I was carving my anger on a brick, so then I learned to write it in the dirt and I felt much better, and now I etch it on the sea shore and waves of divinity wash it away.'*

18

Lust: The Second distortion of love

Lust is aggressive, love is submissive, lust is a demand and love is giving and caring, lust is feverishness, and in love there is a sparkle of joy. A person lustfully makes you an object of their enjoyment, in love you elevate a person to godliness. Lust is nothing but stimulation of the body, love is stimulation of the soul, of the heart.
—H.H. SriSri Ravishankar

Love and Lust lie on opposite ends of the same spectrum and while the latter is feverishly centered on satisfying a desire, the former is about caring and giving selflessly. In every society, there are conservative and liberal approaches to sex. In certain pockets exist very strict taboos regarding sex, while others believe in free sex. Both extremes result in an obsession with sex. The Sanskrit word for lust at the gross level is Kama.

Kama, Purusharthas and Prana

Kama is the third of the four guiding principles in Hindu philosophy—the *Purusharthas*—which are pointers on leading your life such that you reap maximum benefit from the enjoyment of the senses. SriSri says that there are two things we have done for sure in this lifetime and in all our previous births, whether we were humans, animals or insects. We have eaten and had sex. For sure. Since procreation is a natural instinct, it was never denied in the ancient scriptures. At the same time, it was prescribed in combination with the first of the Purusharthas, following the path of *Dharma*, or righteousness. The enjoyment of sex was welcome as long as no other person was hurt in the process. In other words, sex between consenting partners was prescribed.

Sexual practices and tantric rituals have long been associated with the awakening of the *Kundalini*, corporeal energy, a libidinal force or *Shakti* that is envisioned as a coiled serpent at the base of the spine. Through meditation and other esoteric practices, the Kundalini is awakened and made to rise through the body via a network of nerves called the *Shushumna Nadi*. The Kundalini is located in the *Muladhara Chakra*, an energy nexus at the base of the spine which is also connected with the reproductive system. This is why *Tantric* sexual practices were sometimes used to awaken and raise this energy. The idea was to lift the self to a higher plane through these practices.

Madhu Bhardwaj does workshops in Mumbai on sex education as part of the Art Excel and YES courses she teaches. Teen years are fraught with relationship problems but the main relationship that is dysfunctional is between teens and their parents. They can't communicate with their parents, boyfriends and girlfriends are taboo, but primarily it is important to understand that teenagers have sexual issues and no one to talk to about them in a non-judgmental manner.

'We deal with it from physical and emotional viewpoints. In the circle of life we are all at different stages and at each stage certain behaviors are appropriate. Teenagers need to focus on education. The same energy that is used for creativity is also used as sexual energy. When prana (subtle life force) flows downward you think too much of sex and you cannot be creative and if that happens, you won't have career success. This is how it is explained and then the choice is clear.'

When teenagers understand the flow of breath in their bodies, it is almost as if a light bulb turns on in their brain. Suddenly lust and sexual exploration converts from being an instinctive, hormonal trajectory to one of personal choice. Prana or the life force is what drives the body to action. When this energy ascends, it is voiced as creative energy and when it descends, it expresses itself as sexual energy. This is the reason you feel elated when you finish a painting or a research paper. It also explains why you feel exhausted and wasted after a sexual act.

Sexual choices

Sexual tendencies are a product of culture and modern day media glamorize sex. Uma Berlin, while working in America's inner city high schools, has observed that most teens do not know how to handle their own minds. Overwhelmed by the stress of unstable homes, overcrowded classrooms, school bullying, and peer pressure, they cannot clear their minds. Many feel disconnected from themselves, with superficial relationships with their peers and teachers. Without tools to find deeper meaning and belonging, many cope through drugs, alcohol, and sex. Explaining IAHV's YES! For Schools program (International Association for Human values) Uma says:

'Guruji's knowledge is applied in a practical way to real-life situations that teens face. It is about consciously making choices. Schools expose students to the physical consequences of drugs and sex through health education. But what drives students to this risky behavior? YES (Youth Empowerment Seminar) provides a safe space for students to examine why they drink, get high, or have sex, and how these actions negatively affect not just their bodies, but their self-esteem, and their state of mind and emotions.'

The YES teacher models for teens a healthy way of handling one's own mind and emotions. She is a role model, non-judgmental, just there to support and guide her students. Many young people lack such a figure in their lives, and are heavily influenced by media messages and pop culture celebrities as so-called role models.

Uma recalls one particular case that demonstrates the success of the program. After the course one young man had a huge turnaround in terms of taking responsibility for his own body and seeing his own life as something sacred, not to be casually thrown around. He got in touch with her three years after the program. He was in college, something unheard of from his background, and he had turned vegetarian, something unheard of in the cultural context of his life. He still practiced the breathing and was pleased to say that his life had changed.

'In Haiti, our youth leaders wanted to address the problem of sexual promiscuity, which is rampant throughout communities. Without ways of coping with their stress and trauma, many Haitians have sex to feel some level of human comfort and intimacy,' shares Uma. Through Nouvelle Vie, she created a Sexuality Education program based on Guruji's knowledge, addressing sexuality at its core.

'The program emphasizes the repercussions of casual sex on the mind and emotions in a completely nonjudgmental way. It's amazing what difference the knowledge can make in terms of one's sexual choices and sexual health. It is such a gift to bring this program to these people.'

In the refugee camps of Port au Prince, almost a hundred women are raped every day. Since August 2011, Nouvelle Vie's new Haitian teachers have taught over two hundred women survivors of sexual violence in Wharf Jeremie. For the first time in months these women report sleeping through the night, feeling relaxed and being joyful. Instead of feeling the isolation and shame, they can connect with and support each other. 68% of these women continue to join follow-up sessions.

Transcending sexual desire

While lust is understandable during teen and young adult years, as one grows older, wisdom and maturity are supposed to control it, channeling it to its subtlest form: love. It is regrettable many do not transcend, remaining instead at the level of the Muladhara. *The Time Magazine* (Health and Family section) published on June 23, 2010, spoke of a Dutch study conducted on a group or geriatric swingers published in the *Journal of Sexually Transmitted Infections*, where more than 55% of sexually transmitted diseases were identified in aging swingers. This is an unfortunate phenomenon in that even as people age, the desire for sex doesn't wane. Meditation, prayer and other spiritual practices are supposed to elevate you from lust. The mind reaches that space where there is only peace and love, and lust falls away. Our expectation is even higher for people who are supposed to be beacons of spirituality and it is disappointing to see priests, bishops and other holy men involved in sexual scandals.

When anything is taboo it is definitely much more interesting. As SriSri says, '*whatever you resist, persists.*' In an Art of Living Part II course I attended, the instructor told us about an interesting session conducted by SriSri where he asked the group to meditate with the only instruction that they could *not* think of a monkey. Well, as it turned out, monkeys, baboons and orangutans were leaping around the room. Not a single person was able to push the monkey out of their thoughts. When something is prohibited it is the nature of the mind to linger on that thought, and as the mind returns to such thoughts with increasing frequency it becomes an obsession.

When I taught Bala Vihar, a class on Indian culture, to a group of children, I noticed that youth brought up in strict, conservative homes were more likely to lie and cheat their parents, have boyfriends and do what was generally unacceptable in their home. The very fact that it was taboo, made it exciting. Those with teenage sons know about *Penthouse* and *Playboy* stashed away under mattresses. Many parents on checking their children's YouTube history are horrified by what they see. Teenage years are rough, and while adolescents struggle to know and understand their maturing bodies, they experiment with sex. Unfortunately at this stage, their emotional and moral behavior has not matured at the same rate, and the lack of emotional processing and moral policing leads them into lustful behavior. After all, it is natural to be attracted to forbidden fruit.

The Middle path

SriSri always speaks of a middle path for the demonstration of affection. In the East, people do not express their love with words. I have never heard my father-in-law telling his wife he loved her. She knew he did, and they never openly spoke about it, at least not in front of others. In the West, people hug and kiss others even when they meet for the first time. It isn't uncommon to see a couple locked in a passionate embrace in the middle of the road under a blistering, afternoon sun. No one spares them a second glance. Asking your wife if she loves you is not odd or uncommon, and everyone ends their telephone conversations with *I love you*, making it just another apt ending to a dialogue, just as hello is appropriate to start one. Too much of expression doesn't permit the love to permeate the being and take root. It remains on the surface and words remove any remaining traces. Not expressing love at all leads to regret. After my mother-in-law passed away, I know how much my father-in-law regretted that he did not tell her how much he appreciated her and loved her. There needs to be a happy medium, one where you permit the love to fill your being and then prudently express enough for others to feel and appreciate it, but that requires awareness of emotion and consciousness of spoken words.

Love and Lust

Lust is Kama at the grossest level, while love is its subtle and most sublime level. Lust can only be combated with awareness. The moment lust arises, we search for ways to quench the fire. No one actually pauses before committing a lustful act. If they did, the act may never take place. The more you attempt to control and rein in lust, the bigger it becomes and greater is the compulsion to satisfy it. This then leads to a cycle of guilt and blame, creating anxiety and tension and resulting in cunning and manipulation to satisfy just one narrow desire that springs up at intervals with regularity and increasing depth. In lust, there is a narrow focus only on one person, with little or no regard for the means necessary to possess that person. Inability to do so results in an upsurge of the darker side; frustration, violence, and degradation imprison you. While promiscuity may give the illusion of freedom, it actually binds you and destroys you from within. One sexual act may feel exhilarating in the moment, but what follows makes the act regrettable. Emotions are dark and confused, and satisfaction is momentary, leaving you spent and listless until the feverishness begins afresh.

The only way to handle it is to understand its nature. See what you feel as lust arises in you and realize how it prevents you from feeling love. You have a choice.

You can live with lust and the tension and anxiety it brings, or you can relax in love.

You can drive yourself crazy manipulating and planning to satisfy your lust, or relax in the ease and restfulness of love.

You can obsess with possession and grasping even though there is nothing to own but a few minutes of pleasure, or you can surrender in timeless and ever expansive, divine love.

You can wrestle with violent thoughts and actions or sacrifice and surrender to a higher energy, freeing you from the bondage of base desire.

When I interviewed Harry, I asked if he knew of people who had experienced problems with anger, lust and greed, and his response made a lot of sense. *'Everyone for certain has had some issues at some point; they are just not willing to share it with others.'* This is true. If we examine our lives we surely have had some issues with the distortions of love, though varying in degree. Accepting lapses would bring shame and people would rather keep their indulgences private. Either that, or they are simple unaware of what is happening. But that wasn't the case with Harry.

Harry was brought up Jewish. Age 15 was a turning point in his life because his father died. He was devastated, and hated God for that, and as a result became atheist over the next seventeen years, doing his best to seek revenge on life that had cheated him of security and happiness. The distortions of love don't make their appearance in isolation. With anger comes lust, arrogance and delusion, and that is what happened with Harry. He was so angry at what life had to offer that he became a drug addict.

'I initially got into drugs because I saw it as a form of recreation and of acceptance by my peers. It was a cool thing to do. I was never a popular kid and I felt accepted with the drugs. Nothing mattered. I felt great, I loved the feeling; it enabled me to talk with girls and get sexually involved. Off drugs I was shy, but drugs made me more outgoing and drop all inhibitions.'

Not being part of the popular group in school can deal a devastating blow on your self-esteem. Being reticent to begin with, Harry could not battle with his raging hormones and he longed for girls to want him. He wanted to feel he was attractive and popular and these thoughts consumed him. Getting into drugs made his inhibitions drop and he was able to connect with his peer group. Suddenly he had friends and under the influence of drugs, sexual promiscuity was at an all-time high. Harry felt great. He was floating in the clouds and had more sex than he could handle and for the first decade, life was idyllic, or so he thought. But then he crossed the limit. *'I was in hell. I was in my own jail and I used when I didn't want to use.'*

Long term drug use had its natural consequences. The penalty of drug use was tolerable in the beginning, but after a while he got tired of losing jobs and relationships. He was fed up with the life-threatening illnesses, overdosing and being rushed to the hospital, wrecking cars and disappointing his family. *'I was drained and wanted to stop, but didn't know how.'*

Meeting SriSri for the first time was momentous. Harry signed up for the Part I course and did his Part 2 course with SriSri in the Montreal Ashram. He has since taken 15-20 courses.

'I work to stay on that Path and it's been easy. I was actually born again and have started living again. Acknowledging the divinity in myself has given me a constant high that no drugs and sex can offer.'

SriSri says, *'love liberates you, it sets you free, it is effortless and leads to timeless happiness.'* Knowing the nature of love and the benefits of steeping your soul in love, why would you choose lust? Drop it now. Let it go. Reach within you for that fountain of bliss that can give you incomparable joy. The rishis say that a moment of *Samadhi* is equivalent to '*Sahasrarathi*', a thousand simultaneous orgasms. Meditation and Sudarshan Kriya are doorways to that Samadhi. As you practice, over time, lust becomes less and less important and then simply fades away, leaving behind shining and brilliant love.

19

Greed:
The Third Distortion of Love

There is greed inside us that we don't recognize. One is when we want to accumulate so many things in life and the second greed is for experiences.

—H.H. SriSri Ravishankar

The *Bhagavad-Gita* talks of three gates to hell: anger, lust and greed. Let's examine greed and how much it controls us. Greed is what drives economies and people; it is what makes large corporations and 'success' stories. We encounter greed every day, whether it's as mundane as watching the person ahead of us at a buffet line take the last two pieces of chocolate cake, or as critical as experiencing the economic aftereffects of wars fought for oil.

When Hurricane Wilma hit South Florida, we lost power for almost a week. After a couple of days we heard that the neighborhood Publix Supermarket had opened, and of course we rushed there, only to find that the queue of people waiting to enter had wrapped itself around the building and parking lot. After an hour of waiting patiently, talking to people who had driven ten miles to get water, milk and bread, it was my turn to enter the store. As I walked past the checkout, I noticed a lady filling her cart with six gallons of milk and a dozen loaves of bread. I couldn't believe what I saw. There was no refrigeration, so how was she going to drink six gallons of milk in a day? It was sheer greed, resulting from fear, generated by confusion.

Greed and the Self

Greed is destructive because it is a self-centered tendency. We all know we cannot live in seclusion. Our lives are inextricably connected with those of others. We need the mailman, garbage collector and mechanic more than they need us. Imagine for a moment that you lived in complete isolation. What would your life be like? Would you be happy with no one to share your experiences, no one to talk to and comfort you? Initially it might be liberating, but with time one would feel the vacuum closing in. Greed is like living in seclusion. It cuts you off from others, for their needs pale in comparison to yours. At first, as you feed your greed it may feel good, but more and more of the same will devastate you. In the long run, greed becomes destructive and can never lead to happiness. When we seek love and can't find it we get greedy. We find other things as a substitute to compensate for that feeling of being loved. It is in the end a surrogate and an illusion.

Guruji always asks, '*How much can you stuff into this one orifice called the mouth? How many pizzas can you eat at one sitting? One...two... after that you have to run for Pepto Bismol to fight the heartburn. Eat a whole bag of candy and your blood sugar will go through the roof, drink a few gallons of soda and your immune system will break down.*' Greed arises because of the illusion that only after obtaining something will we be happy. So we become crazy in our desire to accumulate and we collect and buy until our homes overflow. Still there is no happiness.

During the construction boom in Florida a friend of mine thought he would cash in, so he quit his job and bought a dozen apartments. Of course his lifestyle changed. Then came the BMW and estate home. Like all waves this, too, came crashing down and suddenly he was on the verge of bankruptcy. His wife had to take two jobs to make ends meet and his daughter quit school and started working. There was no happiness here. If he had invested in one, maybe two apartments, maybe he would not have faced the stress of financial ruin.

It is important to note that desire or greed is not only for objects but also for experiences. In our short lifespan we want to cram in as many experiences as possible even if it means sleeping only for a few hours a day. We have to attend every party, every concert and every picnic, join several organizations and push our kids to do the same. We do this consistently, not pausing to enjoy and savor. Soon, given the entire sensory overload, there is burnout.

Happy with what you have?

Frederick Koenig, the German inventor of the printing press, said, *'We tend to forget that happiness doesn't come as a result of getting something we don't have, but rather of recognizing and appreciating what we do have.'*

When you are happy where you are, with no feverish desire to acquire more, that is true bliss. Only with self-awareness can you control yourself from hankering after what you do not have and save yourself from burnout. Just pause and see how rich your life is. You have what you need, right here, right now. You don't need to have one more thing to be happy. Your happiness exists right here right now in this present moment.

Greed, Ambition and Inertia

Absence of greed should not be confused with a lack of ambition. Ambition drives you to achieve and is a necessary force for you to act. When greed overpowers ambition and you want to succeed at any cost, without caring about others around you, that is when ambition becomes detrimental to yourself and to society. Ambition is positive only to the extent that your needs are met and in the process no one is hurt.

Absence of greed should not be confused with inertia. Inertia is when you do not act at all. It is laziness and a cop out. We need to act and be part of the world we live in but, at the same time, not let greed to dominate our actions. The ability to do this is the art of living and it comes only with self-awareness and with practice of right action. For that to happen, it is necessary to retreat to the Self, to the pure and untainted silence that is true joy. It is only in this refuge that you recognize greed as a distortion of love. Once there is self-awareness, it is easy to make the change.

I always wondered what it would be like to be rich, until someone sent me a quote which read, *'Don't covet what others have; you have no idea what their journey is like.'* They may have wealth, but no peace of mind: they may have achievements but no one to share it with. On the outside they may appear to be afloat while you struggle. But you cannot compare your journey. Happiness is a state of mind. It lies within you and is not connected with any event, object or phenomenon. It is your birthright, an invaluable mental state which cannot be quantified. Don't let greed spoil it.

20

Jealousy:
The Fourth Distortion of love

Jealousy towards someone can happen because of four reasons; money, fame, wisdom, or their partner.

—H.H. SriSri Ravishankar

Jealousy and envy sprout from seeds of a basic desire for bigger and better things, usually out of one's reach. It is natural to want to improve the quality of one's life, but important to recognize when the want becomes unrealistic. Desires arise within us all the time and vary in degree. How we deal with them can determine whether we allow jealousy or envy to overpower us or flow through and out of us. Great souls like SriSri allow desires to rise and fall without focusing on them. It is the lesser desires, like that for food or water, and the greatest of all desires, one for knowledge, which such souls focus on. Lack of self-awareness makes the rest of us hold on to desires, magnifying our needs and making the small mind control our thoughts and actions.

Envy prevents you from being in that state of bliss. The minute you envy something, it creates restlessness within you, an agitation that leads nowhere. Recognizing that jealousy leads nowhere is the first step in eliminating it from your life.

Jealousy is interconnected with greed and lust, and all the other distortions of love. When jealousy arises, it is because of lust (when you covet someone's partner), or greed (when you covet someone's possessions), or delusion (when you covet someone's fame).

SriSri clearly defines the arena of jealousy. Most of us are jealous for money and fame, a few for someone's partner and an even smaller number for another's wisdom.

My struggle with jealousy

In my feverishness to be a published author, I found myself looking at other author websites with a twinge of jealousy and envy. What was it that made them so successful, while I had to struggle? Why was it that they got an agent so easily, while I couldn't find one? Was my writing not good enough or was it my Karma? Why was my wait interminable? Was I ever going to reach my goal?

Not only was I jealous of their journey which, to me, seemed an apparently easy one, but it raised self-doubt on my own ability, lack of appreciation for my present state and feelings of inadequacy. The whole day I would be focused on my own sorry state, catch myself snapping at my husband and children and finding fault with everything around me. Even the food I cooked on that day would be tasteless, with no prana.

I don't know exactly when the realization came. It came in waves and at first I could do nothing but observe. At least I was able to see how jealousy and envy were destroying my happiness. No matter how much I wanted to be published, I knew that my desire would never become a reality until it was time. I could look at author websites night and day and long and hope, and be miserable, but that would not help me realize my dream. Then one day, I just decided that I was not going spoil one more day with feelings of hopelessness. In the beginning I forced myself to change my thought patterns, but soon it became more natural. As soon as I recognized feelings of envy and jealousy arising, a smile lit up my face as I converted the envy into a hope for a better and more prosperous tomorrow. I knew in my heart that their journey was so rich because of their past good deeds, and so I celebrated their success instead. That may sound impossible, but let me assure you that it's just like flipping a coin. On the other side is happiness and bliss and if you have to fake it initially, do that, because soon it will become part of your nature.

Suddenly, I was no longer a separate entity envying something outside of myself. I was able to feel a sense of belonging and participate in their success, almost as if it were my own. *Almost,* because even now, I do catch myself feeling that feverishness and that spark of jealousy, though most often it fades almost as soon as it rises. I don't really want to duplicate someone else's journey. My path is beautiful. I have everything I need, and I am everything I could be. My happiness lies in the here and now, and I am not willing to allow a few moments of envy rob me of that happiness.

A sense of separateness

As you read this, I am sure you are thinking of at least one situation where jealousy or envy consumed you. Perhaps you wanted that job, and if you had that job, perhaps you envied the BMW, and then if you owned one, then perhaps you wanted the three-car garage that merited housing the BMW, and then maybe you wondered how lucky the driver of the BMW was to live in that estate home. Stop the thoughts right there. Envy infects your mind and spreads all round you, affecting everyone you come in contact with. It arises because you see yourself as being separate and not part of the cosmos you live in. It comes from not appreciating your present moment, your present situation, and your present fortune. No matter where you are and what you own, there will always be someone who has a little more and someone, who has a little less.

Controlling Jealousy

How do you handle jealousy in others? Guruji says you need to recognize that emotions are just passing clouds. Such feelings rise and subside. When you sense jealousy in others, use superlatives to praise them, create a sense of belonging. Do something for them that makes them feel at an advantage. If they see you as being inferior, the jealousy will fade. Be humble with your talents. If only people had this awareness, hundreds of corporations may still be intact, countries united and families not bitterly torn apart. Try these techniques: As Guruji says, *'If everything fails, take a pillow and go to sleep. Your actions can help avert some jealousy, but ultimately you cannot control the world, only yourself.'*

Besides, what you see is on the surface. A good job, a fancy car, a brilliant website do not define a person or his situation. You don't know what the other person's journey is like. Life is full of challenges: health, money, fame, family. Everyone has a different basket of fruit. Everything is transient. It doesn't belong to you, it never did and soon you will have to leave all of it back here on Earth, so why be jealous and crave someone else's misery?

Nothing rings truer than a quote I read a few years ago that has stuck in my mind:

'Jealous people poison their own banquet and then eat it.'

21

Arrogance:
The Fifth Distortion of Love

So what if somebody recognizes you: "Oh, you are a wonderful person." So what? In that person's mind that thought came and went. It is also finished. That mind has gone. Maybe they have an attraction for you for some days, some months, so what? That also goes... it also goes.

—H.H. SriSri Ravi Shankar

All of us have confronted arrogance in the workplace. At some point in your career you might have encountered the power the boss wields over you, making you feel small, ingratiated and subservient. Arrogance destroys both the doer and the beholder, because it distorts reality, placing the ego on a false platform of superiority, imagined excellence and bogus rhetoric. Arrogance is born from a false sense of achievement, when the doer makes a claim to greatness above everyone else. It is that power which corrupts the mind and totally eclipses the love within. Arrogance creates sycophancy in political circles, obsequiousness in corporate ladders and blind adulation in spiritual platforms.

Arrogance and Pride

Arrogance must not be confused with pride, although in my humble definition, pride is the first hint of arrogance waiting to swell. Spreading the joy of your achievement allows others to participate in your success and be part of your expanding horizons. Taking pride in one's work and in one's achievements are essential for personal growth, but when you take that giant leap into arrogance, you cease to *share* your self-pride with others. You become obsessed with your accomplishments, which you see as yours and yours alone. Then you brandish your position of power like a lethal sword that keeps everyone at bay, ensures their fear of you and their apparent admiration for your success. Arrogance is pride without belongingness.

Arrogance and Self-Esteem

Self-esteem is that feeling of wellness that comes from a sense of accomplishment. It is the feeling of being useful in this world through accomplishing or contributing something. Self-knowledge leads to self-esteem contained and secure in itself. It doesn't need anyone else or anything else to remind itself of its completeness. The moment you look outside of yourself to develop a sense of who you are, you begin to tread dangerous ground. In order to move away from the arena of arrogance you require self-esteem. You need to value yourself in the first place before you take that leap into comparisons and contrasts.

According to Timothy Wong, an AOL teacher from Hong Kong, '*Everyone who is arrogant is actually missing self-esteem. They go hand in hand and arrogance is good as long as you learn your lesson by realizing it is the opposite of having self-esteem. Arrogance comes from the space that others are less valuable than you. You see your value as immeasurable and that of others as measurable. Self-esteem is that of acceptance and arrogance is that of non-acceptance of yourself and others. When you have high self-esteem you may or may not be perfect, others may or may not be perfect but you are okay with it.'*

When self-esteem develops via a process of self-knowledge, it leads to acceptance of others whether they are better or worse, good or bad, arrogant or humble and it is this essential quality that differentiates self-esteem from arrogance.

Arrogance and the Arts

Arrogance emerges when a person believes he is the master of his craft. I have never seen an artist openly praise another. After sitting through a compatriot's concert there is always a conciliatory remark about how something was amiss. A scathing review from an art critic can bury a budding artist's career in minutes. The famous movie critic, the self-styled expert in cinematography, can determine if the film will be a blockbuster or a failure. Renowned book critics can diminish a writer's career in one derisive review. Having such power makes them feel infallible, almost as if they have power to control life and death and this builds within them an arrogance that is insupportable.

My Father referred to his arrogant boss as the *'I specialist'*. That phrase jumps to mind every time I come across arrogant behavior. Arrogance is not just the shallow creed of corporate giants, political bigwigs and media gurus. You come across it every day in life. You must know someone to whom you were pouring out the deepest secrets from your heart, and in mid-sentence, they got bored, turned away to pick up a conversation with someone else. For all you know, you might be exhibiting arrogant behavior and are completely oblivious of its existence.

Arrogance and Awareness

It is humbling to remember everything you say or do has been said or done before. This life and this soul are ancient. It has been and will continue to be. All your actions are a mere flash in the context of the infinite cosmos. You are here today and gone tomorrow, and once you are gone, it doesn't matter if you are remembered or not. As SriSri says, *'Even if someone praises you, so what?'* Once the moment passes the thought is dead, and he has moved on to something else. The only way to understand whether your own actions or words are arrogant is through reflection and awareness, and that only comes from the silence of meditation. Practicing meditation allows a hundred percent awareness of word and deed.

Religion on Arrogance and Humility

Every known religion praises humility and warns against arrogance that leads only to delusion and disappointment. Here is a quote from the *Bhagavad Gita*, where Krishna warns Arjuna about the dangers of love's distortion, calling it the heritage of demons.

'Hypocrisy, pride, self-conceit, wrath, arrogance and ignorance belong, O Partha, to him who is born to the heritage of the demons.' ~ *The Gita, XVI. 4*

Muhammad warned people to watch out for arrogance, an impediment in creating loving and caring relationships. He gave it a divine reprimand by saying that Allah did not care for those who were haughty and arrogant.

The Almighty says, *'Do not avert your face from people out of haughtiness and do not strut about arrogantly on the earth, Allah does not love anyone who is vain or boastful.'*

The Bible says that, *'Blessed are the meek for they shall inherit the Earth.'* And I do believe they inherit the Kingdom of heaven right here on earth. SriSri speaks of this in one of his commentaries, where he praises Jesus for overturning popular concepts of strength conquering all, by saying that the meek inherit the earth. When you are encompassed in love you are the weakest. It allows the gentle and more nurturing facets of your nature to surface. Even Samson cried when overpowered with love for Delilah. Love can reduce the most powerful to tears. Yet it is love which belongs to the kingdom of heaven. In love there are no distortions, no anger, greed, lust, jealousy, arrogance or delusion. In pure love, your joy is free from blemish, and to get a glimpse of this kingdom of heaven we have to polish the tarnish that covers us and allow the burnishing gold of love within us to shine through and illuminate our path.

SriSri, using a contemporary analogy, says, '*It's like going to a car rental agency and choosing a car. Once you have picked a car, leave the parking lot and get on with your journey. Don't spend your time trying out different cars, because no matter which one you pick, it will take you to your destination.*'

22

Delusion:
The Sixth Distortion of Love

The mind is the hub around which this vicious cycle revolves, creating delusion in the minds of the deluded.
—Swami Venkatesananda (*Yoga Vasishta*)

The mind exists only by virtue of being nourished by prana, the life force within each one of us. When the prana disappears on death, the mind vanishes and the only traces carried are impressions created by our desires. The mind has a focused purpose of perception and unchecked, the mind strays into world illusion. (Maya)

In infancy the mind is attached to bodily needs which become the main priority. As we enter childhood, the concept of the ego develops and this ego sense feeds into the mind, setting the stage for delusion. Objects and people become vehicles of self-satisfaction; as time goes on, the child develops a connection to providers of food, nourishment and play. She sees the world as instruments to satisfy her needs; as caregivers we encourage this line of thinking until desires completely run her daily activities. The strong sense of '*I am*' converts into '*This is mine*' by teenage years.

Delusion and Desires

We are conditioned by the mind into believing what it presents to us as reality. The lifelong struggle between the Self and the mind begins in early adolescence. The mind, fired by the senses, cajoles you into believing you need something without which you will remain in a state of restlessness and misery. As we follow the dictates of the mind we get buffeted between choices and inevitably give in to overindulgence of the senses which ultimately leads to delusion. This distortion of love presents a plethora of situations and objects as desirable and then follows the downward spiral into greed, jealousy, lust, arrogance and anger, all of which signify dominance of the deluded mind.

A piece of chocolate piques the taste buds and is an apt end to a meal but overindulgence leads to breakouts or stomach upsets, yet the mind convinces you that the entire bar needs to be finished. Desires can become so powerful that they take control of your life, guiding all your effort towards satisfying the craving. Once the lustful desire is met, you are filled with regret and are left wasted, with little energy to do anything else. That moment is not one of happiness.

Delusion and Duality

Delusion by its very nature brings in the concept of duality, where you are separate from the world. The focus of a deluded mind is on satisfying urges. Your needs, values and principles trounce those of people around you. This is sometimes evident in relationships between lovers. Love itself is an exquisite emotion and fills you with a sense of completeness, taking you to your core. But what often happens between lovers is the need for one to own and control every emotion, feeling and action of a loved one. This results in fights and arguments, tears and anguish. The need to possess the other and own every aspect of the other demonstrates the duality of the deluded mind. If you were content in love and did not feel your partner was separate from you the need to possess would never be an option.

Similarly, parents believe that by virtue of giving life to their children they own every action and emotion of the child. Some parents are so overprotective and controlling, they organize every aspect of their child's life, from clothing and food to play dates. They insist on making career choices and choosing marriage partners for their children. It doesn't matter what the child needs or is capable of doing, or even what she wants to do: such parents think they know what is best for her. This strong attachment and need to control warps the relationship, resulting in severe and lifelong emotional and psychological effects on the child. Instead of embedding core values in the child and allowing them to flower, parents stifle the growth and beauty of children, believing that this child belongs to me and has to do what I want for her. If you could see the divinity in your child as being the same divinity in yourself, the need to manipulate would never arise. The connectedness and sense of belonging would be so strong that, automatically, the child would reflect their parents' values.

Delusion and *Moham*

The deluded mind makes you see separateness from people objects and situations. In order to have control over your actions, you develop attachment to people, situations and objects. The delusion here is that the attachment will make you happy. This attachment is known as *Moham* in Sanskrit. This mental conditioning appears to give a sense of pleasure but in truth is the carrier of grief. Delusion created by the mind is self-sustaining and grows in size, fed continually by the senses. It merely creates an illusion of pleasure by veiling self-knowledge. In spite of having temporary existence it deludes you into a sense of permanence and perverts all relationships and experiences. This river of delusion created by the mind is self-sustaining and grows in size, fed continually by the senses. There can be no liberation from the mind until this veil of ignorance is lifted to reveal the sole existence of that one supreme consciousness that exists in the present moment, mirroring the essence of the Brahman. As long as desires created by the mind are satisfied immediately without any evaluation, the mind will continually create world delusion, presenting objects and people and experiences for attachment. This results in misery when it becomes an obsession.

Life, then, is an endless struggle for control and meaning in a quest for harmony and peace. In reality it is this very attachment that binds you, destroying your peace of mind.

It is said in the scriptures that humanity was created from a tiny germ of love. When love is the core of our very existence and exists in the nucleus of every cell of our body, we spend lifetimes in search of love hoping that a fleeting embrace, a draught of Morpheus and whiff of fame, or glimmer of gold will provide that elusive moment of love and happiness. The wise and the fortunate turn inward and in a single moment of true bliss realize they are the love they seek.

23

Fears, Anxieties and Worry

What are you afraid of? What do you think you will lose? Just wake up and see you have nothing to lose in the first place. And even if you think you have something, how long can you hold onto it?
—H.H. SriSri Ravishankar

SriSri narrates a beautiful story that demonstrates the nature of fear. A man was given some seeds for a plant and he dutifully planted them. Then every day he watered it and, while doing so, he dug up the seed to check if it had sprouted roots. Every time he noticed there was no change, he felt anxious, thinking he had done something wrong and then the fear of *'What if nothing happens?'* arose in his mind. From this niggling doubt, his misgivings became even bigger. *'Maybe I should have planted the seed in a pot. Perhaps I am giving it too much water. Maybe I should move it to the front yard where it gets more sunlight.'* The mind became fixated on the seed and now he was worried what would happen in the event of the seed sprouting. *'What if it grows into a big tree, blocking out all the sunlight? Perhaps the roots might go under my small cottage and destroy the foundation.'* All of these thoughts turned towards the negative aspects of planting a seed and he was in a constant state of stress, doubting nature and his ability to nurture a plant. Nor was the mind at peace with the tree growing, for he also worried about the downside of having a large tree. All of these disturbing thoughts were sown by one little seed. That is all the mind needs to fester and blow out of proportion.

A little Fear is good

Total lack of fear, according to Guruji, is possible only in utter chaos or in utmost orderliness. It is this absence of fear that prompts the bravest of actions, when primal instincts kick in as the body is on high alert and survival mode. This is what allows you to apprehend a shooting gunman or save a drowning child. Every survivor of 9/11 has stories of remarkable bravery in the face of catastrophe.

A little fear is good as long as you don't hold onto it and make it the focus of attention. It is fear that allows self-preservation which is necessary for survival. Guruji says fear of death preserves life, fear of wrong maintains right, fear of sickness encourages hygiene and fear of misery makes you righteous.

Bringing the mind into the present moment allows you to pause and examine the depth and seriousness of your fear. It allows you to observe if it's justified and evaluate the extent to which you need to focus on it. Is it life-threatening for yourself or someone you care about? Or is it a small worry at the back of your mind that can be solved another day? You need one split second to make that analysis. If you see your fear as critical, you need to act at once. Do what is needed to thwart the danger you face. If the danger from your fear is not imminent, then just put it away. Realize that nothing is going to change by focusing on an unrealistic fear. Perhaps what you fear might never manifest.

The best remedy for combating fears is reposing in the faith that the Divine will never let you down and you will be cared for. The more you take comfort in prayer, the less threatening the fears. Just know that fears are mere shadows of the mind and most often have no real basis. They are developed from impressions you gather and from experiences of others. As Timothy Wong explains:

'Fear is also not accepting the present situation or the reluctance (resistance) of letting a situation go; positive or negative. It is a very subtle phenomenon in the mind that often derails our best intentions of doing something positive. Having a clear understanding of yourself through self-knowledge supports you and prevents you from being totally incapacitated by fearful thoughts. A distinction must be made between a fearful thought and a fearful situation. The skill is to distinguish between a life-challenging moment and a life-threatening situation. Clarity of mind and settled emotions in self-knowledge are very supportive for commanding fear and this is only realized through meditation.'

Doubts and worries

Worry is thinking about events that may or may not take place in the future.

—H.H. SriSri Ravishankar

Doubts and worries always center on the positive, never the negative. We always doubt the likelihood of good things happening in our life. *'I will never become a successful author'* or *'I can never find the right marriage partner'* or *'that perfect job will always elude me'*. There is never a hint of doubt about anything negative. If someone claims to hate you, that is believable, but if he says he loves you, your natural response would be *'Really?'*

Past and Future

Fears are generated by impressions from past experiences, projected onto the future, making the present moment stress-filled. Traumatic experiences from the past remain imprinted in the mind and convince you that in the future too, this pattern will prevail. One broken relationship does not mean no marriage is in store for you or that you will never get that second chance of finding the ideal mate who understands and loves you. Just because you got knocked over by an ocean wave does not mean swimming is not for you. It is how we condition our mind that dictates how we feel about situations in the present moment. Mental conditioning is so subtle yet so deep-rooted that, without a spark of awareness, we can never rid ourselves of doubt. We can never have faith that such actions and incidents occurred in the past and may not be the template for future events and experiences.

Worries, the Ego and eternity

Worry is a product of loving something that is not eternal.
—H.H.SriSri Ravishankar

Doubts and worries bind you to the ego and blow out of proportion the size and impact of possibilities, leaving you in a constant state of fear. The focus then becomes, '*What about me? What will happen to me if I never get a job? People think I'm useless so why try and make friends? Why does God choose me for his experiments with misery?*' One becomes so consumed with plight that self-pity becomes the only salve to heal the uncertainties of the mind.

The knowledge that past and future are connected by the present moment is a realization that helps eliminate these unnecessary fears. While you might have had problems in your relationships in the past, in this moment you are reborn. This is your opportunity to die to the past and create a new future. You have no idea what the future holds in store for you. It is totally in your hands and depends on the actions you take now. Be aware that you are holding onto thoughts and concepts that are fleeting. In a sense you are nurturing the shard of glass that causes the wound and rubbing it further into your injured flesh. Accustomed to being in a space of worrying, you have not tried surrendering and leaving things to the will of the Universe, because that requires a leap of faith:

Faith that nothing happens without a reason.

Faith that every experience is a learning experience.

Faith that the choice you make opens up your opportunities.

Faith that the universe knows what you need and provides for you.

Detecting thought patterns

One disastrous relationship can leave an impression so strong that it fills you with fear of forging new ones. There develops in all relationships and in life situations the underlying insecurity and fear that you are not good enough and will in all certainty be abandoned. There is deep-rooted fear of being judged and rejected. Bringing the mind into the stillness of the present moment allows you to examine your thought patterns and evaluate how this is currently impacting all your relationships and behaviors. Once you recognize the pattern, the awareness allows fear to be released and softened so you have no need to assign blame. Things happen; sometimes good and sometimes bad, and that's the flow of life.

Dialogue with the mind?

When you are blinded by fear, you lose perspective and sensibility. Fear creates separation. In separation we feel disconnected from the environment and with everyone around us. This feeling of being alone and unsupported further deepens our sense of fear, leading to an intense doubt of ourselves and our abilities. The irony is that by conversing with the mind you cannot soften the fear. Dialogue with an unsettled mind leads to even more confusion. The only way such fears can be addressed is by returning to the breath. In a state of fear your breathing gets ragged and uneven, your blood pressure rises and your body's faculties go on high alert to prepare for any eventuality. Slowing down the breath and the pulse with *Pranayama*, especially with *Ujjai* breathing, allows the mind to settle and secure itself in the present moment. Almost immediately the pulse slows down and the moment of panic lifts.

I had a recent experience with the efficacy of this technique a few months ago.

I was getting my nails done when my manicurist Olga got a call from a relative in Colombia. By the expression on her face, I knew something was not right. She looked very upset and when I enquired, she told me it was her nephew calling from Medellin, Colombia. He had faced rejection all his life and battled with his parents who, he felt, hated him and so he wanted to kill himself. In five minutes the young boy Juan called again and I could hear Olga pleading with him not to do it. I was horrified, expecting any moment for her to say he killed himself. What anguish and anxiety could cause an 18-year-old to commit suicide? This was the moment where he had a full life ahead of him and was on the threshold of bigger and better things; an education, a prosperous career and loving relationships. I knew I had to do something. However, never having been in this predicament before I had no idea what to do. I closed my eyes and asked myself what Guruji would have done and prayed for his guidance. Then I instructed Olga to make him lie down and I began the deep Ujjai breathing, instructing him to follow. Olga translated into Spanish and as we proceeded through a guided meditation with a beam of healing light passing through each chakra, I could hear fewer tears. When the light reached his heart center, the one that monitors love, hate and fear, he broke down once again into heart-wrenching sobs. In another five minutes he seemed calm and disconnected the call. In the meantime, I called someone in AOL Bogotá to get in touch with him. Ten minutes later, he called back saying he felt much better and the feeling had passed. It was really a miracle. I knew that his call to kill himself was a deep cry of anguish, a desperate search to reach out for help.

The Universe provides in strange ways and I don't claim any responsibility for doing anything other than what occurred to me naturally. The rest panned out according to what was intended for him. But in that moment I realized the amazing healing powers of the breath, the strength of thought and transmission of energy which earlier, I did not believe possible. My faith and belief was now set in concrete.

On the path with no anxiety

Sonia Mehra, from California is so grateful she came to the Path. She is filled with a sense of purpose and while she has no idea what the future holds, she has no worries:

'I have zero anxiety about the future; I am in the most contented time of my life wherever I am. I know I will survive, I will serve others and I don't need anything, I have so many tools and services to offer. The universe takes care of me. I will always have food to eat and a place to sleep and I will do Guruji's work. That's all I know.'

She attributes her peace of mind to the Grace of the Guru. Her job is stressful but she lives in the present moment with no worries about her future.

Ramakrishna from South Africa attributes his fearless state to his Sadhana. (Practices of breathing and meditation) *'The element of fear has left me. I can die this minute and nothing bothers me. I have learned more in the last four years than in the thirty years before. When I stop Kriya, the fears come back. The antidote for fear is kriya, satsang, seva and sadhana.'*

Anirvachan from Nigeria whose battle with cancer I described earlier, now has a stress-free life. He has become a full-time teacher filled with a higher sense of purpose and is dedicated to caring for this world. Every time he needs something the Universe provides. He recalls a time when he wanted to attend the 30th anniversary celebrations in Berlin but had neither the money nor the means to get there. But temporary work turned up and against all odds he got his visa. With less than a $100 in his pocket he reached Berlin and found a Bed & Breakfast free of cost! And not one night did he sleep hungry.

'I went with no care in the world and was taken care of. Fear about the future is nonexistent for me. Guruji is sending me to Nigeria and people have warned me about the violence on the streets but I have no fear. I know I am completely taken care of. It is so precious to live your life this free.'

24

The Greatest fear: Death

Death brings you in touch with the reality of life.
—H.H. SriSri Ravishankar

Perhaps the greatest fear we have is that of our own mortality. Once born, surely we will die; yet, in the interim, we immerse ourselves in the impossible task of delaying the inevitable. Most of our actions in living are designed to avert death and many of our cravings and desires exist because in this short lifespan we want every conceivable experience with maximum enjoyment. In many ways this fear of death is caused by a complete lack of understanding of the laws of nature. It just seems so final. We have so much attachment to the body that the thought of dropping it fills us with gloom. As Pawan Mulukutla explains:

'Behind every fear the only fear is that of death. When you learn to meditate you realize that life prepares you for the inevitable. My fear has reduced so much. When I meditate, the mind becomes so still, the body has completely dropped and there is only silence and stillness. You become part of space. When you realize that is the death experience, your fear drops.'

Death Meditation

In every Art of Silence course there is a death meditation. Attending such a course, when I was told what we were about to do, I went ice cold. I was terrified. What if I died and never returned? Moving with the in-breath and out-breath, the inhalation and exhalation, Guruji guided us through the birth and death process. Instead of the panic I expected to feel, there was serenity, a merging with a sense of vastness much bigger and more peaceful than I ever imagined. I was in a space, with no room for the mind. Immersed in meditation, I had dropped the body and couldn't feel anything but peace, hear anything other than Guruji's serene voice, see anything but inky blackness that simultaneously seemed illuminated. My senses ceased to exist and with it the mind shut down. I had the experience of leaving the body while still in it. And there was not a trace of alarm. When I opened my eyes I was actually relieved. The fear in my heart had just vanished. The earlier panic at the thought of death was not there.

Sleep and Death

SriSri explains the dynamics of death during his discourse of *Kenopanishad*. He explains that moments before leaving the body, the sense of touch wanes and numbness embalms the body. The senses fade into oblivion, the last to leave is the sense of vision. The self then snaps out of the body. The feeling is similar to descending into a deep sleep. In sleep, if you pay attention, the last thought before sleep is the first one when you awaken. Similarly, in death the final thought before leaving the body is the first one on re-entering the next one. This is why suicide is so misguided. The exact circumstance you wished to escape will present itself on rebirth, because you need to burn the Karma, undergo the trials presented to you and come out of it with learning and fewer impressions. It is also why your last thought should be of the divine. As Mahatma Gandhi fell after he was shot by Nathuram Godse, his last words were '*He Ram!*' (Oh God!) If a man who personified non-violence met his end in such a violent manner, how can we ordinary mortals escape from the path carved by Karma? In that moment, when Gandhiji recognized he would leave this earthly existence he had already merged with the divine.

According to Shalin Desai, an AOL teacher, understanding death gives a new perspective to life. '*You realize that things happen, life happens, that is all a part of creation. Life and death is the phenomenon but it's not just happening to you.*'

His recommendation? '*Feel love but put life and death in perspective. It helps people deal with loss in a better way.*'

Loss of a loved one

Sometimes this is easier said than done because the fear of death is not merely for oneself; the greatest fear is in losing a loved one.

Dr. George Lavrelashvili from Georgia had to deal with the death of his parents. His father had died when he was much younger. It was a traumatic memory because he had been talking with his father at the moment he died. So naturally, when his ailing mother was at death's door, George was terrified; he didn't want it to happen:

'*About a month after the course, just listening to all the knowledge and doing my practices there was an inner transformation. No doubt a loved one is no more around you but you know that their journey continues. I now even believe in Karma and reincarnation, and this gives me solace.*'

Through sadhana Pia Lahdenpera was able to shake off this burden from the past and accept death if it were to come her way. Her cancer, which she battled for a few years, is now in remission and while she goes for annual checkups, the fear has vanished. As an AOL teacher she teaches many groups of cancer patients, hoping to share with them techniques that released her from the bondage that the fear of death had created.

'I taught a course of 20 cancer patients, all of whom were terrified of death. One girl was brought in by her mother. Her whole body was a shout of pain. Her mother didn't want to leave her. She couldn't fly because her wings were broken. Step by step with the breathing and the processes, her bondage and pain was released. The last day she was soaring like an eagle. I can never forget that. All her pain, her suffering vanished.'

Near Death Experience

Death it would seem is inevitable but if it is not your time, miracles can happen. Dushyant Savadia joined AOL in 1999, and has been a teacher for 11 years. He said he had a movie-style life. Born in Orissa, at 15 he started drinking and smoking. At 18, he was almost an alcoholic drinking virtually a liter of rum daily and smoking 30-40 cigarettes. With both parents working in the family store business, from a very young age he and his brother were raised by servants. Alone at home after school, it was easy to slip into bad company and, unfortunately, Dushyant had easy access to money. He would go to the store and put his hand into the cash box and take what he needed and then do whatever he wanted with that money. Chasing girls and partying became his pastime. He was such a violent and angry person that at the drop of a hat, he wouldn't hesitate to beat people up. He was also a gang-leader. Anyone challenging his authority saw the rough edge of his anger. Being an extrovert got him into trouble all the time.

As time passed, his parents got fed up of bailing him out of trouble and literally threw him out of the house, that too in the middle of the night. He had no choice, so he went to the train station and decided whichever train came, would be his destiny. Reaching Delhi, he started doing odd jobs and eventually got a decent job in a company, but his bad habits remained.

Soon, a family friend very forcefully suggested he take the course. Even though he enjoyed the course he continued with the drinking and smoking, though in lesser quantities. Nine months later, he met Guruji in Kerala for the first time, and that was the moment of transformation, when Dushyant realized he was born to do Guruji's work. Though Dushyant never completed his graduation, within the year he became an AOL teacher. He claims his real education was through Guruji.

For three years he was not in touch with his parents. When he went back for the first time dressed in a traditional *Dhoti Kurta* they were shell shocked. They couldn't believe it. In fact they dissuaded him from following a Guru, but he didn't budge.

'*Had I not gone through these events, if I had not gone out of control, my father would not have let me leave home ever and then I would not have met my Guru. I don't see my colorful past as something adverse. That was the path laid out for me to leave that town and merge with my Guru, for whom I was born.*'

In the year 2000, Dushyant was declared physically dead. He was in Chennai, India at the time and contracted a rare virus called Guillain-Barre Syndrome, a very rare virus that attacks the nervous system. As he drank water it dribbled out of the side of the mouth. His fiancée, who was a doctor, noticed the beginning of paralysis and rushed him to the hospital. Within two hours the virus progressed and paralyzed his limbs and back, and he went into complete paralysis. The virus paralyzed his optic nerves and respiratory muscles and would soon paralyze the heart. The doctors said they had no hope and it was now in God's hand.

His fiancée was expecting him to die any minute. He was on a respirator and his pulse was almost nonexistent. She called his uncle in Delhi to inform him, who then immediately called

Guruji, who was in Germany at the time. Guruji picked up the phone and the first thing he said was *'Haan kya hua Dushyant ko?' 'What has happened to Dushyant?'* His uncle informed him that Dushyant was no more, that he had passed away in the hospital, to which Guruji replied, *'Nothing will happen. I am here now and he has plenty of work to do.'* He then instructed him to have someone whisper the mantra, *'Om Namah Shivaya,'* in Dushyant's ear. *'Wake everyone up and have them chant the same.'* In the middle of the night his uncle gathered a group of friends in satsang and they chanted, praying for Dushyant.

Dushyant, at the time, was aware of his surroundings but couldn't move. His fiancée told him what Guruji had said and that was a transforming moment for Dushyant. In that instant, there was a revival of strength in him and a feeling of confidence. He knew nothing would happen because it was the Master's wish that he live. *'I felt the sensation of a wheel revolving between my brows and then I saw a bright golden light and just dissolved in it.'*

Forty minutes later Dushyant woke up at the hospital. He had left his body, seen the other side and returned. The paralysis had disappeared and his pulse was normal. He was able to move and suddenly sat up. The doctors were shocked. A person who was in total paralysis just a while ago was perfectly alright. It was a miracle. He asked for the feeding tube to be removed because he wanted a drink. They brought a stretcher for him but he refused, preferring to walk twenty meters to the adjacent room. He walked out of the hospital a week later.

The first thing Dushyant did was to go and thank Guruji for saving his life. Guruji looked at him and said, *'I didn't do anything, I just gave a mantra and I supposed it worked.'* Guruji never claimed any responsibility. When Dushyant and his fiancée shared this experience in Chennai in Guruji's presence, the Master just listened and smiled. Then he said, *'The power of Sudarshan Kriya was more potent than a virus. It is the one pointedness and the devotion that caused this miracle.'*

Death and Karma

After listening to Dushyant's story I was convinced of the power of Sudarshan Kriya. Every story and interview I conducted revealed the same transformation—that life was rough before coming to the Path and Sadhana made everything alright. I couldn't imagine that death would come prematurely to people who were on the Path. I forgot about the powerful role that Karma plays and that while the Master can avert some tragedies, others are beyond his control. So when I spoke to Lekha Chari and Paramita Bhatt, both AOL teachers, and heard their stories, it threw me into a whirlwind of confusion. I couldn't believe anything so traumatic could happen to a devotee as she held Guruji's hand. It took me a while to process this experience and realize that death is inevitable. Coming to the Path, doing Sudarshan Kriya and meditation helps us not to hold onto the form and grieve neither for the dead nor the living. It gives us the unique ability to accept and surrender to the inevitable and maintain equanimity of mind.

Lekha Chari's closest friend introduced her to the Art of Living and had been her spiritual guide. Two years later, this friend passed away from cancer. She wanted to live and was so enthusiastic but that's what was written for her, and she came to terms with this destiny when she did her last Silence course. Lekha, however, was devastated when she heard of her terminal illness. She kept asking, '*Why? Was this because God needed me to have the strength to handle her loss? To understand that life is bigger than what we think?'* It was difficult to accept that in a few months she would leave this world. But time was a great healer and, slowly, understanding dawned within Lekha, giving her the strength to bear the loss.

'*I was no longer angry. I prayed for a miracle and then slowly when I realized the inevitable, I accepted it. I felt this was meant to happen. She was instrumental in getting me on the path so I might have the right attitude and strength. Each day improves my mindset. Every time I breathe out a minute particle of fear leaves my body.*'

Paramita Bhatt joined AOL when it was still in its infancy and has known Guruji intimately through the years. Living in the D.C. area she was instrumental in promoting the knowledge, hosting courses in her home as well as weekly satsangs. Her whole family is deeply spiritual and devoted to the Guru. In fact they epitomized the Art of Living, leading normal lives and holding well-paying jobs in a spirit of dispassion.

Paramita really wanted to attend the 30th Anniversary celebrations in Berlin and her husband encouraged her to go. In hindsight it was almost as if he pushed her to leave along with their son and her mother, saying he couldn't accompany them. It seemed as if he wanted to be alone. She spoke to him from London and then flew in to Berlin. After speaking with her he went to work on his motorcycle and was hit by a truck that instantly killed him.

On reaching Berlin, her son logged onto the Internet and saw a message from his sister informing them about their father's demise, urging them to return immediately. Paramita reacted to the horrific news in a strange manner:

'*I was really serene and calm, no tears. My facial expression didn't change and I wondered what to do.*' Her son was crying so much he couldn't breathe and her mother was in a semi-coma. This was like an earthquake; her life was finished. She called her friends to book a return flight and told them she needed to speak to Guruji *right away*. Guruji called her and fifteen minutes later he was in her room.

'*He sat in my room and very few words left his mouth but his presence was so powerful. I was feeling abnormal and I wanted to stay here and then leave after the celebrations, if that's what Guruji wanted.'*

She was shocked at her reaction. Had she gone crazy? Why was she not reacting like a normal person? Was Guruji just removing all her pain? Her consciousness was at such a high level that events were not touching her. She thought of the very first knowledge point in the Part 1 course, about the present moment being inevitable. Now she was living the knowledge, the truth of the moment hitting home in such an inconceivable manner. She had lost her husband and realized that this event had nothing to do with her mental state. Her mind was focused on what to do next. She was with Guruji, the closest she could be to the divine. What else did she need?

'Everyone thought I was in denial, that it had not hit me yet. This event was supposed to happen and He kept me in his lap. The most earth-shaking event in my life and I am in the physical presence of the divine. How many people can have that fortune?'

He kept saying *'aisa nahin hona tha.'* 'This should never have happened.' Nothing else. He insisted she return and do the ceremonies and that he would call her on the 13th day.

They returned home, completed the rituals and today Paramita is just moving on. Her son was very angry with Guruji who, he believed, could have prevented this from happening. The trauma of losing his father affected him deeply. There was physical pain in his chest and he could not understand why his father had to go in this harsh and cruel way.

Guruji was to come to the D.C. center three months later and her son Fenil wanted to meet him. He was perplexed about death and by now completely broken. He had so much anger and so many questions. As usual the crowd was milling around the Master and there seemed little chance of seeing him but Fenil insisted he wanted to meet Guruji one-on-one. This was going to be next to impossible. The Master knows when a devotee needs him and Guruji asked everyone to leave the room except Paramita and Fenil, who stared in disbelief.

They spent the next fifteen minutes pouring their hearts out, going back and forth between gratitude, disbelief and distrust in the Master and the Divine. She was sobbing and falling in weakness and Guruji put her head on his lap and allowed her to cry.

He said her husband would take a form in her family and in reality there were no answers. And at this point Paramita ranted: *'Guruji, I don't trust you anymore. No knowledge point makes any sense to me. I just don't care, I don't trust you at all. Where were you and what were you doing at that time? I want him back. I'll believe in you if you can bring my husband back.'* He didn't answer. She waited and continued. *'For whom shall I live? What have you done to my life? I devoted my entire life to you and is this what I get? My husband was a gem. What did he do to deserve such a death? Why such a miserable end to this physical body? What is this Karma to find death under a truck?'*

Guruji was quiet, listening and allowing both mother and son to vent. What could he say? In reality there is no answer. You have to accept death and move on with life. He could not get him back.

Paramita has not yet resolved her grief. She has not yet accepted her fate. She is angry with her husband for leaving her alone. When I spoke to her she said of late she had stopped her sadhana, the only thing that could conceivably give her the strength to carry on. The following excerpt is a direct transcript of my words to her.

Paramita: *'I just exist now. I cannot talk of love I can't even do my practices.'*

I listened to her in silence and then I spoke. I hope my words gave her some solace.

Kanchana: *'Nobody should face this but if this is your Karma, you just have to face it and then you need the tools. You have to continue with the Kriya. Life goes on and you have to go on. You have a role to play and many more things to do. Much more is coming your way. You are there to show people what it is possible to be.'*

'Be with the feeling and it will pass. Things will change. There is too much emphasis and delusion with the physical. The loss is ours, not that of the spirit which has found release.'

'Be with the formless, don't focus on his physical body… be with the spirit. By asking why or how, does it solve your problem? It is what it is. Don't search for answers. Focus on yourself and the children. What's happened is over. Now what can we do? You didn't ask to be born; you didn't choose the people to walk the journey with you. Your journey is alone. This, too, shall pass; everything does. You have a force within you and plenty to do. Be in this moment, accepting everything and move through it. When you feel, "why did this happen to me?" remember; it is what it is. You are still alive and breathing. You will find the motivation and zeal. It takes time processing it. You will be angry and shouting and going through the seesaw of emotions but in the end it will pass. Kriya and Sadhana give you the strength. The mental resistance asks questions. It has to be dropped the only answer is that there is no answer. No one knows why you were chosen to go through this. You have to find within yourself to become the supreme source of inspiration for others, you cannot give up.'

Paramita listened silently and my prayer is that time has helped heal the wound and she has found the strength to move on. Death is difficult to deal with. Many emotions overwhelm us, anger, a sense of abandonment, fear of solitude and uncertainty about the future. Refocusing on the formless allows the emotions to go through and burn out. There has to be a period of grief; it is only natural, but after that, you have to let the departed spirit continue on his journey. It helps to imagine you are saying goodbye at the airport and watching the plane soar into the sky, bound for another destination. In your heart there is sorrow but you know you will see him again. And it may be sooner than you think.

Avoiding Death: the greatest Delusion

The biggest of all delusions is thinking that death will never visit you. Remembering you are not the only one who faces loss helps put things in perspective. Each and every one of us will have to face the death of a dear one at some point in our lives. We will grieve and then learn to move on. The mind deludes you into *moha maya*, a feeling of attachment with the departed loved one and it tells you that life without that person is not worth living. It brings back old memories and makes you believe that those past images are better than anything that could possibly take place in the future. This mental conditioning has to be broken. You have to recognize that the past is done with. It's over. All you have is the now, the present moment and this is the time to use the knowledge to break away from the grief. Recognize that bigger and better things await you and that you have to get into that stillness of the moment for intuition to take over and guide your future activities. The Grace of the Divine is always with you; your mind just never allows you to see it. Drop the mind for one instant and see that the Universe is aligned to your desires. Ask of the Divine and it shall be done. If you ask for your loved one to be returned, that, too, might happen, but he may appear in another form. Then will you be able to recognize him?

The only salve for healing the wound of loss, is time. As time moves on the pain lessens to a dull throb and after some time it becomes a distant memory. You can never forget the person but the wrenching and torture of absence disappears.

Yes. Death is inevitable, yet the deluded mind cannot see it. We don't want to think about it and don't want to dwell on its certainty.

I will leave you with a couple of verses from the *Bhagavad Gita:*

Jatasya hi dhruvo mrtyur dhruvamjanma mrtasyacha

Tasmad apariharyerthe na tvam sochitham arhasi

Death is as sure for that which is born, as birth is for that which is dead. Therefore grieve not for what is inevitable.

—Bhagavad Gita Chapter 2. Verse 27

Sri Bhagavan Uvacha

Asochyan anvasochas tvam pragyavadams cha bhasase

Gatasun agatamsum cha nanusochanthi pandithah

The Lord spoke

You have grieved for those that should not be grieved for

Yet you speak words of wisdom.

The wise grieve neither for the living nor for the dead.

—Bhagavad Gita Chapter 2.

25

Drop Your Expectations

Act without expectation, it relaxes and rewards.
　　　　　　　　　　　　　　　—H.H. SriSri Ravishankar

No act is ever committed without expectation. From important events like marriage, jobs and education to trivial actions like brushing your teeth or eating breakfast, we expect a result from action. That is how the mind is conditioned and this habituation prompts action. When you brush, you expect clean teeth and when you eat breakfast, you expect to feel full. Such acts are undertaken through the day, with little or no attention attached to the fruit of such actions. If a little plaque is left on the teeth, the next trip to the dentist will take care of it. And if you are still hungry after breakfast you can always pick up a snack later. There is little emotion attached to such acts, and therefore little importance given to them. But our priorities change with certain activities we believe are crucial for survival, to a feeling of well-being, or that give status and add to our feelings of importance.

For me, it is education and cooking. When I went to school I had to get that A. I worked hard and expected results. Similarly when I cook, I do so with a hundred percent effort, because I believe that food provides essential prana, and my cooking performs a vital service. I am proud of my cooking and I love being complimented. It gets disappointing when there is too much or too little salt in the food and someone passes a disparaging comment. No matter what, I cook with love, a fundamental ingredient which transforms the taste of food. At times the fact that my family expects me to always cook brings a scowl on my face. I can't help wishing someone else could take over the kitchen even if it is for a day. Frankly I can't decipher whose expectation is misplaced; mine or my family's!

Every person has a different list of priorities where their expectations are high. For one it could be dress and punctuality, whereas for another it could be job performance or money. When some event rises in your esteem, you attach emotional links to it and success or failure in it determines your state of mind, dictating ensuing happiness or misery. For an entrepreneur it is monthly profit, for the artist it is a sale and for the writer it is publishing success. As adults we are aware of expectation in our sphere of interaction. Children are not born with expectation but learn about it very quickly: '*If I cry I will be fed; if I scream, I will get the candy and if I throw a tantrum, Mummy will hug me.*' Adults also build expectations based on their interaction with their offspring. They train and get trained to expect results with specific actions. They expect obedience, discipline and above all gratitude from their children.

While we have a set of expectations for ourselves, it doesn't stop there. Our expectations extend to others around us. We have expectations of and for our family and friends, for political figures and spiritual leaders. Everyone is expected to behave in a certain way and when they fall short, we demonstrate disappointment. Such expectations are a byproduct of socialization, group norms affected by family, society and media. We are hardly aware of the number of expectations we have regarding almost every facet of our lives, until we face disappointment. Only then do we become aware of all the preceding built-up hope.

Expectation and disappointment have a direct correlation; the greater the expectation the greater the disappointment and vice versa. It is impossible to live in this world without expectation. But it is possible to dissociate oneself from getting emotionally involved with the fruits of action. For this to happen, it is necessary to have awareness, to be in the here and now and to understand that with expectation comes disappointment, which is then followed by overwhelming guilt, preventing you from functioning normally and robbing you of happiness.

My daughter had imposed very high academic standards on herself, which stemmed from her association with high performers in school. She checked the school website for updates on her grades twice a day, and was frustrated when her scores did not match her expectation. While I as a mother wanted her to succeed in school, I knew it would not happen if she did not focus on the means to the end: the coursework, the tests and the learning curve. It was important for her to enjoy the process and I told her that repeatedly. This year she was blessed with excellent teachers, and chose subjects she loved. She brought her work home and we discussed US history, politics and economics continually. She enjoyed the process so much that, without realizing it, she reinforced what she learned in school, and so the 'As' came seamlessly.

What happens when we get caught up in results is that we lose sight of the process. Our mind constantly hovers over possible events and eventualities which could play out in the future, over which we have no control. So how can you stop the expectation? *By bringing your mind back to the present.* When you catch yourself feverishly involved in future plans that is the time to bring yourself back to the present. Do what you have to do with intention and faith and know that the Universe will align itself to your objective and realize your dreams and goals.

As a teacher in a classroom I always expected more from the high achievers and almost nothing from the students at the bottom of the class. The more you achieve, the higher the expectation. In India because of paucity of good schools, children are enrolled in tutorials to pass entrance exams for a handful of elementary schools. The need to secure admission is crucial, and the disappointment and shame from failure are overwhelming. Children are at a heightened level of stress, and this interferes with their natural performance and masks their true abilities. Here in the United States, I have noticed Indian parents generally want their children to only become doctors, lawyers or engineers. This stifles their natural talent preventing them from flowering in new and unexplored avenues. As September approaches the phone calls begin to find out whose child scored what on the SAT's, and which college accepted whom. Your children better win the Spelling Bee, get the National Merit Scholarship or at the very least, be recommended for the Silver Knight Awards. This becomes a major source of stress for children and parents alike. Ask me. My daughter in the 11th Grade was caught up in the swirling and raging currents of tests like the SAT's AP's and ACT's. I refused to be drawn into the game and wanted my child to prepare for college free from expectation and external pressure. At the same time she needed to realize her maximum potential. This meant, on a daily basis, I walked the fine line between creating stress from expectation, while being nurturing and encouraging. Every day was a challenge to focus on the present; on preparation and intention without creating fears with '*I told you so*' and '*if only*'. I was not about to convert college entrance into a scary monster looming over her future.

Parental expectation added to societal anticipation makes failure unacceptable for the child, who feels she has to succeed at all costs. It doesn't stop there. Once you enter the portals of Ivy League or state colleges, you are thrown into a peer group of high achievers. Now it becomes even more difficult to maintain your GPA, and the stress mounts until it becomes intolerable. With her vast experience, Dr. Neelam Raval believes that in

India, depression is not as common amongst the youth as much as in middle age. However in total numbers, suicide amongst youth has definitely increased. The stress of having to prove themselves in their studies and education drives them to it. Kids go to school in the mornings and for tuition classes in the afternoons. From infancy we teach children to be competitive and prove themselves. Though the middle class has more money, with it has come fierce class competition. This unfortunately has had a deep impact on the student's psyche.

Most students cope, but some succumb to the pressures and either drop out and accept their failure or graduate with low grades. A few unfortunates, unable to handle the stress, commit suicide. It is regrettable that our unreal expectation drives our children away from life and creates unnecessary stress and fear of failure. Instead, how wonderful it would be to navigate them to success by accepting them in totality and being completely happy.

Gurpreet Singh is a volunteer with the Art of Living from Pune, India. After completing his schooling from Jamshedpur in eastern India, Gurpreet went to pursue higher studies in a prestigious college of engineering—the Indian Institute of Technology (IIT) in Mumbai. The entrance exam was rigorous and the curriculum exacting on even the most brilliant and studious. With only 9000 seats available for all engineering colleges, 1 in 61 is selected for the IIT's. For Gurpreet, pressure to merely pass the exam was overwhelming. He was aware that only the fittest survived. Students slept little and spent most of their time studying. With few recreational outlets, the pressures mounted steadily. Many students buckled under the stress, succumbing to drugs and alcohol. Others fell deep into depression. This was what happened with Gurpreet.

'When I joined professional college after my 12th Standard (A level), I was drained with all the effort it took staying up nights to study every day. Being an introvert, I made few friends in two years,

which were mostly devoted to rigorous engineering college preparatory study.'

His college experience was quite contrary to his initial expectations and the study routines and constant pressure of tests and exams dulled his senses. He was sucked into a hopeless situation, mounting academic pressure, lack of outlets for the emotional buildup within. The only escape seemed to lie in ending his life.

Entering the second year, the rungs began to give way and he scraped through the first semester with scarcely passing grades in all subjects. After this, things went further downhill as he had a backlog of classes, little or no motivation to study and no spirit to kindle interest in life. Two students committed suicide on campus and Gurpreet also contemplated the same. With no spiritual guidance, the mind wandered to cheap pleasures which only momentarily satisfied, leaving him with even more prolonged periods of guilt, blame and despondency. He could not share his failure with his parents because he was their only hope and their disappointment would compound his depression. It seemed as though his degree was floating away from him and there was no end in sight.

There were weeks where he just attended two hours of classes. (out of eighteen) He stopped running or jogging, a passion earlier. In fact he ceased all activity, and lost all sense of time and space. He stumbled through the day satisfying his basic needs and would eat when hungry, and sleep when tired. All interaction with the outside world stopped and Gurpreet was boxed into a lonely, dark and incomprehensible world.

Somehow Gurpreet went through those two grueling years. The following year, he was forced to take a semester break from school. His parents took him to see a psychiatrist. He was diagnosed with depression and prescribed antidepressant medication. Initially, he had little or no relief from the pills. He could not tell the difference in his behavior and mood whether he took the pills or not. Over the next few years he changed several medications and doctors, but the despondency and lack of vitality remained. The medication allowed him to function, but he was still not happy. Gurpreet's parents were ashamed of his condition. They feared Indian stigmas attached to mental conditions in social circles, and did not encourage him to appear in public.

Gurpreet had heard about Art of Living in his first year of college. It was a reasonably popular movement in college but, like most young adults his age, Gurpreet believed he was in control of his life. When he heard that Sudarshan Kriya was a set of breathing exercises that brought inner transformation, he was fiercely skeptical:

'I felt like I didn't need a guru or anyone else to tell me how to lead my life, let alone instruct me how to breathe!' In all my interviews, I have seen this identical initial reaction to AOL and Sudarshan Kriya in particular. When life carries on smoothly no one cares about an option that could better their situation. How could it? In their opinion, life is as good as one can hope for. It is only when people are faced with a situation they cannot handle, and their life spirals out of control, that they begin searching for a solution and take solace in spirituality. After his third year, when Gurpreet rejoined school after a semester break, he was on anti-depressants. When a friend suggested he try the Part I course, he took it.

'The course was great and I loved it. The sessions were very interactive and just what I had been looking for.' The Kriya gave him a momentary high but he did not continue his practice and so did not benefit from the effects of prolonged Sadhana. The medication was working. He felt normal and occasionally when he felt low, he used the Kriya to boost his mood. In his fifth year he started attending the weekly Satsangs at a friend's house.

After graduating from college, he took a momentous decision and spent a memorable four months at the Bangalore Ashram during which he did TTC1. (Teachers Training Course –Phase I)

Living close to the Master changed many things for Gurpreet. *'Guruji was very warm and supportive and that I think was the basis of my recovery. I felt I belonged. I felt I meant something to him and other people.'*

He has moved on and has several achievements under his belt. It was as if a ray of sunshine had broken through rainclouds and he relinquished his turbulent past like a bad dream.

'It is a wonderful, new and beautiful sentiment, quite distant from the feelings of uselessness and helplessness I used to have. There are still many milestones to achieve before I can say that I belong to the mainstream but I truly believe I am on the right path. It is just because of the Art of Living, Gurudev, people, satsang, sadhana, service, silence and smiles, that this was possible.'

Gurpreet was forced into a stressful situation without being equipped with the appropriate mental skills necessary to face his daily problems. Suicide was really not about to solve anything. Such escape is illusory, an act committed in a moment of insanity leaving behind a trail of tears. Gurpreet would have had similar dilemmas in past lifetimes and if he had succumbed to the temptation the saga would have continued. But he is fortunate he found a safety net and meaning in his life, transforming his future choices and destiny. As long as he was in the grip of depression nothing could make him see the clear and beautiful prospects the future held. It was a long and painful journey but eventually he was able to overcome his problems and walk on the path to self-discovery and unlimited joy.

26

Self-esteem and Confidence

Have respect for the Self and no one can take your self respect.
—H.H. SriSri Ravishankar

Self-esteem, self-concept and self-worth are all used interchangeably to describe the mental picture we have of ourselves and how much we value that image in the context of the world we live in. Those comfortable with their vision have high self-esteem and others tend to possess a diminished view of themselves. Since self-esteem is really an assessment and not an absolute value, it is very much a product of socialization. It is a comparison and contrast against a backdrop of societal norms, family values and the existing culture we live in.

Most often we use yardsticks like a good job, a good relationship, success in school and career to measure how we feel. Low self-esteem results in a lack of confidence and has a negative impact on all our interactions. As Timothy Wong, an AOL teacher from Hong Kong has pointed out earlier, self-esteem is a necessary foundation, but when misplaced it can lead to arrogance. The difference between the two is that arrogance elevates oneself above and beyond everyone else whereas self-esteem, being more inclusive, is a state in which you feel good about yourself and can recognize worthiness in others. A healthy self-concept is essential to feel enthusiasm about life and develop motivation for all activities. A lack results in depression and suicidal tendencies, stemming from commonly expressed, '*I am not good enough and don't deserve any happiness.*'

Dynamics of Low Self-Esteem

The need for reinforcement of behavior results in a lack of confidence in your own actions. Many of us go through periods in our lives when someone or something takes precedence, controlling all our thoughts and actions. It could be your boss, husband or mother-in-law. Rani has a long history with her mother-in-law. From the time she was married, all she wanted from her was approval and love, which she never got, no matter how hard she tried. In the beginning this made her try harder. Yet, each time found herself falling short of her mother-in-law's *expectations*. She was just not good enough for her son. Over a period of time this subliminal desire for approval controlled Rani to such an extent that she was always in a heightened state of *stress*. She made mistakes and when reprimanded, it led to *guilt* and tears, followed by a sense of *hopelessness*. No matter how hard she tried she never got the love and approval she craved. As a result she had *no confidence* in anything she did or said. Whatever she did seemed doomed for failure.

It took almost ten years for Rani to disengage and break away from this cycle. Her release came only after she moved to live in another country. For Rani, lack of self-esteem resulted in *fear of mistakes, hypersensitivity* to everything, *overwhelming guilt* and a need to *compensate* in unacceptable behaviors. For others it can lead to *isolation* and *withdrawal, depression* and *neurosis* and the need to control virtually every aspect of their lives often resulting in serious *health repercussions*. If you examine the neurosis of battered women you will notice this chain of behaviors tying them down to the marriage in spite of knowing that they need to escape their predicament or face more abuse and even death. The shackles are so strong, and self-esteem so low that such women cannot find within themselves the courage to break free.

Knowing the Self

Guruji believes that self-respect is critical and once you are comfortable in that space, the needs, wants and expectations of others cease to control you. In order to begin that process of respect, you have to understand and recognize the Self. When you have no inkling about who you are, what are you going to respect? When you have the realization that happiness is your birthright and your only duty and responsibility in life is to be happy and share happiness, then the Self stops being object-controlled. It stops the mental conditioning that deludes you into believing that the outside world manipulates how you feel about yourself. Your self-image, in other words, stops being a reflection of the world mirror. The Self just is. It neither wants nor controls and this concept has to be internalized at a deep level. Practices of meditation and pranayama take you beyond the body, the senses and the intellect and a sense of vast comfort dawns. No matter what you are, how you look, where you live, what you have achieved, the capsule of happiness at your core remains unchanged. Once you realize you are the happiness you seek and you are the Self, you can appreciate others without feelings of inadequacy or superiority, envy or disdain, fear or disregard. Your self-worth is at a constant and does not change according to how your day progresses. This is a process of dropping the mind and breaking away from the shackles of expectation and performance.

This requires awareness, knowledge and change. Awareness about your state of mind, unconnected to the outside world; knowledge about what needs to be done in this moment to get back to the self and the ability to affect this change in your life to bring harmony within yourself and with the world you live in.

Self Image and the Body

Depressed self-esteem can result from a combination of factors affecting your life. Sarika was brought up in a family consisting of internationally well-known doctors and scientists who had reached the pinnacle of success in their chosen fields. As a result, Sarika perceived her father's strictness and concern for her successful future as an imposition of high standards of achievement and behavior. This, coupled with a low body image, had severe psychological and physical ramifications.

Sarika is doing her PhD in Law and currently lives with her husband and child in Singapore. She did the AOL course at a very young age, encouraged by her parents who were also very spiritual. She was an extremely insecure teenager, and felt she was just not good enough. Her self-image was completely caught up in how she looked and when she saw her reflection in the mirror, it did not meet her standards.

She had several anxieties. *'I don't look so good, I can't dress well, my skin color is too dark, and I look like a boy.'* All of these perspectives of the self gave her an inferiority complex. She kept it from her parents, who always believed she was a highly successful and balanced, young girl. Very soon this disgust with her self-image converted into bulimia and within a few years she had lost 6-7 kgs. Yet she thought she was extremely fat, when in fact she was super-skinny. Outwardly she appeared very confident, even bordering on rebellious and her parents could never have guessed that she was wracked with anxiety. She went to law school and was a high performer but was never satisfied with herself or her achievements. She had built unrealistic expectations for herself and just could not live up to them. Only her best friend knew but he, too, didn't take it seriously. He helped her cope with the continual panic attacks but didn't really know how serious her condition was. Common triggers were exams and presentations, when her insecurities became insurmountable obstacles. This in spite of the fact that she was a National Level '*mock court debater*' and had also won awards and scholarships at the national and international levels. Outwardly she seemed to be this successful intellectual but inside she was a jangle of nerves. This continual, high level of stress ultimately affected her health. She had bronchitis and a permanent sore throat. There was no apparent reason, yet she was deeply unhappy.

Seva as a form of healing

The turnaround came when she enrolled in the Art of Living's DSN program (a second-level program for self-development) and joined up with a group of likeminded friends for voluntary service in the slums of Delhi. The mentors in the DSN program would skillfully convince her to do her Kriya every day and soon she became regular in her spiritual practice and the combination of Sadhana and Seva performed miracles for her self image.

'*I stopped looking at myself and thinking I was fat. I can't recall the day I stopped throwing up. It just happened over the course of time and it didn't strike me that I had to throw up my food. I was so busy; I ate and then ran out because I had so much to do. It has now been nine years since I got a bronchitis attack. I stopped being insecure about so many things. The focus of my life stopped being about me and I started working for others around me.*' Afterwards she learned about chakras or energy centers. All the anxiety in the chest and depression in the throat region affecting her in the form of throat and bronchial conditions, were cleared by the '*hollow and empty*' meditations.

Guruji says that your mental state can lead to any number of physical ailments and that is what happened with Sarika. Through service and knowledge she was able to find release.

Self Image, Culture and relationships

Anand Kumar was born and raised in Mumbai, India. Life for him had always been fast paced and after completing his Engineering degree, Anand came to America in 2002, for further studies. The huge disparity in culture, financial burden, difficulty in forming meaningful relationships and adjusting to school caused a lot of stress. He felt that he needed to become someone else, perhaps more American, in order to fit in. Anand soon found himself becoming more private, starting to judge others and consequently he developed an inferiority complex. His way of dealing with his own inadequacies was by isolation and withdrawal from society. If he didn't have to be in the company of others, who he felt were better than him, the whole situation of feeling undervalued would not arise. It was also easier to blame others and though outwardly he did this, it sprouted from a bed of inadequacy:

'My friends were okay, they were having a great time at that point in their lives. It was me who was seeing things differently and not in a pleasant manner. I knew that I was a nice guy and I wanted to do things for others, but there was this tremendous lack of confidence in front of people and this, coupled with a high speed highway in the mind, made me thoroughly unhappy. Outwardly I always felt I was okay, I was cool, yet inside I knew I was far from cool; I was totally in denial.'

This resulted in low energy and self-esteem and that really encapsulated his mindset. Nothing felt oriented, everything was haphazard, and he didn't feel connected to people. In addition there was a broken relationship (which I have described earlier) and all of this made him plummet into a downward spiral. He lost interest in everything—girls, relationships, school—and didn't really bother to job-search. In 2005, he did his AOL part 1 course and, for Anand, that was the turning point.

'The moment I entered the venue I sensed a shift in my mood. Suddenly I was so happy. I even had the courage to go up and talk to a girl who was attending the course and this surprised me.'

Something very profound happened during the Sudarshan Kriya and from that day forth, his life changed. Suddenly he found himself organizing a course and there was no looking back after that. His life was full of joy and it became all about Seva. Things just started happening. With almost no effort he found a great job and the earlier relationship with his girlfriend rekindled. The fear of other people's reactions stopped and he could accept people as they were. There was a new found confidence and relaxation. He finally had both feet on the ground.

'The world was the same but the way I started feeling about the world changed. I felt much more connected, I started feeling things where earlier there was a disconnect.' His life has become about serving others and while life has its problems, Anand reveals that from somewhere the strength, relaxation and guidance appears and life unfolds seamlessly.

Veena Narayanan hails from a traditional Hindu family and currently lives in Bahrain. Before she did her first course she felt a lot of heaviness in her heart and complications in the mind. She thought the worst about people and their intentions about her. Unsure and completely lacking confidence in herself made her relationships very unstable leaving her heavy-hearted and pessimistic.

'I was a very nervous person, always worried how people think of me. I always felt the need to prove myself as a good person. I don't feel this way anymore and my actions and seva speak for me. I am much more confident than ever before and focused on my goals which get blessed by Guruji automatically.'

Self-Image and Academic Achievement

Anirvachan,an AOL teacher is currently the Marketing Manager for Sumeru (an AOL organization) in Nigeria. Anir was a very average student in school. As a young scholar he sat on a backbench, and was part of the 'cool gang' who never took life seriously, always roaming around and having a lot of fun. A natural corollary to this was a waning of interest in his studies and a lack of value for education.

His close friend Siddharth suddenly started excelling and scoring higher marks than Anir in exams, and this was difficult to accept because Anir had been faring better than him all these years. Suddenly he noticed that Siddharth was going and talking to girls! He was filled with envy because this was the age with so many inhibitions, so much shyness. It baffled him because all this while he had felt like the group leader and now he was lagging behind in everything, including talking to chicks! This chipped away at his confidence and somewhere at the back of his mind was the growing feeling that he was not good enough.

In the meantime, he failed in four out of five subjects and his father had to beg the principal to let his son be promoted to the 12th grade. Anir remembers that his father was a very proud person, and to see him begging on his behalf was very disappointing for his father and shameful for Anir.

Academic failure destroyed Anir's confidence and he started stammering. This speech impairment was so bad that he almost never spoke in public. The earlier happy-go-lucky boy was replaced with a stuttering, nervous and unsure adolescent.

In the holidays after school, he took the AOL course and on the first day he sensed that something was going to happen. When he did Sudarshan Kriya his energy was unlocked and he was knocked out cold. The next few days went by in a haze. When he came out of the course it was a revelation on what life could be.

Academically he began doing really well in his college, where he enrolled in a Bachelor's in Electronic Science and even taught class in his first year of college. In his second year, he was one of the youngest students to be selected into the 'Students leadership council'. The third year saw a setback as he had to battle cancer, his experience of which I have described earlier. As a result he had to miss school for half the year. But that didn't deter Anir. He was so revved up and so confident; he made up for it in the last six months and was awarded the 'best overall outgoing student.'

'From seeing my parents beg for my future to seeing them standing up and clapping for me when I got this award... this was all because of the course.'

Issues and treatment surrounding self-esteem constitute a vast stream of inquiry for psychologists. Each person faces issues with self-esteem based on their unique situation and while I cannot speak for the multitude, in my experience it requires that momentary transfer from head to heart. In that instant you realize you deserve to be happy. Then all issues become non-issues, all hurdles surmountable and problems convert to lessons. Because you have reached that calm and serenity, you can recognize your opportunities and carve your destiny. Life simply unfolds and when you devote your life to creating happiness, it is joy all the way.

27

Desires

Desires do not allow you to relax in the peace of your being. Unless you let go of them, you can never find peace, you can never rest in divine Love.

—H.H. SriSri Ravishankar

The ultimate goal of all desires is love, yet desires kill the very joy you seek. Behind every desire is that deep need to find happiness. No act is ever committed without a goal of happiness. But the nature of desire is a projection of the confused mind urging you to be object-centered, taking you away from the core. Every desire that is satisfied leads to ten new desires. The adolescent wants to go to college where he can be free from controlling parents. When he is in college, he can't buy all the things he wants, so he looks for a job. Now that his money is surplus, he wants to buy a car. Once he has the car, he wants new Bose speakers. Now the cost of petrol is too much, so he needs a better paying job, or, even better, he thinks he can ask his parents for more money. Once he has borrowed money from them, he is in debt and once again his parents are in control—the very control he wanted to escape.

Desires move you away from your center

When you are centered and calm you want nothing and need nothing. Your mind and body are in complete harmony in that moment and the world around you feels perfect. There are many moments like that, most often when you are surrounded by nature. Sitting on the beach watching the waves crest and crash, or examining the colors of the clouds at dusk, or basking in the even calm caused by the steady drone of summer rain. At such moments we experience the peace of a meditative moment, a moment that needs nothing more: it is perfect in itself. That is the gift of the Universe to us. The moment a desire rises, it creates within you a certain restlessness that cannot be stilled until that longing is met. In that period of restlessness you have moved out of your self and are in the grip of mind delusion that is object-centered.

According to Ramola Prabhu, a doctor and seasoned AOL teacher, *'We desire for things that are outside of us. You'd never feel discontent if there was no desire. Even to be enlightened is a feeling of hankering, which takes you out of yourself. You seek peace outside, because you don't think you have it and you don't realize you are peace. Your mind takes you to another place because at the time the heart-mind connection is broken. It can be an emotion, or an object, or a state of mind—and therein lies the difference between what you think you are and what you are truly.'*

Desires symbolize a period of development.

Each one of us has a different basket of desires depending on our upbringing, cultural background, economic sufficiency and past karmic impressions. So while one person may have an overwhelming craving for ice cream, another may have a chronic addiction. By giving in to and satisfying certain cravings we reinforce the mind to continually present certain temptations. Every time you give in to invitation, your mind is taught a little more on what you require to feel happy and you now believe that you can be content if and only if that desire is satisfied. Desires are specific to certain stages of development. As a baby it may be for nourishment and warmth, in infancy it becomes forms of stimulation. In adolescence it typically centers on sensual pleasures which generally become less important when you enter the work force and economic needs take priority. At every stage of life our desires manifest depending on what we hold as our priorities.

Someone asked Guruji why he had this overwhelming desire rise in him when he saw beautiful women. Guruji smiled and said, 'I'll tell you a story. On a family outing, a father, son and grandpa went to this wonderful resort where everything was provided. The setting was beautiful and at the end of the second day the young son thought to himself. "*I am so happy; I can eat whatever I want, any number of ice creams and burgers with no limits.*" The father thought to himself, "*this is such a feast for the eyes. What beautiful women are here! Just seeing them makes me feel complete.*" The grandfather smiled to himself, thinking "*Ah! What a perfect day. I had such a smooth bowel movement*".'

At each stage of life we become obsessed with different things. For the boy it was food, for the man it was women and the grandfather could only think of how well he slept after his digestive system cleared. We need to lighten up about the urgency with which we attend to rising desires. This allows us not only to put our desires in correct perspective but also makes our attitude less judgmental. The next time a friend is obsessed with sensual enjoyment and you are disdainful, remember this story; and try to observe without judgment. Desires are temporary and change according to our priorities in life. At least that is how they are supposed to work. Of course some of us get stuck in some desire and then life goes off-track and hinders personal development. Sometimes desires are so strong that they result in foolish acts of insanity.

Desires and crime

Jakob Lund works in the Prison Smart program in Denmark. He believes that crime is a result of strong desires resulting in insane actions. The breathing techniques help to channel this desire into something bigger and more beneficial. As an ex-criminal he speaks about desires from experience:

'Criminals have the courage to go really deep in this path. Their acts require a lot of courage used in a wrong way. They have strong desires and this becomes overwhelming and thus far they have used this for crime. When this is channeled, the practices go really deep. I know; I have felt this. A desire is when you want something in exchange for something else, because of a strong need. Then you lose yourself in that which you want and this can become very painful.'

To some degree all of us give in to desires and commit acts we are not proud of. For the criminals Jakob meets, this might involve killing and raping but for others it could be something as harmless as eating a whole chocolate cake. It's a matter of degree.

Julia Tang from California has experienced this very shift from the material to the spiritual and for her this has worked well. She is cognizant of desires rising within her and through awareness and mindfulness has made the mental shift:

'Desires keep coming but shifting desire from material to spiritual, is the art of living. People want reach that place that's deep, they want to be happy.'

Desires are a gate to temporary joy

Desires by their very nature leave you unsatisfied. The happiness you feel is transitory till the next desire pops up. This reinforces mental conditioning because you long for that brief period of pleasure. The mind gets accustomed into believing that you can be happy only if the desire is met. Aversion is the flipside of desire. Here the mind tells you if you stay away from something, only then can you be happy. This mindset can stem from one isolated incident. You might have gone kayaking and fallen into the ocean and panicked. Now the same panic rises if you have to go on a cruise organized by your office. You refuse to go. The very thought of being near water fills you with aversion. Yet in your heart you know that this would perhaps be a fun filled day. Your mental conditioning creates strong likes and dislikes and you are now hopelessly trained to follow the dictates of your mind. Life then becomes like a pendulum as you are buffeted between cravings and aversions

Erjet Malaj from Albania realizes that: '*not knowing what they want makes people unhappy. You have new desires and run to fulfill it without satisfying the previous one. That makes for suffering. Added to that is the lack of knowledge and impressions from the past.*'

You cannot escape desires. The nature of the mind is such that desires will rise and fall. All you can do is be aware of them, observe as they rise and dissipate. You can decide which desires to pursue and which to ignore. Through reflection you can recognize when a desire becomes a craving and control the feverishness that follows. In the present moment acknowledge your desires completely and then decide if they are worth holding onto. Therein lies your path to happiness or misery.

28

Cravings and Aversions

If there is love, there is bound to be longing, and if there is longing know that there is love.

— H.H. SriSri Ravishankar

Through the day we are buffeted by alternating cravings and aversions, leading us to pleasure and pain. This takes away happiness.

Mothers would probably understand uncontrollable aversions because during pregnancy women get very sensitive to smells and tastes. Added to this are strong cravings, as the body hankers for what it lacks. Most of these are connected to food and nutrition but some women have a lot of sensitivity to their environment as well.

The First Lady of the Unites States, Michelle Obama, has been a huge advocate for reducing obesity in America, a problem where eating disorder is an offshoot of mental health. Food is used to calm the spirit and very soon it becomes a crutch and the frequency between cravings becomes smaller, the indulgence of which results in obesity.

All cravings and aversions are deeply connected to sensual satisfaction. If we believe a smell, a taste, or a sound is pleasurable or distasteful, we hanker after or avoid its source instinctively. Over time the mind gets conditioned to strong reactions on presentation of certain stimuli.

Desires (Cravings) and Feverishness

A knee-jerk reaction to such stimuli upsets the equanimity of the mind as you alternately ping-pong between things you intensely like or dislike. This results in a feverishness of the mind, an unsettling feeling or sensation that is called *Vasana* in Sanskrit. Feeding each and every feverish desire, takes you away from the peace of the present moment into a whirlpool of dissatisfaction, truncated with periods of brief bliss. Buddhist philosophy focuses on the removal of vasanas, which are the cause of sorrow.

The whole process can be quite exhausting and if you are winded at the end of the day it is probably because you spent a chunk of your time chasing cravings and dodging aversions. Awareness of the day's proceedings, however, requires some reflection. An awareness exercise I use several times a week is attempting to recall every event of the day, beginning with brushing my teeth in the morning. I go over every thought, feeling and sensation that crosses my mind and put those thoughts into baskets. One basket has actions prompted by my deep desires and the other has routine actions with no particular motive attached. Of course the first basket is still overflowing, but the more I am aware, the less the feverishness. The first step towards channelizing your desires is awareness. If you don't have the presence to recognize the motivation behind your actions, you are on a path to misery. Sridharfrom Washington D.C. insists that, '*It is feverishness and cravings that make people lose the present moment. One scoop of ice cream is never enough. You don't enjoy what you have and the more you have the duller it leaves you.*'

So how do you reduce the intensity of vasanas? Guruji says that you can do this by replacing it with Sankalpa (intention).

Sankalpa and Vasana

Sankalpa is that gentle intention in you without feverishness but with confidence. Attend to every part of your body with honor—all feverishness will be transformed into love.

—H.H. SriSri Ravishankar.

The only thing standing between *Sankalpa (intention)* and *Vasana, (desire)* is feverishness. It is not wrong to want things. We all want happiness, harmony, health and that is a natural corollary of living in this world. If you want desires to stop being feverish, you have to approach life from the space of gratitude. When you are content with what the Universe has provided you, gratitude flows into every aspect of your life.

Madhu Bhardwaj from Mumbai believes: *'For me, no desires come in a feverish way; I think about it, then I drop it. All desires are either fulfilled or they vanish. It is just the Grace. It comes from a deep sense of gratitude. In terrible situations when others misbehave with me, I am still grateful to them. If I didn't have them I would be stuck in the world. I am now so free I can go right now.'*

Just being on the path has changed Madhu's perspective and calmed her feverishness for achievement and success. Yet, on a daily basis she achieves and is successful. She is so content with her life that she needs not one more thing to complete her, which is why the Grace just flows in her life.

Being in gratitude does not mean you have no plans for the future. In fact Guruji believes the power of the breath lies in being able to lay the foundation for your future without hankering for results. Taking a Sankalpa is having that gentle intention in your mind and then letting it go. It involves a strong sense of purpose and action geared towards walking the path towards your goal. Intentions that are self-seeking and egocentric tend to convert quickly into desires because there is no thought outside of yourself. But an intention that is inclusive involves others and comes from a space of sharing and caring always gets actualized.

As Ramola Prabhu puts it, *'Intention for upliftment of yourself and others will drive you from a place of love, belongingness, sharing and caring. Intentions that are not all inclusive driven by the ego alone—like a quest for a million dollars—inevitably lead to stress.'*

Jill Smith lived in Surinam and Curaçao and took the AOL Part 1 course at a time when she was resolving relationship issues in her life. She was on another spiritual path earlier and had been seeking a Master for a while. She didn't know about SriSri but wondered if the moment were right, would she ever get to see him? Attending the 30th Anniversary celebrations in Berlin, she participated in a course. In her mind was a strong intention to meet the Master but he was just a dot on the stage and she was losing hope. Yet the intention was strong. In her mind she had the Sankalpa that somehow, somewhere she would meet him. By chance a lady stopped her and told her which hotel Guruji was staying in. The next morning Jill was up at 5 a.m. and, in spite of the rain, waited in the lobby for the Master to arrive.

'We waited and as he came out of the elevator I said to him, "I am here" and he looked at me and he touched me. On the train ride back I slept peacefully. My search was over; I had found my master. I was left with peace and bliss. I had arrived.'

Dr. George Lavrelashvili described a simple incident that clearly demonstrates the difference between a Vasana and Sankalpa.

'We were going for a course in the German ashram. I had bought my return ticket for the day it finished. The course was to be followed by another one. There was another lady there who was very excitable and didn't speak English. She kept talking about the return tickets and she said she had an expensive ticket and could change the return at no charge, unlike me. I had a cheap ticket with fixed dates. She called me three times about her departure date and signaled to me

and talked to me even in silence. Throughout I kept telling her to relax.

When the course ended, Guruji invited the Georgian delegation to stay for the next course and they needed me for translation. The next day was my flight. I spoke to a teacher and he told me to ask Guruji. I explained to him the situation and he answered, "Do whatever is possible."

I called the airline and they changed my return at no charge. I was astounded. And I attended the second course. This lady also wanted to do the next course and when she called the airline they told her she could change her date but had to pay $100. She was also astounded. This was a great lesson. I was calm and things worked out and she was so feverish and had trouble. This is the difference between Sankalpa and Vasana.'

Letting go of desires, or letting go after taking a Sankalpa, comes from a space of gratitude where you see that the Universe has more than provided for you. The more you hanker after fame and money the more it will elude you, and the feverishness will take you away from your center. When you are completely satisfied this moment and nothing can add to your happiness, then grace and gratitude will flow in your life. In order to feel that gratitude you need one more addition to your spiritual treasury: Faith.

29

Faith

Consolidation of your energy is faith. Faith brings totality in you. It pulls together the loose ends of your consciousness. Doubt scatters and destroys you.

—H.H. SriSri Ravishankar

Faith, according to SriSri, is the core of existence. Without a foundation of faith it is impossible to move ahead in life. It is what grounds you and gives you a sense of purpose. Interwoven into your being is a faith in the Self, in the world you live in and in the Universe, or divine faith. You can realize this faith either through experience or knowledge and it is what keeps us strong in the face of problems. If your faith is shaken by some trauma or negative experience, you completely break down and this has ramifications on your physical health as well. In the face of challenge if you have faith, you will be able to see the silver lining in rain clouds.

Faith is that which allows you to look into the future, knowing everything will pass, everything will change and the situation can only improve. It is this inner strength, rooted in divine faith, which allows you to move through life, surrendering to every challenge thrown at you. Even those who claim to be atheistic have faith in something; in their own words, if nothing else.

A deep-rooted knowledge, that you are blessed and someone is taking care, is what guides us through life. Your faith is never challenged in good times but every time you are down, it is your faith that helps pull you back up.

When times are rough, miracles can take place and if you have a strong intention, the universe aligns itself and realizes your dreams. Kiki from Chicago has seen rough times and good ones and understands at a deep level the power of faith in tiding over choppy waters:

'Faith is what gets you through the bad times. Since opposite values are complementary it's a 50-50 deal. It's not going to be good or bad all the time and faith is what sees you through the bad times. It's not Guruji who is testing you and making things happen in your life. No one is doing anything; it's like knowing the seasons will follow one after the other. He reminds us that the sun will come out tomorrow. Faith just makes remembering that easier and joyful.'

Umberto Sartori a devotee, is very academic about life and everything in his world needs to be ordered. Faith for a chaotic mind is inconceivable. Tapping into his own self and being honest, helps him get a better vision of his life and the world around him. When you are beset with problems, thoughts swirl in your brain and doubt clouds your vision. Meditation helps settle the mind and when that happens, the dynamics of your problem become clear. At that moment, your faith kicks in and you can rest in that space assured that the future will work out. As Umberto says:

'Faith is about clarity. When something is very clear to me I have faith because I know exactly what it is. Clarity of your nature, of the layers within you, the nature of your teachers, that is the realization that you are immortal and this world is a playground. If things are clear you know where you are going. If there is no clarity no matter which angel walks with you, you will be lost.'

Miracles or coincidences?

Meena Krishna moved to live in Bengaluru, India, and had no idea that school admissions were next to impossible. In her heart she just took a Sankalpa for her kids to get into a good school. In May, all schools and admission offices were closed and every school asked her to come back later. But in Bishop Cotton Boys School there was a teachers' meeting and she waited to meet the Principal, but there was no sign of him. Suddenly the guard said the Principal was leaving for the airport. As she ran up to him at the gate, he asked why she was there. She explained her situation; her children needed to be in a school that taught French. He turned to his assistant and asked for her forms to be filled and she got admission for both her children, seemingly effortlessly.

Reshma Kurup studied Architecture in India and wanted to do her Masters in the US. The Frank Lloyd Wright School of Architecture was her first choice and they were picky about whom they selected. She didn't have good GRE scores and was grateful they only needed TOEFL scores. This was after September 11, the Twin Towers tragedy and it was tough to get visas for USA. She went for her visa interview with a lot of trepidation, aware there was a history of rejection. All ten people who went before her in the US Consulate in Chennai, India, had been rejected. Reshma was silently muttering '*Jai Gurudev*' under her breath hoping for a miracle.

The lady at the counter sternly asked for her GRE scores and Reshma's heart sank. But then the lady suddenly left and returned with the officer from the next cubicle. He had a smile on his face as he scanned her documents. This man was a student from the same school of architecture Reshma was applying to. What were the chances that a visa officer, sitting in Chennai, graduated from the very school that took such few students? It was nothing short of a miracle. He gave her the visa and then went back to his cubicle. The lady looked at her and said, '*Girl, you are so lucky!*'

Reshma says: '*It might be a coincidence. It's not a big thing. Actually everyone is taken care of but when you get that realization then faith takes over.*'

Hansa Dave had been on the path for a while but was unsure if she wanted to give up a lucrative job to become a full-time teacher. One time, Rajshri Didi, a respected AOL teacher, informed her that until her youngest finished her education Guruji would not let her teach full-time. Soon after Guruji's' visit, her contract with her company was terminated and she was unemployed. Ironically, she was happy and attributed it to Guruji's manipulation of the Universe. She knew the time had come for her to become a full-time teacher. This was also the day after her youngest daughter's graduation. Three months later her husband got a job so Hansa became a full-time AOL teacher, but was still scared and confused. Her husband was fully supportive of Art of Living but not of her giving up her career. Besides, she was used to having money and there was a lot of hesitation and misgiving. She was not resting in her Self and doubted the divine. Two hours later she received a gift in the mail: a magic lamp in which, when lit, a picture of Guruji popped up. This was the same picture she always used for meditation. The card read: '*when you surrender to the Divine, every step of your way is set by the Divine.*' Hansa was elated: '*This was just what I needed to hear. The timing was perfect.*'

On a flight from New Delhi to Kolkata, Meena Lakra was sitting next to me. As the plane was about to take off I heard her mutter to herself, '*Jai Gurudev*' which is the Art of Living signature mantra. I turned to her and asked if she was an AOL devotee and then interviewed her on the flight.

After Meena's marriage her mother had a paralytic attack and since she had no father, the whole responsibility was on her and her sister.

'*That was a difficult time. I had little support and had to keep flying to Delhi. I was disappointed with Guruji, asking why this had to happen in spite of my devotion to him.*'

On reaching Delhi her sister told her that the neurologist was not good or approachable and they had to fight with the hospital administration for a new doctor. The new neurologist came and saw Guruji's photo next to her mother's bed and his face changed. Meena was sure he was thinking why qualified people had so much faith in 'false' saints. Three weeks later, on discharge, her mother's EEG was also favorable. When Meena took her mother to see the neurologist he looked at her and said, '*Jai Gurudev*'. Meena recounts: '*I was stunned. I realized that Guruji was with us through this time. We were part of the same universal family (Vasudeva Kutumbakam) and help had come to us from nowhere.*'

Faith is to sink inward

Without faith the journey lacks grounding. Faith is like the roots of a tree. When you allow faith to take deep roots within you, the universe allows the tree of life to grow and the flowers and fruits become yours to take joy in. Reshma Kurup has let go of her fears, secure that a divine presence cares for her. She believes that faith does not reside in outward manifestation of religion. The strength is not in a mosque or temple, but within you.

'*I can be anywhere and I know I will be taken care of. To have faith, there has to be inner silence and peace and that comes from spiritual practice, and then everything becomes magic.*'

30

The Universe and you

There is some power, someone who is really caring for you. There is only One in the whole Universe.

—H.H. SriSri Ravishankar

The Universe is there to serve you. All you need to do is ask and it will be given to you. Maybe not immediately, perhaps not in the way you envisaged but ultimately, the Universe provides if your surrender is unequivocal and innocent. When you believe you are in control, things do not work out according to your plan, because in reality none of us control anything. We are mere actors on a stage and react to situations as they pan out. Yet most people believe they have control over their lives and are in charge, so when plans get disrupted they are thrown into disarray. When you have the realization that you are nothing and want nothing, the Universe embraces you and provides for you in ways unimaginable to the cognitive mind. If there is hankering in your mind, your goal will elude you, whether it is for money, fame or success. Dreams get realized for those that are persistent, who relinquish control and surrender to the will of the Divine.

Being on the path for a while has made Uma Berlin reach the stage in her life where she has figured out her equation with the divine:

'*I am a vehicle for Divine Grace. I allow it to move through me. I am not the doer. What I see as obstacles are just opportunities the Universe is providing for me to grow and learn. I am part of this vast universe and am always supported by it. Because my intention is pure and is to serve, whatever I need will come. The Universe has a far more sophisticated plan than I can ever comprehend. Into this faith, I surrender all my actions.*'

2004 was a bad year for Sridhar. There was stress at work and very soon he was laid off. He had the burden of mortgage payments and was also paying for his wife to complete her Master's degree. Money was just not enough. His expenses far outweighed his income and he began budgeting on a daily basis.

The following year he took a Part-2 course where he met a young girl who was desperate to go to the Canadian Ashram to do her TTC and become a teacher. She was in college, had health problems and no money. Although Sridhar himself wanted to become a teacher he felt this young girl's need was greater. She needed $1500 to do the course, which was exactly what Sridhar had in the bank. He emailed her, saying he would make the payment directly to the Canadian Ashram for her to do the course.

A few months later, Sridhar was still struggling for money and he forgot about what he had done. Soon after, his wife finished her Master's degree and on Christmas day received two interview calls for jobs. She accepted one and obtained her H1 visa in a week and was soon earning twice what their annual income had been.

'*The girl called to return the money in installments. She was so grateful, but I never took it back. I just told her to finish her degree and get a job and to give the money to someone else who needed it. I felt compelled to help her. It's beyond comprehension. By then my wife had a job I was already taken care of.*'

The Universe provides in ways beyond mortal understanding. When you have faith and you reach out to help others you receive in unfathomable ways. Having deep faith helps to go deeper in prayer. In situations beyond our control, a moment of complete surrender to the Divine is where we let the Universe guide us. It's that moment of relinquishing control that heralds humility and faith.

Amit Kumar Vyaghambare from Chhattisgarh, India, was planning to go to the Bengaluru Ashram when his father fell ill. Being the only son, taking care of his father was Amit's responsibility. That evening, Amit wrote to Guruji an email asking him to take care of his father. But things took a turn for the worse. His father's EKG was abnormal and his blood pressure high and they had to shift him to the ICU. After two hours the doctor said he had suffered a serious heart attack, and wouldn't survive. Amit received this news calmly but in disbelief. For the next 72 hours he chanted '*Om Namah Shivaya*'. The wait was excruciating. Several thoughts ran through his head but it was a moment of surrender when his faith had taken over. He was 35 and had never done enough for his father. Now, with a better paying job, he wanted to care for him. He knew that death comes and was ready to accept everything in his destiny. The next day his father was better. He was so lucky to have had the attack while in the ICU:

'Thank heavens I did what I did and took him at the right time. I don't know how the Universe works but it has a strange way. After a bypass surgery he's fine.'

All the while, Amit prayed to Guruji and believes he caused the miracle in his life. But Pawan Mulukutla thinks of Guruji in another way:

'Guruji is not here to make our life sugary. He is here to help us move through tough times. Guruji is not a physical body alone but an existence; that is why we call it Guru Tattva; something that is in

nature all the time and it is up to us to get in touch with that and be in tune.' Pawan thinks this way because he has seen miracles in his life, inexplicable events that defy logic, like the time his nephew had a speech problem. His sister was disillusioned with what modern medicine had to offer and had even stopped praying to God, she was so miserable. But in 2008, they went to Tampa. She had cooked for Guruji and they had no appointment and no hope of meeting him. Yet the intention was so strong that Guruji called them in and said, *'don't worry your son will be fine.'* And he is. As Pawan explains:

'How do these things happen? It is not that I run after miracles. It is just that I am in touch with him and myself and things just happen, intentions just materialize. When you are in that mode of working for the highest, everything comes to you as a gift. There have been days I was so involved in seva and have been so hungry and someone just knocks on the door with food. These are simple examples that take place all the time.'

Ru Wan was born and raised in China and came to the US when she was 16. Moving to the US was a big cultural swing for her. She spoke and read a little English but having to use a second language for everything was a huge shift. Academically she did quite well but was disoriented and wondered how her life would turn out and whether all the effort she was putting into her studies was even worth it. Doing the AOL course brought a huge modification in her faith. She stopped doubting the future and the present and learned to submit to the divine.

'I am not confused and lost anymore. I know that I can just go forward. I have visions of my future. It's like being on a river that just flows, at some parts the water doesn't know its course but the path is already carved out. The landscape is different but that too changes. A river changes direction and at the end the water reaches the same ocean. My life is like that.'

Dropping the Effort

When problems crop up in life, the small mind takes over. You continually search for reasons why some incidents took place. *Was it me? Did I say that to her intentionally? How could he do that to me? Has he no sensitivity to my feelings?* And if you see the error of your ways, such questions are closely followed by a period of guilt. Or, you see the other person is at fault and then you blame them. Ultimately the feelings of sadness and misery are in your own mind. Awareness about your train of thought allows you to simply drop the effort. Sometimes things happen; situations occur. Seeing intention behind mistakes only causes hours of tears, blame and guilt.

When we are caught up in the small mind the focus become 'me', 'me' and 'me': you forget that problems happen to everyone. The divine is not sitting in the clouds with a telescope, choosing you to test his new emotional thesis. It is a momentous realization when you figure out that you are not the only one suffering. It is true that when you are in emotional turmoil, you lose the sense of belongingness and don't want to hear about other people's pain. But as the emotions settle, you can elevate yourself into the bigger mind. Take a deep breath and let go of all the wretchedness, fear and misery you are clinging onto. The process of moving from the sufferer to the observer is walking the path: The Art of Living.

It begins with awareness and moves towards developing the ability to use knowledge to assist through life. In the beginning this involves conscious effort as the mind has trained you to react to stimuli. It presents the ego and mental concepts that accompany it and likes you to be unhappy, because that way, it traps you in its clutches. You are so used to be being the victim and love the attention it brings to you. At such times you have to stop, take a deep breath and say: '*Drop the effort. This is my mind entrapping me. This is not happening to me; it is just happening.*' Initially, it may require effort; over time, it becomes more natural. Even for AOL teachers, while promoting courses the sense of doership creeps in and it requires awareness and effort to recognize this and drop the effort and ownership. Timothy Wong was very excited when he first became a teacher and plunged into organizing courses:

'I felt the onus of growing the foundation was on me and then I realized it was all unnecessary. Doership is inherent in any action that has results. As long as we recognize this, it's fine. I am in a different space now where I don't have a compelling need to do anything but at the same time can roll with it if it comes along. I'm in a very free space. There is some doership but I see it as the nature of things.'

You do not require knowledge when you are happy and life is smooth. It only becomes important when you are in a predicament. Practicing reconditioning of your thought process with small things becomes very advantageous as tools to utilize in a real crisis. In order to move through the process you have to leach the tendency to get stuck in blame and guilt in order to ultimately surrender. Only then can you go through life as the observer.

31

The road to Surrender: Blame

The ignorant person says do not blame me because it will hurt me.
The enlightened person says do not blame me because it will hurt you.
—H.H SriSri Ravishankar

Assigning blame to others gives you temporary exoneration from an action committed in error or by intent. Guruji says assigning blame to mistakes only leads to misery. If you have made a mistake, acknowledge it, take responsibility for it and apologize *once*. Sincerely. Then forget about it and move on.

Assigning blame increases your negative Karma and that is why the enlightened say, *'don't blame me because it is bad for you'.* Holding onto that one incident and allowing it to fester in your mind puts you into a cycle of guilt. You feel bad and wish you had done things differently. When you are blamed unjustly, feelings of being mistreated arise and negative emotions churn within you. For your own mental sanity it is better, in such cases, to assume the other person apologized and move on: otherwise it becomes the case of an unstoppable force against an immovable wall. No one wants to acknowledge their mistake, to accept responsibility and maybe no one apologizes. The end result is hours of misery filled with guilt, blame and regret.

Preity Thomas from Vadodara shares knowledge sheets with the Art of Living world and for her, the one knowledge point that has been most practical and saved her from months of agony is, *'Don't see intention behind people's mistakes. This allows me to accept people. Take a mistake as a mistake, not as mine or yours or hers. Look at the bigger picture.'*

Once you learn not to assign blame, life becomes much simpler. People around may be rude, pushy and disagreeable but that doesn't bother you. You don't get into the small mind of *'how dare you?'* and *'I am so hurt'*, and just move on. You cannot control other people and what they say. You can only manage your own mind and emotions. You can observe these (i.e. your own mind and emotions) and respond to the situation or completely lose it and react. I would suggest the former. It may give the appearance of being submissive and a walkover but, ultimately, you will be the winner. Awareness about your own response to others allows you to stop, think and respond. You can choose to retaliate or you can choose to let it go. Trust me, it will save you from hours of guilt. Mrinalini believes this knowledge point has helped her deal with people at a non-judgmental level:

'I don't blame others for anything going on in my mind and surroundings. I immediately go inward and make the change and when I do that, the circumstance changes for sure. This helps me deal with any type of people; nasty, rude or highly competitive and not very agreeable. As a result I can even continue an unstressed friendly relationship with them. In fact, I have noticed that changes in my behavior, positively affect a large number of connected people.'

32

Guilt

It is easy to become attached to feelings of guilt, even over small things. This feeling of guilt is usually damaging and unhelpful. We are not saying we should ignore our conscience – far from it. What we are trying to do is let go of unnecessary feelings of guilt and move on with our life.

—H.H. SriSri Ravishankar

A little bit of guilt keeps you on the straight and narrow, where you function from conscience with a sense of belongingness. You don't want to commit acts that deliberately hurt others. It helps to preserve your own sense of purpose in the long run. Guilt takes place when the mind, like a broken record, gets stuck in the same groove and can't move on.

When Rani's older daughter was nine months old she conceived again. She had a difficult first pregnancy and this time, too, had a bit of spotting. Her husband was between jobs and they lived with the in-laws at the time, which was stressful enough. Her sister-in-law was to be married the following month and one day her mother-in-law called her into the kitchen and suggested she postpone the baby. Rani was unhappy about being pregnant to begin with. She had a small child, no home and no decent means of livelihood. Once her mother-in-law planted the seed in her mind, she was so susceptible and so tuned in to her mother-in-law's needs that her mind swerved in favor of an abortion.

Her husband opposed her decision but she went ahead and had one. She was spotting anyway, so she thought at 35 days she was doing no harm to the unborn child. The timing was all wrong and she was just in no mental state to have a second child. Deeply unhappy about living with in-laws, she was just miserable about everything. Ten days later, she began hemorrhaging and they had to repeat the procedure. She was scared and certain this was divine retribution. But she recovered and three years later wanted another child. Her older daughter longed for a sibling but Rani was not conceiving. Again the fears came back. '*Had she made a huge mistake? Would she have to pay for it for the rest of her life?*' Then miraculously she conceived. In 40 days however, she had a spontaneous miscarriage. Rani was devastated!

Now all she could think of was that scene where her mother-in-law asked her to abort the baby, but now the images and memories were distorted. Rani was convinced she had demanded it of her. She blamed her mother-in-law and blamed her weak mind and blamed her destiny. Twice more she suffered miscarriages, and the guilt and blame became overwhelming. Not one day passed without her thinking evil thoughts about her mother-in-law and blaming herself as a baby killer. Not only so, her husband also blamed Rani and she constantly had to hear, '*I told you so*'. In the meantime, she had a bawling toddler who was demanding a sister. The stress from the guilt was overwhelming and she just could not conceive after that.

When she moved overseas, the joy of being away from her in-laws and the freedom it gave her relaxed the mind and in a few months she found herself pregnant. The time was right and she had another lovely daughter. She never realized that when the move to Singapore took place, she had resigned herself to having only one child. She sold the pram and cradle and gave away all the baby clothes. Unknowingly she had surrendered to the divine. In that surrender her deepest Sankalpa was realized. But it was only after she did her AOL course that she forgave her mother-in-law. In fact forgiveness is a wrong word to use. Although the facts could never be altered, the abortion was Rani's decision. The moment she took ownership of that decision, she stopped seeing her mother-in-law as a perpetrator. In fact she stopped seeing herself as the perpetrator; she had taken a decision in the past which she thought was for the best. It was over; she had another child and needed to move on. The release and freedom she got from her own acceptance of responsibility freed her from the shackles of hatred, revenge, guilt, blame and a host of other negative sentiments. All of this came from that one moment of unequivocal surrender.

Crime and Guilt

Jakob Lund knows that prisoners have a lot of guilt. Alone in their cells, they relive those moments of insanity and regret their actions. Hours of solitary confinement leads to a lot of mental flagellation but that moment of surrender never really takes place. Violence by its very nature is contrary to mental peace and even soldiers who are trained in warfare suffer the effects of PTSD (Post Traumatic Stress Disorder). However much they believe their motives were clean and they killed for their country, the act of taking someone's life leaves a scar on their psyche, the consequences of which they have to suffer. Memories haunt them as visions during the day and as nightmares at night. There is almost no escape. The Art of Living techniques of breathing and meditation allows them to reach that inner space and release the pain that racks their body and spirit. Jakob tells us:

'Prisoners have guilt about the past. To overcome guilt for some time they punish themselves and then they are ready to commit the

same crime again. We encourage them to feel the effects of their actions right here and now and feel the effects fully, only then can they be free from them. Many course participants have been successfully integrated into mainstream society. Not only have they given up their life of crime but they help others and they can reach that section of society that normal people can't reach. They become real role models because they have lived a life of crime and have been able to give that life up.

With soldiers they are still traumatized by their actions. They kill for the country still the very act of killing leaves an impression. They repeat themselves in an evil cycle and the practices cut the cycle and break the chain.'

Homosexuality and Guilt

> *Every form belongs to the Divine. When you adore the form, you adore the Divine behind the form.*
>
> —H.H. SriSri Ravi Shankar

Homosexuality has been recorded throughout history and often misunderstood and shunned, rarely accepted in the mainstream of society. Men and women attracted to the same sex conceal their preferences and cannot reveal this lifestyle to their parents and loved ones because of homophobia and social reprisals. They live trapped sometimes in a double-life unable to express themselves freely and openly. I have known several men who live a heterosexual lifestyle, marrying and having families while having a homosexual boyfriend.

J. Allen Danelek in his book '*The Mystery of Reincarnation,*' offers a theory which made me ponder. He says that in many past-life recorded regressions, people recall belonging to the opposite sex in their lives prior to their present one. If the impressions they bring into this life are strong enough, the attraction for the same sex might remain dominant. Of course this theory cannot be proved but it definitely is food for thought.

In America, gay and lesbian rights are gaining legislative recognition, but we still hear of harassment, assault and other hate crimes arising out of homophobia. This is why I was pleasantly surprised and happy to speak to Timothy, who had no reservation about his homosexuality:

'I was quite involved in Asian Pride. I was not out and proud shouting from table tops. But I was in a different position. I was not afraid to hide it. I had career, money, background, position and confidence within myself. I promoted Asian Pride because I saw that stereotypical image of a homosexual Asian as an effeminate, weak individual. That was not the case with me. The circles I moved in had strong, muscular, good looking people who are gay and we took pride in that. We wanted to show the world the positive side of homosexual Asian men.'

Timothy knew this about himself growing up but it wasn't until he started working, that he embraced it. He hailed from a Christian conservative background where you had to do the right thing; go to the right school, be with the right group, see and be seen; he could never really be himself. Belonging to an established, Chinese family with highly educated parents, Timothy had high standards to maintain. Once he broke the news to them, they were supportive yet concerned and scared of the blackmail that sometimes takes place when people know you are gay. This made Timothy focus aggressively on education and career. Being highly successful in the corporate world gave him the confidence to be open about his sexual orientation.

'Just because your sexual orientation is different it doesn't mean you can't be good performers at work. Your working life is seen as an expression of your individuality. My Gay Pride and my pride in work grew and went hand in hand.'

A friend of his tested positive for HIV. Hong Kong society is conservative in many ways, even more so when they find you have AIDS and you get ostracized from the community and often lose your job. By chance, Timothy came across an AOL course and thought it would help, so he suggested it to his friend and ended up taking the course himself. His attitude at the time, being a corporate, hard edged person was: '*If you can't work it out yourself, crawl under a rock and die.*' When he went on the website Srisri's photo popped up and that scared him. He didn't want to get caught up in any cult. Coming from an Anglo-Chinese culture the whole concept of a Guru was foreign to him. He decided to attend for an hour and ended up staying for all four days. There was internal resistance during Sudarshan Kriya and he would occasionally open his eyes and see others having deep experiences, knowing it wasn't going to happen to him. On the fourth day when he woke up from bed, something had changed inside.

'*I could not pinpoint what it was but it was like everything I was searching for my whole life was answered. It was like an epiphany. I went back and said to them "I have to meet this man SriSri Ravishankar." So from a huge skeptic, I became a devotee and disciple.*'

Timothy went to meet Guruji at the Canadian Ashram and the very first thing he asked was, '*Is it against the Divine to be Gay?*' He was homosexual and he needed to know what the Master's views on the issue were. This was perhaps the most important question he had ever asked and everything hinged on the Master's answer.

Guruji looked at him and said, '*You shouldn't think like that. Do you like pumpkin?*' Timothy was puzzled. What was this question and where was it leading? He just stared blankly and Guruji repeated the question. Timothy stuttered saying he really didn't mind eating pumpkin. Then the Master asked, '*Can you imagine eating pumpkin every day?*' Timothy shook his head saying no. Guruji smiled. '*Look around you, there are so many different types of vegetables out there. Divinity likes diversity.*'

Right that moment Timothy knew he was in front of a real Master, one whom he now accepted as his Guru.

33

Acceptance to surrender

Acceptance brings calmness to the mind.
—H.H. SriSri Ravishankar

The Art of Living is an organization that accepts people regardless of background. At the Bengaluru Ashram you will see the business tycoon taking a course alongside an auto-rickshaw driver. This is particularly refreshing in a society where caste prejudices are deeply embedded into the fabric of society.

I always believed I was evolved to the extent I had no caste prejudice. When I took the Part 1 course in India, there was a young man who was a peon in a company, a delivery boy, and his work made him travel in the hot sun. When he came to the course he smelled of body odor. To make things worse he never changed the shirt he wore for all four days. The smell was so offensive to me I avoided him as a partner during the processes. I was aware I was doing this but felt justified for his body odor offended me.

On the last day of the course we were at the Bengaluru ashram and, after the group processes, had broken for lunch. We were making our way to the dining hall and there was a shortcut which involved scaling down a steep slope. Very bravely I thought I would take the shortcut and be ahead in the lunch line. As I took my first step, my foot slipped and I lost balance. In that moment I knew I was going to land in a heap at the foot of the incline and I screamed. This young man was right in front of me and in an instant, turned around and held me tight. I looked into his innocent, concerned eyes and tears of shame welled in mine. In that moment the utter wretchedness of my thought process, my lack of belongingness and my internalized prejudice stared at me in the face. The boy I was avoiding, because I thought he smelled bad, saved me from a treacherous fall. The irony of the situation changed my tears into laughter and waves of gratitude cascaded over me. In that one instant Guruji taught me the basic tenets of acceptance and the foolishness of the small mind.

Veronica Niyazova is of Russian origin and is a teacher in South Florida. She believes that this acceptance is part of the organization because SriSri is pure love. When there is only love, acceptance is natural and all encompassing.

'One thing that resonates with me is that he does not reject anyone. It does not matter what religion you are, what color you are or if you are a terrorist or prisoner. He accepts every single person with so much love. He is pure love. I just feel at home when I am with him.'

'Accepting people and situations as they are', is a very taxing knowledge point to apply in your life. In all your clashes and disagreements with people if you have some awareness and are able to reflect, you will notice an internal resistance that does not permit you to see only the positive. The mind always goes to what is not perfect. You probably are, or know, the person who has a negative comment to say, no matter what you talk about or whom you discuss. *'Be careful, she is evil'* or *'don't be friends with her, she tortures her mother-in-law'* or *'have you seen her unibrow?'* or *'She got a 1600 in her SAT but she really needs to shave'*. Such comments are inane and demonstrate your small mind and the meaner and more envious side to your nature.

Being around such people make you less aware and I find myself making many negative comments that are so unnecessary and take away from that sense of belongingness. It requires effort to stop and realize that the words leaving your mouth have power and carry sentiment. When you take the Happiness decision you realize that your job is to be happy and spread happiness and hurtful comments do the opposite. It makes me very contrite and small when I catch myself making such comments or passing judgments on people and I realize that all it does is create a distance between myself and the other person.

Having good intentions is not enough. When I have acceptance at a cellular level the option of making hurtful, negative and judgmental comments will become nonexistent. That is my goal and I am on a journey. Every time I catch myself, I am just a little happier and just a tad evolved. It's a process, one that needs awareness and practice.

Marita Andreassen also took a while to understand that acceptance of people and situations saved her own mind.

'You can't change others, you can only change your own mind. I stopped getting irritated by others and got out of the small mind where I had been wasting energy and time thinking of what others had said and done to me. The conversations in my head stopped and I was finally able to relax.'

Mrinalini taught me a technique that works really well if you take the effort to practice it whenever you are in a disagreeable situation or come across rudeness. It saves you from hours of small mind chatter.

'Guruji says if someone is behaving towards you in a strange manner, as a first step, just smile, as a sign of acceptance. For some reason I decided to try it. I went back to school. One of my teachers was always very taunting and demeaning to students, especially to those who weren't particularly good at studies. I looked at him and decided to politely listen and smile and within me there was silence.

I didn't judge him anymore and whatever he said to me in class stopped affecting me negatively. As a consequence, I started focusing more on doing well in my studies which at the time was much more important.'

Another technique Guruji suggests has worked wonders with me. He says if someone is rude to you or hurts you or if you have hurt someone, go out of your way to say something nice to them or do something special for them. This helps to break the cycle of hurt and retaliation and frees the mind from bondage to the negative. Just the other day I was annoyed at having to cook three meals for my father-in-law and I caught myself being short with my husband. I knew that I felt some resentment for being forced to cook instead of spending time writing my book, while everyone else was watching the Olympics on TV. The next day I made every food item my father-in-law liked. Just seeing the joy on his face as he relished his favorite dishes made everything alright. Perhaps the next time I will catch myself before the words leave my mouth, be able to resolve my sentiments internally and be free even before I respond rashly. It's a process and it requires awareness and practice.

Acceptance is a prerequisite for surrender. According to Umberto: *'The present moment is inevitable. Everything that happens good or bad is what it is, and in order to make it work for you, you have to surrender to it. Embrace everything as an honored guest without getting too excited about it. Accept and work with everything. Surrendering is observing, realizing, feeling and letting go. All this as you enjoy your life. It's simple but not so easy to practice because of past habits of reacting and worrying and thinking that the world around me is the only reality.'*

Surrender

Surrender is not an act; it is a state of your being. Whether you acknowledge it or not, surrender is there. The wise wake up and see this, the less wise take a longer time. Know that you have no choice; you are in a state of surrender deep within you.

—H.H. SriSri Ravishankar

Surrender comes with acceptance at a deep level. It occurs in two situations. One is you have abundance, more than you ever need and in that moment of gratitude, you surrender. The other is when the situation is much bigger than you and there is nothing more to think, say or do. Such moments culminate in deep surrender.

Surrender is your very nature and when you reside in the Self, surrender just happens; it involves absolutely no effort. If you have the thought that you need to surrender to something, then the moment of surrender is further than you think. Surrender will only happen when you have no option. You surrender and the mind is incapable of labeling the moment as one of surrender and in that instant there is only One, when you are the Self, where you are the Divine, there is no other, therefore the mind ceases to exist.

Surrender is that moment of prayer when the silent inner cognizance opens up in true humility. It is the feeling that you are nothing, have nothing and mean nothing. When you close your eyes in prayer, you drop the ego and offer everything, good or bad, to the divine. It is a private and personal flash where two entities converge and become fused in devotion. It is that epiphany; when you hold onto nothing and offer that space to the divine. In that moment of surrender is a feeling of space, of vastness, of union with the Brahman. That space exists within the emptiness of your body yet it reaches beyond the confines of mental constructs.

In surrender you give nothing and that's what makes it *the biggest illusion.* You are nothing, so what is there to give? You have nothing, so what have you to offer? You surrender to the divine but that divine is you and therefore you surrender to yourself. The divine is One, only One, so when there is no other who are you surrendering to? Surrender is really the easiest act; you commit and in that moment the power of the future becomes tangible. Nothing can hurt you because you have accepted at the deepest level and returned to your source. Your source is the very divinity that humbles you and from that germ of humility comes freedom. Freedom beyond the imaginable. Freedom from the mind, the body, the world, the problem and dilemmas. In that moment of relinquishing you soar to unchartered heights of liberation.

Edina Atic has survived the genocide and trauma of war-torn Bosnia. The pain existed in her life at a subliminal level. The Art of Living has helped her to release this accumulated stress and just surrender to the divine:

'The ability to let go helped me to stop this movie going on in my head, and to just do nothing. This has been powerful. Knowledge points usually come up when they're most needed...but still, for me it is not so much about remembering them in my mind, it is always about the heart and being connected with the Divine, the Life Force, with Guruji, and people who surround me on a more subtle level. It is about sharing that which is beyond words.'

34

Coming to the path

Once you are on this path know that you are purified.
—H.H. SriSri Ravishankar

Becoming spiritual and beginning a transcendent journey occurs spontaneously for some, for no apparent reason. This is a sign of an evolved soul and the truth remains hidden until some historic instant when the veracity of life just gets revealed or a Master presents himself. Such was the case with Swami Vivekananda who was a known agnostic until a chance encounter with the Master Ramakrishna, who recognized him and gave him a glimpse of Samadhi. Following this, Vivekananda's enlightened soul was simply exposed and his journey across the seas to *'the Chicago Conference of Religions,'* became the first glimpse that the West received of an enlightened Guru.

Sonia Mehra heard about AOL through her mother. After marriage, Sonia came to live in the United States and always looked forward to receiving paper cuttings on Guruji's talk. She grew up with many gurus but did not really believe in anyone in particular, yet was spiritual. She listened to her mother talk about AOL but was still skeptical. Her mother and sister met Guruji and, while returning to the city, met with a severe accident. It was a miraculous escape and everyone felt it was the Guru's Grace that saved them.

'This was very momentous for me because my mom and sister were everything for me and that's what made me attend the course. The very first moment I entered, I was sold. My Kriya was just waves of love.'

Dr. Neelam Raval is a pediatrician, and on her sister's recommendation decided to take the course in September, 1993. Entrenched in a scientific world she has always been plagued by the occurrence of terrible events in the world. Her job and her life brought her into close proximity with sickness and misery and the advent of these universal questions spontaneously arising in her mind demonstrates that she was priming for spirituality. The answers science could not provide were given to her from the final day of her course. She claims: *'On the last day of the program I had an experience from within as if I were being spoken to.'*

Meeting Guruji in 1994, cemented her relationship to the path and ever since there has been no looking back. Just a few sentences from the Master in response to a query gave her a whole spectrum of answers. After Guruji blessed her as a Basic/Part 1 course Teacher in 1996, Dr. Raval has been conducting Art of Living programs very successfully. She also conducts 'GEP' Courses—Government Executive Programs, Sri Sri Yoga Courses and AOL Programs for Excellence at the workplace and is currently the District Teachers' Coordinator in her area.

Many others arrive at a time when debilitating illness reduces their zest for life. Marita Andreassen's illness was chronic but not really life-threatening. In the summer of 1997, Marita was learning some healing techniques in Norway and there were girls in the same group that attended a meditation group. She asked to join them, and was informed about the AOL course. Two weeks later she signed up and attended the course. Marita at the time was a student studying law, and had trouble with chronic sinus. The problems accompanying sinusitis left her with symptoms of a permanent cold which interfered with her state of well-being and her ability to focus on studies.

'After practicing Sudarshan Kriya for a few months, I was able to reduce the allergy pills and now I don't use them anymore. As long as I do my Sadhana regularly I have no sinus problems.'

Throughout the book I have recounted stories of people arriving at a low point in their lives where they needed the lift of a spiritual journey. They are here because of depression caused by loss, death, financial problems or a relationship crisis. Until you reach that point in your life where nothing answers your questions, no amount of information or seminars can convince you. If your mind is open, only then will certain solutions jump out as your unique deliverance. It doesn't matter which path you choose or who your Master is; if you are on a journey and are on a pathway with spiritual guidance, then you are indeed blessed. The need to go inward does not come to most in one lifetime and the soul needs to evolve through several lifetimes until it discovers its true identity and realizes that the only option is to go inward on the road to deliverance and enlightenment.

All of us are on a journey although we may be at different points. Anand Kumar recounts an interesting video on YouTube with Guruji. At the location, several courses were taking place simultaneously and people were arriving from different corners of the world to take the TTC. (Teachers Training Course)

Talking about the journey, Guruji mused, *'Haa, advance course kaisa hai?'* How is the advanced course progressing? He paused and continued. *'Kuch aa gaye,* (some have arrived), *kuch aane waale hai* (some are about to arrive), *kuch pahuch gaye hain* (some have reached), *kuch puhuchne vale hain* (some are on the verge of reaching), *aur kuch pahuch rahen hai* (some have almost reached), *kuch pahuchaa rahen hain* (Some are helping others reach). *Teacher ka kaam hai pahuchaana* (the teacher's job is to help you reach). *Voh khud pahuche na pahuche baat alag hai,* (whether they themselves will reach or not, that's another matter)'. Guruji laughs heartily and then as the audience settles he continues on a more serious note, '*Hain kuch jo pahuch gaye hain* (some have reached). This is how he summarizes the world.

Some have arrived, some are about to arrive.

Some have reached, some are about to reach.

Some have almost reached, some are being reached.

The teacher's job is to help you reach;

Whether they themselves have reached or not is debatable.

But there are some who have reached...

35

What is the Art of Living?

My vision is of a stress free world, a disease-free body, violence-free society, confusion-free mind, inhibition-free intellect, trauma-free memory and sorrow-free soul.

—H.H. SriSri Ravishankar

Art of Living and Religion

The Art of Living Foundation was instituted in 1981, by spiritual and humanitarian leader SriSri Ravishankar. Ever since, the program has grown and is now present in over 150 countries worldwide, where people of all faiths have embraced the practices and transformed their lives. More detailed information about the organization can be found on the website at www.artofliving.org.

Whenever people come across a new undertaking and one spearheaded by a Guru, there is internal resistance and skepticism. So far in most of my interviews I have encountered this as being a first reaction and objection to taking the course. People do not want to get involved in a cult and fear losing their religious and cultural identity. Newspapers in India are quick to expose a fraudulent Guru and this has led to a lot of spiritual refrain on the part of the community at large. Based on a handful of past experiences, they shy away from being duped by false saints.

Though the evidence confirms a majority of great, authentic and learned Masters teaching human values across the subcontinent of India, the resistance to try something different is very high. Following a movement and accepting a Guru is a leap of faith and many are not willing to take it. This, in spite of evidence supporting the techniques as proven stress relief.

The Art of Living has followers of every creed and faith and in no way interferes with or prescribes any religious belief. All my meditation teachers have so far been Jewish and though steeped in the Art of Living, they observe the high holidays and remain as Jewish as the day they were born. The only flavor added to their religious beliefs is one of acceptance, belongingness and tolerance.

Bhushan Deodhar from the Washington D.C. Center was never a religious person. He never really understood religion and stayed away from it. Even as a child when the family would visit temples, he never went in because he did not understand why he had to pray and why he had to ask God for everything. Going to a temple, mosque or church made no sense to his analytical mind.

Over time he began pondering why he was here and what life was all about. These types of universal questions started bothering and preoccupying him. Having fun and excelling in a professional career or having a family didn't add up. He felt that there was something more and so the quest began. He started searching, enquiring and reading and began with the works of Swami Vivekananda which served as an eye opener. It gave a very plausible explanation of spirituality and how it actually complemented science: *'It all started making sense. The philosophy started resonating very much within me and I started looking for a technique. I wanted to meditate and experience it myself.'*

At a Vedanta Society meeting on a friend's recommendation, he attended the Art of Living course which turned out to be exactly what he was looking for; an experiential process of applying knowledge. What religion could not satisfy, the Art of Living provided for Bhushan.

What Veena Narayanan likes about Guruji is, *'he explains spirituality in a very modern way. I am a very spiritual person but I am not orthodox. I don't like the rigidity in our orthodox South Indian manner that we have been following for ages. Guruji explains the essence of why certain rituals are done. We people hold onto the banana skin, and drop the banana. The younger generation should know the essence of spirituality, not just about religion. It is about tapping into the inner beauty.'*

Personally I identify with what Veena says. Hailing from a similar background, I have been following certain rituals for years. Having taught *Bala Vihar,* a class for culture and religion, for twenty years, it was always important for me to understand the reason behind Hindu rituals. This became much more significant after moving to live in the West as the children began questioning what we practiced. Meditation has transformed my person, my home and my surroundings into my temple and I need no rituals to access it. All I need is to close my eyes and descend into the sanctum of divinity. Yet I respect tradition and participate whenever I need to. Sometimes outward manifestation of faith is needed to give a spiritual foundation. It really does not matter what path you take to begin that inward journey; all of them lead to the divine.

Family resistance

Ronnie Newman started meditation in 1972, and for nearly 30 years her parents were unable to accept it. Graduating from Harvard, she could have found a well-paying job in the city. Instead she chose to become a Transcendental Meditation (TM) teacher and later an AOL teacher. But ironically, she is exactly what her parents wanted her to be; somebody with a social responsibility, able to listen to her own inner voice and chart her own path. They just wanted that to happen while she married a nice Jewish doctor had two kids, a stations wagon and a dog.

There needed to be acceptance by both parties for the relationship to become amicable. Ultimately the first step was taken by Ronnie, but only after she realized this axiom of acceptance.

'By me insisting they accept me, I wasn't accepting them as they were. They're first-generation Americans, half the family was killed in the Holocaust, and they are so invested in tradition. And their brilliant, beautiful daughter who is ready for the marriage market is busy running around the countryside teaching meditation.'

In addition to personal resistance there is a lot of opposition from family members who see such people as *'weird.'* Twenty years ago, yoga was viewed with such suspicion but today, there are yoga centers at every street corner and this ancient science is widely accepted as beneficial for both mental and physical health across continents. Strangely enough it is not considered 'weird' to drink alcohol, chase women, do drugs or be a debauch.

A novel glimpse of Divinity

Lucas Ejchenbaun lives in Argentina and was born into a Jewish family, a not overly religious household. His grandfather escaped from Poland in World War II and found refuge in Argentina.

'My family doesn't believe in "God". After seeing the religious persecution they escaped, I pray not to become religious. I always thought the idea of God was a lie, and I was praying to someone I didn't know. I don't believe in anything, I just live. Guruji has given us such an experience it is not anymore a belief in divinity but my very reality.'

I was brought up in the Hindu tradition and believed that God was up there and watched and heard everything you said or did and you had to ask Him for what you needed. With the Art of Living, my whole concept of divinity has shifted within. Divinity has grown beyond images, idols and rituals and has become more about who I am and how the consciousness that flows within me is the same one that flows within everything else. My perception of a personal God has morphed into this expansive, limitless ocean where there is only love and bliss. The journey into the present moment completely alters your views on divinity. My interviews brought the realization that we all share a common view on what we consider divine, whether you live in Albania, India or Argentina.

Fer Frassia a student from Argentina, felt Divinity was too big to describe with words: '*For me the Divine is what the world is made of and it resides in every heart. When you realize that, you can never think of saying an ugly word or hurt someone; you have no choice but to love them.*'

For Umberto Sartori, Divinity was a word signifying reality: '*To me Divinity is nothing more than what I am living. There is reality behind words but for me, Divinity has to do with honoring myself; that I am alive, that I have so much, that I grow in a positive way and that I learn so much each day. It has everything to do with who I am and that is sacred. Everything becomes divine by paying attention to things, appreciating it and seeing the grace flowing.*'

From Albania, Erjet Malaj says: '*When I met Guruji I felt nothing; that's a good thing. It's an experience of joy. When you see him it all disappears, no questions enter your mind. Everything is divine; it is that which keeps everything going on. Divinity is everything; the self, the ego, the mind. It's like when you make a hole in a paper you can see something. As the hole grows bigger your view keeps expanding and you see more of what it is.*'

As for Divya Mehta a teacher in the Bay area: '*Having that freedom to be in peace of mind is everything in life. This is my Art of Living where I have the tools at hand to carve my freedom!*'

Ganesh Nagaraj is a student in medical college and feels: '*People are looking for happiness outside of themselves. For me it's connecting to my inner peace and happiness, that's my divinity.*'

'*I mirror Guruji's concept of divinity. For him it is in the beauty around him. He sees every aspect of creation as a work of art and basks in the beauty that enshrouds him.*' Declares Kaushik Bhaskaran, who sees art and artistry in divinity.

Julia Tang reflecting on her spiritual journey holds that: '*I was always spiritual. It has just deepened; it's constantly changing; I see divinity as beauty and love. I am still enjoying the journey.*'

Bhushan Deodhar sums up this novel glimpse of divinity: '*AOL just made me realize that divinity is inside. It is not out there or somebody external. That whole concept changed. I understand that creation has come out of divinity. It needs a different state of mind to realize that everything is divine.*'

A practical guide to Life

Ru Wan was raised in Communist China and never really believed in any religion per se. Growing up in China there was no religion, a result of their culture and recent history. Ru's impression of religion was deeply connected to superstition. When she was in Middle school, she noticed that her mother started reading spiritual books. However, her mother didn't want the family to know and only read after everyone was asleep, which made Ru believe that this was some mumbo-jumbo. Subconsciously, this lack of spiritual awakening left a vacuum within her, one that longed to be filled. Nevertheless, Ru grew up with good human values of righteousness and being good to others. Basic human principles existed although not formatted in any way, which is why from a practical point of view coming from a background that was entrenched in doing the right thing, AOL appealed to her. Ru feels: '*AOL is so practical, contrary to popular belief,*

*this path improves your contact with the outside world, and you can
function more efficiently. We nurture virtues in a positive way.'*

AOL and Knowledge

The Art of Living is not just a set of breathing exercises followed
by a period of sitting and doing nothing. The breathing and
meditation prepares the body and mind to receive and integrate
the knowledge so that you can apply appropriate action to
improve. At the same time, comprehending the knowledge at
just a cerebral level does not bring about any change. This is
because the transfer from head to heart has not occurred and so
the knowledge cannot become a way of life. The Art of Living is
a symbiosis of breathing, meditation and knowledge all of which
seamlessly merge into one another.

Divya Mehta did not get hooked into AOL till she attended
Knowledge sessions on the *Bhakti Sutras* offered by an Art of
Living volunteer: *'It is only when the practice becomes amalgamated
with knowledge that awareness dawns of what has happened and is
present in every state; in sleep and in an awakened state.'*

Being religious and from a conventional background she had
always heard all this knowledge but till now it meant nothing
more than following tradition. *'When you hear the same things from
Guruji, it soaks into your nervous system and you start experiencing
it and it leaves you feeling amazed.'*

AOL is beyond religion

Jesica Tirado is a traveling teacher with AOL, currently based
in Madrid, Spain. She is Catholic and studied in a convent. She
talked about a course she had the opportunity of teaching a group
of nuns in Spain. Jesica went in expecting resistance but was
surprised to see how much they welcomed the practices, which in
no way interfered with their personal relationship with God.

'It was nice for me to teach them for a change. The talk compared the AOL knowledge points to the Bible. Guruji says to broaden your vision and deepen your roots. Learning about other religions has made me appreciate my own. The nuns do the Sudarshan Kriya and then pray. They say that is connects them so much to themselves, that they connect with God easier.'

Religious cults tend to be divisive and limited. The very definition of a cult lies is its exclusivity. It prescribes redemption only for members and does not embrace all ethnicities, religions and faiths. Joining a cult requires relinquishing your original beliefs and religion and replacing them with prescribed tenets. Art of Living is focused on the individual becoming more centered and happy and from that position of strength being able to contribute to the world around.

Shalin Desai has taught several courses and across the board, people of different faiths enroll and practice the breathing: *'In my experience, people don't really think of it as a cult. A cult is exclusive and AOL is all inclusive. No one is ever turned away. Yes, it does stem from ancient Vedic teachings. Guruji says that people in Saudi or the Middle East cannot claim that electricity was invented by Christians so we won't use it. If they have that mentality they will be left in the dark. It is foolish not to adapt and accept. We eat Japanese food, Chinese food so why not spirituality from India? That is what India is known for... spiritual wisdom.'*

Its very essence is compassion and acceptance, which is why Pia Lahdenpera, an architect from Stockholm, Sweden now believes that AOL is beyond religion: *'We were brought up as Protestants with the Lutheran Church and in the beginning, I may have thought of it as a cult because I had so much resistance. In the Part 2 course I had so many deep experiences, a cleansing of my body and soul and then it was just bliss and love.'*

Erjet Malaj is from Communist Albania. The country was Communist from 1945-1990 and religion was not allowed. After

1990, some chose Christianity and others Islam. Erjet's family is Muslim, but he never really prays in a mosque.

'People in Albania do believe in God who has created this world and personally, I do believe in God. I don't have any Islamic beliefs; I read lots of different books from different faiths. Here in Albania, AOL activities are yoga and stress relief and there is no preaching or conversion.'

Erjet was surprised at my question on his opinion whether AOL was a religion or not. Frankly, not being very conservative in his religious beliefs, he was quite open to anything that helped reduce his stress. He saw the Art of Living as a practical guide to life which saved humanity from the clutches of misery and put them on a path to happiness. He added with a laugh, *'If you breathe then you can be in the Art of Living.'*

The knowledge that Guruji presents becomes part of your daily life and has an effect at different levels. Once the transformation occurs, changes become apparent and these modifications don't come alone, they tend to affect a whole gamut of glitches in your personality, making you better adjusted to situations and people.

Veena Narayan could not pinpoint one area as the focus of change and found that it flowed through every pore of her being, making her float up above petty problems and really begin to enjoy life. *'Its taught me to live in the present moment in a practical sense and today I am living with more ease by living all the knowledge points. It's easier for me to accept people and situations, not being a football of others' opinions, not trying to find fault with others and think positive. This has caused a tremendous shift in my life and helped me progress in my spiritual path. I can feel more love towards all and feel very happy all the time.'*

AOL is Universal

Camille Abgrall was never baptized but was always aware of religion. He truly believes that AOL is a very complete practical technique beyond gender, religion and culture. As a YES! Plus teacher working in the European Ashram in Bad Antogast, Germany, Camille is involved with teaching courses that have been taught through the United Nations to the US and Russian armies, which would never connect with religious organizations. *'After 30 years, so many have benefited from the practice. Coke is made in the US but everyone drinks it. Similarly SriSri Ravi Shankar and His teachings come from India but like the Coke example, spirituality needs to be globalized.'*

What has struck Kiki, a teacher from Chicago about Guruji, is his irrefutable spirituality, his true belief in Vasudeva Kutumbakam, or one world family...*'He accepts everyone and gives them the space to do what they do best and have fun doing it. There is no pressure to be and act. Instead you can be natural do what you do best. Your core and essence is brought out and expressed. He wants you to do and be the best you can. He is like the Father taking care of the "Whole World Family".'*

AOL is your natural self

One of the main purposes of the Art of Living is for each and every one to tap into their true nature and achieve their maximum potential. Mired in the world delusion makes you incapable of discovering your path and this leads to trials and failures, depression and disillusionment; all of these cause suffering and misery. SriSri leads by example and shows how a vision for the world came to realization within the span of two decades. He doesn't want for you that which you don't need for yourself. He makes no demands and your participation is by choice.

Art of Living and Hinduism

Umberto Sartori found the practices novel, yet very welcome. After the first Sudarshan Kriya his body reacted at a physical level, accompanied by mental relief. The meditation was quite a revelation into a state of awareness discovered quite by accident. Now he can bring it back at will in any stressful situation. But Umberto did not recognize its worth immediately, as he was born in a tradition that did not value meditation: '*I thought non-Catholics go to hell. There was very little understanding of humanity and the mind. My first exposure to spirituality was through a cultish organization, so AOL was a revelation. I don't think AOL is a religion; it's a living tradition but there is no conflict. It's more a culture from India and its closer to Hinduism whether you like it or not; the practices, the Ayurveda, and the religious days observed like Shivarathri and Guru Poornima. If you get involved beyond the practice you may decide to practice customs which are Hindu and that's fine as long as you don't judge it. It's like celebrating Thanksgiving. Once you move to America and fall in love with a way of life, your practices gravitate around it.*'

Guruji celebrates with the world traditional Hindu festivals as well as religious holidays from all faiths. I have seen him with a Santa hat at Christmas, a Muslim traditional *taquiyah* and the Jewish *yamaka*. To him it's an act of embracing culture and honoring that which people hold very dear as part of their tradition.

Hinduism is a way of life (*Sanathana Dharma*) and no two Indian cultures, ethnic groups, castes or even families practice the same traditions. The rituals and prescribed participation vary from community to community and yet all of them are irrefutably Hindu. Whether you visit temples, follow rituals, observe high holidays or not, it doesn't take away from the fact that you are Hindu. The essence of Hinduism lies in its capacity to absorb any practice within its fold. There are no prescribed texts which you *have* to read or no fixed time and place for prayer. You can pretty much be who you want to be, pray if you want to, attend temple festivities if you choose to and participate in cultural activities if you care to.

The Art of Living stems from Hindu roots and carries with it this essence of freedom to do what you want and to participate to the extent you choose. If you wish to learn the chanting of mantras you can, if you want to stick with Sudarshan Kriya, that is up to you and if you meditate only you will benefit. There is no concept of social ostracism or exclusion within this fold. People participate in events based on their personal commitment and priority. It is possible to take what benefits you and leave the rest. And no one will judge you for it, which is the beauty of the Art of Living.

Art of Living: Simplicity of Knowledge

The Art of Living presents the highest wisdom in a manner that is easily understood by everyone. You do not need to be a Philosophy major to appreciate and apply the knowledge. No matter what your background, these basic principles reflect core values that every good human being possesses and wants to live by. It merely reminds us of axioms we know but never practice. Reading and thinking about the knowledge combined with awareness, allows application of knowledge points towards overcoming daily obstacles. It allows you to live your life without making any drastic changes. You don't have to give it all up and move to the ashram, although some choose that path. You can be right here right now, given your current circumstance and make the internal change that allows you to go deeper within yourself and yet maintain a lighthearted attitude to life.

Vikas Sinha from Chhattisgarh, India loves the simplicity with which Guruji's knowledge is presented: '*I think he has some kind of contract with the nature's law. He makes us understand and once that happens, we become calm and everything plays out according to what we want. He gives us a positive attitude to life.'*

Shalin Desai says: *'The way Guruji has given us knowledge is like that of a mother and baby sparrow. A mother sparrow chews the food and then feeds the baby sparrow. This is exactly what Guruji has done with the knowledge. He has given it to us in such a simple format that a learned spiritual person or a novice can still get so much from it.'*

Knowledge about life and the Universe is so abstract that sometimes it goes beyond average human understanding. Not all of us are Doctors of Philosophy but all of us live and can benefit from advice on the best techniques to minimize misery and maximize happiness. SriSri has simplified the highest knowledge and presented it in such a practical and applicable way that you can seamlessly move through life with no pain. The knowledge is repeated continually and even if you forget to apply it to life situations, when repeated often enough it resonates in your inner mind. In conjunction with Sadhana, your daily breathing and meditation, the propensity to recall and apply knowledge increases. The first time you apply the knowledge point with good results reinforces it in your mind and, over time, with little or no effort you find yourself using it without any forced cognition. It becomes part of your life, part of who you are. Short phrases remain in the forefront of your thought process: drop your expectation; don't see intention behind mistakes; don't assign blame; the present moment is inevitable; opposite values are complementary. All of these axioms become part of your existence, guiding principles to steer you away from misery. Each day is an opportunity to apply a new knowledge point. Life presents new and more challenging situations to give you the opportunity to grow, to rise to the trial and to overcome hurdles with a smile on your face. The beauty of the Art of Living lies in its holistic approach preparing the body, mind and intellect to collectively combat

life's challenges by bringing everything to the level playing
field of the present moment. In that present moment nothing
matters except your equanimity of mind and inner stillness. It
is then that you realize that nothing is more important than
the love and happiness which is your true nature.

The Symbiosis

Hinduism is a way of life that constantly adapts to new knowledge
and makes room for change. This prevents the redundancy of
blindly applying ancient texts to modern knowledge. Many
other religions, perhaps traditional Hinduism included, don't
move away from what the holy books prescribe. With so many
changes taking place each day in the modern world, people tend
to become close minded and intolerant in attitude, unwilling to
compromise and unable to mentally adjust to such modification
that contradicts ancient tradition. The beauty of the AOL
movement is that it is on the pulse of change and can therefore
embrace any innovation. Because it is nonreligious there are no
'must do's' and 'should haves'. This is what makes it a movement
for the future.

Hansa Dave is an AOL teacher in the DC area. She affirms
that AOL provides all the means, techniques, wisdom and all
that we need to be happy in this modern life; *'It combines ancient
wisdom with modern lifestyle.'*

And Shalin Desai adds: *'It's not that life has no problems and
struggles. You will have situations where you are lost but AOL gives
you the strength to deal with the situations. Like an insurance policy,
by having one it doesn't ensure you won't get into an accident but if
you do have an accident, you can rest assured you are covered.'*

Perhaps Ramola Prabhu with over two decades of experience
practicing and promulgating the knowledge encapsulates the
essence of the movement best:

'*AOL is part of life and a wonderful way of living with knowledge and innocence. It needs to be part of every learning institution and its applications are available in every field. It makes the world a wonderful place, based on teachings that are natural and easy to apply in the way it's taught. It engages people from all walks of life and gives tools for all aspects of living. Learning for change is the art of living. It is the word of God made more diverse and more applicable that improves the quality of living.*'

36

Special programs and successes

Expand your vision and see that inside every culprit, there is a victim crying for help. That person is also a victim of ignorance, small-mindedness and lack of awareness. It's the stress, lack of understanding, lack of broad vision about life and bad communication that leads to violence in society.

— H.H. SriSri Ravi Shankar

The Prisonsmart program was launched in 1992 and is currently available in 32 countries. Over 200,000 people have benefitted worldwide from participating in this program, which has been adapted to suit the needs of particular institutions and varies its curriculum depending on the inmates taking the course. The teachers receive special training in order to qualify to work with institutes and agencies of crime.

SriSri believes that all criminals are victims and behind every act of violence is a history of stress and other exacerbating factors like lack of love, poverty, socioeconomic conditions and mental illness. What happens is that once incarcerated, continual association with criminals does not permit a break from the chain of violence. There is violence and sexual assault in jails and gang association becomes crucial for survival. Loss of liberty doubles the feelings of being a social victim and the combination of isolation, guilt and blame against a backdrop of confinement becomes an inextricable web of bondage. Once released, such people are unable to adjust to the free yet apparently hostile world. With so much opposition and struggle to find gainful employment, they slip back easily into a life of crime, making them an even greater menace to society. The goal of the Prisonsmart program is to break this chain of violence, get the prisoners in touch with their consciousness and assist in assimilation on release.

Prisonsmart

Reaching people deeply entrenched in the criminal system is a challenge, one perhaps much easier for a person who has been in this dark and crooked world and has had the fortune to escape his predicament and find salvation. Within the Prisonsmart program are several ex-cons who have benefited so much from the program that they dedicate their lives to helping others. I had the fortune of speaking with one such person: Jakob Lund from Denmark. His story is deeply moving and demonstrates the power of the Guru, the process and divine grace. Jakob Lund spent his youth deeply involved in the murky world of crime and violence. He was a trained martial arts expert and had a job as a bouncer in a night club. But his addiction to drugs dragged him under:

'It went very quickly downhill as I progressed from marijuana to crack and other drugs. When I took drugs, I developed psychosis and was seeing dead people and things coming out of the walls. Reality was misty and I lost my identity completely and knew I needed to get treatment. I didn't want medication and would leave the hospital as soon as I felt better and soon begin drugs again.'

It seemed that the cycle could not be broken. Jakob had taken the AOL Part 1 course but never practiced the Sudarshan Kriya and pretty soon reverted heavily to drugs and was sucked into the associated sleaze of crime and violence. Eight long years passed. Finally he decided to retake the Part 1 course, which resonated in some part of his brain as a bygone moment of peace. The following week he enrolled in the advanced course and that's when he met Guruji: '*He made a strong impression on me. I felt something very uplifting in my soul and I could see there was something more to life. As long as I was on drugs there seemed to be no meaning, no reason to live. After the course, even though I felt bad about my past actions, at least I had hope, I had a glimpse of peace that I experienced in the course. Even though I was not ready to go into it fully, still it was an impression on my consciousness so strong that in spite of my feeling bad, it followed me like a shadow.*'

It took two long years of determination and extreme discipline to finally kick the habit. The practice awakened something in him and the Master had stirred that which was stronger than the bad impressions carried in his consciousness.

The transformation

'*Earlier it was the surroundings that created the excitement. Now I get the excitement from within me in that beautiful space that is surreal and so warm. The quality of excitement has shifted. The more I am connected the more I find what to do with my life and get all my answers.*'

The addict in Jakob disappeared and very soon he became a teacher in AOL. He began to teach prisoners and drug addicts, people with PTSD after war, and serial killers: '*Guruji realizes that a change is needed and to stop violence you need to go to the root from where the violence stems.*'

Imprisonment is a School of Crime. It doesn't help. In fact it increases criminal tendencies. There is no cure just being locked up, with time in hand and no guidance. In some prisons where Jakob worked, especially in South America and Morocco, the energy was very bad and it was hard to make any headway. In the beginning no one was ready to speak to them. He would invite people from the criminal world to his home and conduct courses. He knew people in that circle and then they invited others and even without advertising it became bigger and bigger. Then suddenly, one of the prisons contacted him and they started a course there. Now with so many participants, they are looking for an even larger place.

'The funny thing is that so far no one has ever stolen anything from me, even if I had money lying around. Literally hundreds of criminals have been here; gang members, robbers and really violent people.'

His mental shackles so deeply connected to crime, were broken, yet he felt the need to return to that world. Only this time, he approached it from the perspective of Seva: *'I had no choice; I had to do this. It was a calling from deep within me. I have been working with hardcore prisoners, murderers, people in the mob, assassins, robbers, organized crime; really tough people. These techniques are so powerful that it is possible to transform them even though they have such heavy impressions. The goal is to reach and connect with that part of their consciousness that is untouched by their history. You give them a tool to raise their consciousness. Such people are victims and when I see them, I look beyond their actions. Actually I never am scared, I feel safe and protected because I am doing the Guru's work.'*

Connecting to the source

Jakob believes people resort to violence because they possess emotions and feelings they can't handle and merely react according to some past impressions. It becomes important to protect honor in the criminal world and they take offence very easily and do what is necessary to maintain their power and position. Unmindful of the price and results, they kill and maim to protect the ego. The course makes groundbreaking changes because, for the first time, they have to examine their actions and the consequences on their own psyche. For the first time the ego is set aside, honor is buried and actions are examined from the standpoint of emotions and feelings. Once they reflect and connect to themselves and others, it becomes more difficult to be criminal.

Karma and crime

The question that has always plagued me is why some people have the propensity to hurt another and others don't. Do people slip into a life of crime because they can't escape their Karma? Are the impressions from the past so deep that they scar the psyche, propelling them into violent actions? Jakob agreed with me on Karma revealing itself as past impressions:

'There is darkness in some people and if that person allows light to enter, change can be affected and you can make the Karma disappear. But this takes time and the person needs to be ready to prepare themselves and that's what AOL does.'

Crime and guilt

Prisoners have a lot of guilt about the past. To overcome guilt, for a time they punish themselves and then are ready to commit the same crime again. The program encourages them to feel the effects of their actions right here and now, be with that and feel it fully, only then do they find freedom. Many course participants are successfully integrated into mainstream society, some even turn vegetarian. Not only do they give up a life of crime but also help others. They can reach that section of society that normal people can't and therefore become real role models because they have lived a life of crime and have been able to give that life up.

Jakob Lund is a living example of this. He also works with soldiers who return traumatized by war. They kill for the country, still the very act of killing leaves an impression. They are haunted by their actions; by visions in the day and nightmares at night and get caught in a cycle of guilt, blame and regret. Whether you kill in self-defense, to protect your honor or the honor of your county, killing is killing and when you shoulder responsibility for taking another person's life, it scars you.

Learning while teaching.

'Some of the most honest people I have met in my life have been in prison. These people have the courage to open up without a mask. They have the time and can be very spiritual. If you want success in prison you have to reserve your judgment.'

Jakob admits that his work does drain his energy and he needs the silence to recuperate. He doesn't socialize much and has to meditate a lot and be vigilant, in order to find his own space and make that space vibrant with energy.

Kiki works in Prisonsmart in Illinois. She was apprehensive at the very beginning but it was such a learning experience and she felt empowered being able to help where it was so badly needed: *'Working the prison program was such a life-changing experience. Teaching the program I realized the inmates were so wise, they were so eager for this knowledge and at times I felt they were teaching us. They were so hungry for the Kriya. Everyone is a victim and the circle of crime has to stop. It cannot go on and on. My prayer is that we can offer and teach our programs at the grade school level. It is critical that we teach children how to handle their stress and negative emotions while in school before they commit a crime and look at a life in incarceration.'*

Ramakrishna assists in prison programs in Durban. He escaped the shackles of bondage to his mind and he understood their captivity at a cellular level: *'To see them smiling and hugging us on the final day, saying if they only had the knowledge they wouldn't be here in the first place, is unbelievable. I identified with*

them because I had been there in my mind. To see the change in them
after one week is beyond words.'

Saving endangered teens

Being a YES Teacher, Mrinalini deals with the most difficult
age group during adolescence when youth are at a crossroads,
trying to become adults while still traversing childhood: *'In*
my experience, teaching youth is a challenge and at the same time
extremely joyful. Children are very natural and have no pretenses. If
you are being fake they will tell you to your face that you are. Their
authenticity makes you more natural.'

The common denominator amongst troubled youth is low
self-esteem, and problems communicating with parents. Some
children come into the course contemplating suicide but after
the course have the strength to face life. Her most memorable
experience was in New York, teaching at-risk youth. This was
taught at a detention center where students who committed
violence or used extreme abusive language, (but not crimes
violent enough for them to go to prison) were brought for a
period of time as a 'punishment' of sorts. These centers were used
to help them to reform their ways and get them reintegrated to
school. She found their entire aggression against societal norms
and challenge of authority streaming from their background,
where they had never received the love and attention due to a
normal child. Even though there was no funding at the time,
SriSri wanted them to continue and do more courses for this
fragment of alienated teens, because he believes that reaching
them at this age is crucial in preventing further degeneration
into a life of violent crime. This was the time to help them access
their consciousness and make better choices for a hopeful future.
With no funding, IAHV persevered with the program, with
unbelievable success. Their rationale lay in reaching one child at
a time. Even one solitary child who chose hope in lieu of suicide

was a step closer to the attainment of the Master's vision of a violence-free society: '*There was amazing feedback from teachers and students. They claimed students were calmer and were listening much more in classrooms and even broke the cycle of returning to the detention center.*'

I have nothing but admiration for these brave Seva warriors who dedicate their lives to helping misguided rejects of society find salvation. The rest of us have judged them, don't want to associate with them and are happy that they are locked away. Such people we condemn, we look down on and leave to rot in their cells. It is easy to have compassion for your near and dear ones and we sometimes feel lofty forgiving a spouse for having hurt us. How difficult it is for any of us to embrace people who have lived and want to escape this world of violence. We want no association with them and with the legacy of crime they carry and have no compassion for them. They are denounced, shunned and left to deal with their own mess. After speaking to these teachers I realized the importance of focusing on criminals as they are the root cause of violence.

It is easy to feel belongingness in a peaceful world but it takes a great person to have this sense for the perpetrators of crime. We by our aversion spurn them and ultimately what they want, like what everyone wants is to belong, to be accepted and to be loved. Do we have it in us to sincerely accept them?

37

Art of Living in Mongolia

The message of non-violence must be loud and clear. We must promote human values–especially love, compassion and belongingness.
—H.H. SriSri Ravi Shankar

The great Khan Temujin was responsible in the 12th century for consolidating nomadic tribes and creating the Mongol state. He was crowned as Genghis Khan, head of the Mongol state and through his lifetime conquered most of the Eurasian steppes. He was known and feared for his cruelty and lack of compassion for the enemy.

The Mongols were raised in a harsh environment and lived off the land, eating virtually anything. Blood from their horses sustained them through the long incursions into Russia and Europe. Their cruelty was boundless and on conquering new terrains they mercilessly destroyed the population, raped the women in a combination of physical and psychological warfare.

In 1921, The Mongolian People's party established a communist regime with the help of Soviet Russia, which was replaced by a peaceful Democratic transition in 1990. In the early 1990s the Communist party had fallen apart, the economy collapsed, shelves in stores lay empty and factories were closing their doors. At this time the Mongolian people lost their jobs, had no money and the environment was gloomy and depressing. Today, more than four million Mongolians live outside the country.

Over time, Tibetan Buddhism became the popular and peace-loving religion for people reeling from centuries of violence. During the communist regime religion was banned and the Russians had destroyed all the churches and temples; high officials and Buddhist monks were killed. This spiritual vacuum coupled with economic paucity made this region prime for rebirth with the Art of Living.

At around this time the Mongolian Health Minister and his family moved to India for a year. Living in Bengaluru, his wife Sarantsetseg suffered from severe allergies. Someone told her that Sudarshan Kriya helped alleviate symptoms of allergy, so she decided to take the course and that's when she found her Guru. Over the next year she took several courses and under SriSri's personal guidance became a teacher.

On her return to Mongolia, young and energetic Sarantsetseg started teaching courses and once people took the course they felt reborn. After the course they wanted to share this transformation and brought their kids, relatives and friends to take the course. At that time Mongolia had a population of 2.2 million people, of which around 1 million lived in Ulan Bator, the capital city, and the rest in rural areas. This meant that the news about the AOL course spread quickly in the city, and the name Sarant became an integral part of every Mongolian's vocabulary.

There was only one problem. During the course, students were not served meat. This was particularly hard for them, because Mongolian winter is usually cold, mostly reaching from -40-45°C and they are accustomed to a high protein diet to keep warm. Sarant had her job cut out convincing participants that it was only for the duration of the course. But the benefits of vegetarianism struck a chord somewhere and after a few years, vegetarianism gained popularity in Mongolia. Another factor which persuaded many to include more vegetables in their diet was the average life expectancy, which is age 55 in men and 60 for women. The breathing opened doors to a healthier lifestyle and many were willing to adopt a vegetarian diet to live longer and healthier lives. Today Ulan Bator boasts of several vegan and vegetarian restaurants and almost a confirmed 10% of city people are vegetarians.

Sarant has worked tirelessly to promote the Art of Living in Mongolia. She began teaching government officials in small groups and the turning point came when the President of the country and the Senate members enrolled in the course. In Mongolia, almost 70% of the population has taken the Art of Living course, a feat achieved singlehandedly by Sarant and the team she consequently trained.

Sarant teaches in Mongolia for most of the year and also has conducted courses in the US and that's where Billy (Sukhbaatar Bilguunzorig) first met her. I met Billy at the Boone Ashram this year and he has been my source for all the information on Mongolia. I had been emailing the center in Mongolia for six months with no luck. Then at Guru Poornima this year, I saw Billy and recognized him from a previous course. Talk about coincidences; I had a Sankalpa and the Universe provided.

Billy came to the US in 2001, as a student. After his studies he travelled around and then settled down in Washington D.C. and was working with a Korean hardware installer from 2003-2005, during which time he somehow injured his lower back. The pain was constant and debilitating and Billy tried everything from Allopathy to Chinese acupuncture, Korean and Japanese alternative medicine, but nothing helped. A chance meeting with Sarant changed everything and she promised that if he learned Sudarshan Kriya everything would be fine. At this point Billy was willing to try anything. There were 55 Mongolian people taking the course led by Sarant, who by now was a household name in Mongolia. Recalls Billy: *'During Kriya, I was releasing a lot of stress and the pain. I felt a shift within me and now I can tell it was part of my transformation. During Satsang, Sarant sang a Mongolian song and it reminded me of summer camps in Mongolia and that brought me to such a happy place.'*

Soon after, Billy met Philip Fraser, a senior AOL teacher and one of Guruji's first devotees. Phillip asked what he did and when he realized Billy was a general contractor, he was thrilled. He asked for Billy's help, as they had taken over a building in Washington D.C. which they wanted to convert into an AOL Center. Billy went to do Seva and in four days redid Guruji's room. Phillip was starting an advanced course right about then and Billy took the first of his many courses. He finished the center and, in 2010, went to the LA center and fixed it in two years and now he is busy working in the Boone Ashram.

Mongolia is one of AOL's success stories. In the short span of two years it went from nothing to more than half the population taking the course. It demonstrated the vision of the Guru and the power and drive of one person changing and forging the spiritual destiny of a nation.

38

The Art of Living in Argentina

Dissolve into infinity, be in the moment and look beyond events.
—H.H. SriSri Ravi Shankar

Back in 1995, I lived in Buenos Aires, Argentina, for a few years. At the time there were a handful of Indians and vegetarian food meant 'pasta with ham' in a city where the people, primarily of Italian and Spanish descent, ate meat every day. It was virtually impossible to find a restaurant serving pure vegetarian food; almost every so-called 'vegetarian' dish was prepared in beef or chicken stock. Argentine Beef being world famous, locals commiserated with you on hearing you didn't eat meat. Around the time I left the country, an economic recession hit the economy hard, and bulimia and divorce were serious social problems. Crime and poverty spiked sharply. Many unhappy, misguided and depressed folk were looking for a way out of their misery.

The movement started in 1997, when Guruji sent a member of the Lions Club, a teacher from AOL, who gave a talk followed by a course. Then Guruji sent a teacher who taught courses for a month, following which SriSri came for the first time to Buenos Aires. There were almost 1,000 people in a stadium and Beatriz Goyoaga attended that meeting. She was taken aback by his presence and in the meditation Guruji guided, found a lot of peace. After that, she took a stress management course organized by AOL and that was a turning point for her. At first AOL consisted of only Beatriz and soon there were 10… 20…a 100. In the meantime Beatriz trained to be a teacher and worked night and day to promote the program in the city. She trained almost 200 teachers who trained another 200 and the organization now has over 400 teachers. Over 4,000 people in Argentina take the course every week and it's just growing every single day. She has personally taught some 42,000 people and 1,800 prisoners as well as Police and Prison system workers.

'You find course participants everywhere. Whether it is a waitress, a hairdresser, a banker, a CEO or a dean from a University, the penetration of the AOL is amazing. We prepare Yogathons, Marathons and intro talks with syndicates. There are 2,000 people working in AOL Seva projects in shanty towns. Everyone is very active and very happy and it is a huge success.'

AOL took off in such a magnificent way because of a mixture of things—proper timing, goodwill, and Guruji's grace. According to Beatriz: *'When we started, we had a group of volunteers working 16 hours a day and we gave everything we could to the foundation and then we were lucky it happened. He saw our intention to spread meditation, breathing and human values and he granted us with rewards. Our Seva was rewarded within a year.'*

Beatriz Goyoaga hails from Spain and is a journalist who has been in politics and economics for 25 years. When she joined AOL, Beatriz was the Director of International Press Services. The pressures of the job left her so stressed: *'I think it was just my time to start helping society with what God had blessed me with. I am a full time teacher and organizer and am extremely happy.'*

Esteban Coll is currently the President of AOL in Argentina. He did the course in 2006, when on a sabbatical he met Guruji at a Satsang in the Bengaluru Ashram. Since 2009, he works on the board with a very nice group of people who are very committed to the cause.

Two things have worked well, according to Esteban. People needed quick and continual access to centers with qualified teachers and a support group. If there was an area where a few teachers worked well, the board supported them and opened a center. It functioned as a community center for Satsang and yoga, where people would meet and enjoy and help each other. Today there are 17 centers in the city and about 30 in Argentina.

Secondly, the organization tries to maintain transparency so people have confidence that the money is being spent legitimately. This transparency is important in gaining the confidence of members.

Youth Movement

Young people have flocked to this movement and currently, 20–30 is a strong group. Word of mouth has been their greatest advertisement and they never need to campaign for any for publicity. As Esteban puts it: '*Society is quite violent at this moment and lifestyle is stressful and the course has a lot of value. Buenos Aires is a trendy city; going green is trendy, yoga is trendy and so AOL has become trendy.*'

Beatriz reiterates the same: '*The youth are looking for a change. They are tired of the same old drugs. Youth like trends. When marijuana was trendy they went for it and now AOL is trendy, they are looking for change. They have fun without the drugs and alcohol. We are not against people having a drink; we try to prevent people getting drunk and violent.*'

Now every year, 40,000 people take the course. The speed with which the movement is spreading is breathtaking. Fernando Frassia is part of the increasing number of youth taking the course and making AOL an integral part of their lives:

'*It's a spiritual revolution. People are realizing that the material world with its fraught relationships doesn't result in happiness and there is this search for something more. When they see other children who are just natural, playful and joyful and who don't need alcohol to have fun, everyone wants to be with them, they hear about the course and do it. They are self-motivated and are making others do it by example.*'

The movement is so spontaneous and the music is what attracts the children. The city has hundreds of nightclubs and partying is a serious pastime for youth in Buenos Aires. Only now they dance all night in pure joy; an expression of bliss, a natural effulgence of their true selves. And Fernando is happy: '*It's so wonderful that they are starting their journey at 14 or 15. When they hit their 40s they would have been meditating for 20 years.*'

Stress and relationship problems

In Argentina the teachers see stress in everyone and believe it is caused by economic and relationship difficulties. In their 40s many people get divorced, jobs are hard to come by and they seek happiness outside themselves. Bulimia used to be a problem but is waning nowadays.

Esteban was in a crisis when he decided to take a year's sabbatical. He was divorced and had trouble with his children. He married very young and by 24 had three children. An engineer by profession, he also did his MBA and had worked in many multinational companies. Life was very generous but at the end he was still not happy. Divorced at 40, he was disillusioned with life: '*It's hard to say why. Everything seemed okay but we were not happy and started distancing ourselves from each other.*'

Although there were no open fights, Esteban and his wife kept avoiding each other. Meeting other persons happened after the break, and really, that's when the fights began. Through all of this the children suffered, especially his older daughter. At this critical juncture in her life, his 15-year-old daughter hated her father and was furious with her mother. Misguided, she became pregnant and through all of this never spoke once to Esteban. It was sheer torment for him, not being able to reach her or work things out with his wife. Naturally with so much mental turmoil, his work suffered and he felt as if his life was falling apart, which is when he decided to take that sabbatical. On his return he attended a course and slowly his life was pieced together again, only this time the pieces were made up of breathing, meditation, Seva and Sadhana: *'I felt a connection. I was touched by his goodness. Guruji gave me back my smile. I remember crying through my first Kriya. I thought these people were crazy, but nice, crazy guys.'*

The mindset of the people was not so favorable. In the beginning many thought AOL was a cult and others thought they were a crazy group brainwashing everyone. Now it is so widely accepted, even politicians and people in the government are talking about the AOL. Beatriz likens AOL to movements like Green Peace, which is for cleaning the pollution on earth and maintaining the pristine areas. Similarly AOL is doing the same but for the mind. It takes responsibility to unravel the stressed mind and prevent clean minds from falling prey to anxiety. It is a non-political and non-religious movement. She is a practicing Catholic and has not and will not convert. Most people she teaches are Catholic (about 20%) and some Jewish (20%) But the main thrust has been to target the intelligentsia: doctors, psychiatrists, neurologists and academicians.

As Beatriz explains: *'It is at a very high level of sophistication in academics and is very respected. We are not a group of hippies chewing cannabis. We have Deans from Universities bringing the program into schools. Doctors have seen their patients improving and are vouching for us.'*

New Innovative Programs

Recently AOL has introduced nonprofit organizations for meditating doctors and medical practitioners, professors, teachers and educators. There are others for lawyers and for business persons and its filling up with hundreds of new members each day.

Marco DiGiano began a new program called SriSri Tango. This is a course which incorporates tango with yoga and knowledge. People come for the tango and stay for the knowledge.

Discovering this course was very natural and the proposal was immediately accepted by the board. Although Marco wasn't a great dancer, he spearheaded and planned the content for the course. In countries like Mexico in South America, they offer tango sessions then do the intro talk, after which participants are encouraged to take the course. In Europe this has become increasingly popular, especially in Sweden, Germany, Italy and Spain. Marco says: *'Always the grace of the divine is there. And it's such a joy to see everyone smiling at the end of the course.'*

Adds Beatriz: *'My view of divinity has been awakened by Guruji. I always had knowledge of the divine but it was only a concept. I believe in the laws of nature and the spirit behind it and Guruji is a messenger. I have met very fascinating people in my life but nobody has awakened me to action like him. He has never demanded anything from me. He just enlightens by example. We become light and happy in his presence.'*

Between the age group 8–80 years, some 170,000 have taken the course since 1998, 60% of them women. Art of Living has mushroomed in Argentina in an incredibly short time and all because of the perseverance of one woman: Beatriz and her team of dedicated Seva enthusiasts, realizing her dream of spreading the happiness. Today the city boasts of several vegan and vegetarian restaurants. Rock bands have sprouted, playing in nightclubs with a difference. They sing *bhajans*! The youth flock to these clubs and enjoy the music without the accompanying alcohol, drugs and sex.

In 2011, Argentina hosted one of the greatest ever events. SriSri led the meditation for the '*The Planet Meditates*,' and this was simultaneously telecast to over 300 cities worldwide. In Buenos Aires they reportedly received a group of over 150,000 meditators.

In a world where violence and crime against humanity grabs headlines, it is a refreshing change to see a country so dedicated to affecting change and bringing a smile to millions of faces.

39

The Journey-Yoga

It is said: "Yogaha karmasu kaushalam", the skill in action is yoga. Yoga itself means skill. Yoga is the skill to live life, skill to manage your mind, skill to deal with your emotions, skill to be with people, skill to be in love and not let love turn into hatred.
—H.H. SriSri Ravi Shankar

The ultimate goal in all spiritual practices is to settle the mind. SriSri refers to yoga as being skill in action. In order to develop such proficiency it is important that you harness the quality of mindfulness. Before any journey inward can bear fruit, the first stop is to honor the body. Proper attention to nutrition and exercise prepares the body to receive the fruits of pranayama and meditation.

The word yoga has Sanskrit origins and literally translates to 'yoking, attaching, focusing attention on'. The practice uses physical exercise in conjunction with the pulse and breath to allow the various organs and systems within the body to be enriched with oxygenated blood for improved functioning. Yoga is the connection at one level of the body and mind; at a more esoteric level it is the union between the soul and the Brahman.

There are several health benefits. Doctors and medical practitioners have recognized this and recommend yoga asanas for alleviation and cure of hundreds of chronic diseases, from lung and heart disorders to bone and muscle repair. The power of the body to heal itself is immense and merely requires discipline, focus and intention to achieve the necessary health benefits. Every minute cells die and regenerate, allowing healthy cells to replace defective ones. I have merely enumerated a few generic benefits from the practice.

Breathing

Yogic breath uses parts of your lungs which are scarcely utilized in daily life. This increases lung capacity and delivers twice the normal volume of oxygenated blood to the body. Though focused pranayama or breath exercises are at the next level, yogic breath brings awareness and attention to the trajectory of the breath and for the first time connects your life force to its source.

Flexibility

Yoga Asanas use different sets of muscles and when practiced over a period of time can herald relief from chronic joint aches and pains. My yoga teacher always told me that: *'You are as old as your spine'*. Those of us who suffer from back pain know how debilitating it can be. Degeneration of muscle and bone may lead to chronic and excruciating pain. Hundreds of nerves emanate from the spine and effect different parts of the body. Injury to any portion of the spine can have repercussions on any and every part of the body. The spine supports the body all day and in our daily lives we do not manipulate the backbone. Yogic spinal twists develop greater bodily strength and flexibility and stretching the spine increases the spaces between vertebrae, releasing pinched nerves. Spinal twists also squeeze internal organs and release trapped toxins. As you move out of the twists the organs receive fresh oxygenated blood and function more efficiently. A good yoga routine should include at least a couple of spinal twists. Yoga is best learned from a qualified instructor as opposed to an instructional video.

Strength

Yoga develops core muscle strength, needed to keep the spine erect and prevent further degeneration. In combination with balance and flexibility it improves posture and increases muscle tone. Daily practice of a yoga routine is comparable to a two hour daily workout at the gym. This becomes significant as you age, because of degeneration of bone and muscle. Yoga maintains muscle tone and allows you to live a longer but, more importantly, a healthier life.

Stress relief

Perhaps the greatest benefit comes in the form of stress relief. When you are in a yoga class, the mind is totally focused on maintaining the postures and does not get a chance to escape into the world of problems and solutions. Just getting into the asana is such a challenge that, often, I don't notice the soothing music till it is relaxation time at the end of class. The mind is set free, attention is focused on the body from within, through the portals of the breath. Research indicates that regular practice of yoga reduces cortisol (stress hormone) levels and is therefore an accelerant to relaxation.

What is Yoga?

Pantanjali's yoga sutras (#29, Book 2) refer to *'Ashtanga Yoga'* (Eight-Limbed Yoga). The eight different steps in yoga are: *Yama* (Moral Commandments), *Niyama* (Self Purification), *Asana* (Postures), *Pranayama* (Rhythmic control of breath), *Pratyahara* (Withdrawal of senses from the external world), *Dharana* (Super Concentration), *Dhyana* (Meditation) and *Samadhi* (Liberation).

The physical aspect of Ashtanga yoga is *asana* or postures. These were said to have been revealed to ancient sages during meditation and are designed to develop mental equilibrium, agility, balance and vitality. Yogasanas are in close conjunction with evolution and environment and poses reflect animals, plants and other aspects of nature. Every asana is synchronized with the breath, making it much more potent than mere gymnastic exercises.

In 1990, after months of aerobics classes, I severely injured my spine and was recommended surgery with metal implants in my upper vertebrae. At the time I hadn't hit 30 and could not even consider such surgery. I had lost sensation in my left side and knew the situation was grim. For two years I was on steroids for pain and visited the physical therapist weekly; I also gained 25 pounds. I had 40% movement of the neck and was almost constantly in pain for the next five years. In Argentina, I heard about the Indira Devi School for Yoga and had a personal trainer from there work with me for two years. It was my first introduction to yoga but I looked forward to the sessions. The stretching of my spine took place very slowly and the teacher was tuned in to the body and breath, quickly shifting gears and switching asanas at the slightest indication of pain. Today I practice yoga regularly, and have been pain free ever since and never needed the surgery.

Yoga was my first body-mind connection which prepared me to receive and benefit from Sudarshan Kriya. My personal experience has convinced me about the efficacy of yogasanas with chronic illness and I highly recommend that everyone take a class. If nothing else it will give you an hour of freedom from the mundane drills of life, leaving you energized and ready to face the next day.

40

Sudarshan Kriya

Breath is the connecting link between the inner world of the mind and the outer world of body and environment.
— H.H. SriSri Ravi Shankar

Sudarshan Kriya was revealed to the Master, SriSri Ravi Shankar, in an inspiration, a revelation in deep meditation, harnessing ancient breathing techniques to connect and channel prana, the life force that drives the human body. Sudarshan Kriya contains a series of cyclical breathing patterns preceded by a specialized form of *Ujjai* (victorious breath) and *Bhastrika*. Practiced with focus and intention, it bridges the gap between the worlds of inner silence and outer expression of life.

Mirroring cycles of nature, sequences of day and night, seasons, planting and harvesting, the body has biological rhythms. Emotions rise and fall and the mind closely follows such patterns. When such rhythms are in sync, we feel a sense of harmony and well-being. Modern day living produces stress which throws these natural tempos off balance, which is then followed by unhappiness, anxiety and discontent, culminating in sickness.

'Su' means proper, 'darshan' means vision, and 'Kriya' is a purifying practice. Sudarshan Kriya is therefore a purifying practice, connecting to the source, leading to a true vision of the Self. This unique breathing practice energizes the body at a cellular level, increasing prana, converting negative feelings to positive and raising levels of enthusiasm and motivation, all of which have natural effects on how we view ourselves and the world around us.

The breath has the potential to leach the body of toxins and beneficially impact hormones that promote well-being and manipulate emotions. Every emotion we experience is accompanied by a corresponding breathing pattern. When we are tired the breath is shallow; with anger breathing is rapid and with relaxation it is long and deep. By control of breath we in effect control emotions. Applied to the real world, the breath can be a powerful tool in moments of anxiety, anger or fear where you can willfully change the pattern of breath and therefore the accompanying emotion.

Ronnie Newman has been connected to research on the benefits of Sudarshan Kriya for over two decades. According to her, *'Sudarshan Kriya is the best-kept secret on the planet for your health, well-being, attitude in life and your experience of moving through this world. As we navigate through life, the knowledge and techniques help in terms of practical tools. It combines everything— cutting-edge Biology, Psychology and Sociology and it does it in the most efficient manner possible. I have been doing research for 20-odd years and I have never seen anything like his. I have been a meditation teacher, researcher and student. From all three perspectives there is nothing more powerful than the compilation of practical knowledge and techniques that these programs offer.'*

Chakras, Prana and emotions

The word *chakra* translates to wheel. A simplest explanation of a chakra is a spinning vortex which creates an aural vacuum capable of absorbing vibrations. According to ancient Vedic knowledge there are seven such energy nexus within the body. Each chakra is connected to specific organs in the body and reflects a different element and consciousness. This is where emotions manifest, sensations emerge and stress is stored.

The First Chakra (*Muladhara*: earth element) is located at the base of the spine. Energy enters the body through this chakra and ascends along the spinal column.

Ascending prana: *Enthusiasm:* Descending prana: *Inertia.*

Physical organ association: Gonads, adrenal gland, the kidneys and the spinal column.

The Second Chakra (*Swadhishtana*: Water element) is located about four inches above the base of the spine behind the sexual organs.

Ascending prana: *Creativity:* Descending prana: *Sexual energy.*

Physical organ association: Spleen, kidneys and bladder.

The Third Chakra (*Manipura*: Fire Element) is located behind the navel (solar plexus).

Ascending prana: *Joy* and *generosity:* Descending prana: *Greed* and *Jealousy.*

Physical organ association: Adrenal glands, pancreas, liver, stomach as well as the nervous system and the bladder.

The Fourth Chakra (*Anahata*: Air element) is at the Heart center.

Ascending prana: *Love:* Descending prana: *Hatred* and *Fear.*

Physical organ association: Thymus gland, heart, blood, circulatory system, immune system, and the endocrine system.

The Fifth Chakra (*Visuddha*: Ether element) is in the throat region.

Ascending prana: *Gratitude*: Descending prana: *Grief.*

Physical organ association: Thyroid and parathyroid glands, lungs, vocal cords, and bronchial apparatus.

The Sixth Chakra (*Ajna*: Light consciousness) is in the region between the eyebrows just below the forehead.

Ascending prana: *Awareness:* Descending prana: *Anger*.

Physical organ association: Pineal gland.

The Seventh Chakra (*Sahasra:* Thought) is at the crown of the head and is connected with bliss.

Physical organ association: Pituitary gland.

If you pay close attention to sensations arising in the body you will see the close link to emotions. This is the reason when you feel grief or gratitude the throat closes or that you knit your brows in anger, or that the chest contracts with fear and hatred but you feel a sense of expansion in the chest area with love.

There are two easily accessible sources of prana; the food we eat and the air we breathe. Prana is the life force that keeps us going and the movement of prana determines the quality of the mind. An upward course brings positivity and the reverse is accompanied by every negative emotion. Sudarshan Kriya reverses the downward tendency of prana which is why it leaves you energized and enthusiastic about life. It clears bottle necks at the chakras and this prevents the onset of disease. It brings clarity of mind and awareness, both of which are crucial as we make choices that shape our destiny. As Ronnie Newman says: '*The higher the prana the higher the consciousness. The more regularly you do the breathing practices, the higher the prana, the happier you are. It has a snowball effect. It's not just for relieving depression, it is so much more. When you make it a priority the universe aligns itself around you to make things happen.*'

First experience of Sudarshan Kriya

Breath is what keeps us alive yet in our daily lives we pay scant attention to it. This is what makes the first experience of Kriya so powerful. In a short period of time there is so much fresh oxygen, prana and grace entering the body and flooding the brain that it both purifies and uplifts you. The experience for each person differs, depending on the baggage they bring to their first course. For some it is memorable, for others it isn't vivid. Every person I interviewed felt different sensations; some were leached of pain while others felt a physical lifting of stress. For some it was waves of gratitude and for others it surged as a sense of belongingness. Kriya gives you exactly what you need at that moment. It aligns your energy chakras and clears the blockage at the source.

Stress management

Ganesh Nagaraj had taken Art Excel courses at the age of sixteen, but it wasn't until the Part1 course that it became a more engaging and spiritual experience:

'Kriya helped me to be happy and deal with the stress, especially in my freshman year. I feel I really have an advantage knowing that I have this unique and useful tool and have inspired my friends to take the course.'

While all his friends had problems dealing with exams and getting organized, Ganesh was more in control and found time to practice his Kriya every day. Both in Undergraduate and Medical School his stress was always academic. The expected activity to unwind after exams was to drink and most of his friends did the usual, not knowing how to deal with stress in a healthy way. Ganesh by his own example has inspired an expanding circle of friends to take the course and use an alternative for stress management.

For many years Goran Popovski from Macedonia was looking to find himself, to release stress, belong and just be happy. After his first experience with Sudarshan Kriya, he believes it is the most powerful yet the simplest technique. Sudarshan Kriya has the ability to remove bodily accumulation of stress at a deep level.

'In the first moments after my first Sudarshan Kriya, I did not know what was happening to me. I felt twenty kgs lighter. All my fears, old emotions and feelings of being hurt, were released. Afterwards, I felt as if I had just recovered from sickness, all the pent up anger collected in my lifetime was escaping. This went on for the next twenty four hours. I could literally feel each part of my body. And then…all that was left was the deep experience of belongingness and true love.'

Increased Energy level

Dr. Alka Ahuja currently lives in Muscat, Oman, and when she did her first course in 1996 in India, she experienced a deep internal transformation. But the real change came after the first six weeks:

'After I practiced my Sudarshan Kriya for 40 days I started feeling very energetic and a different sort of happiness dawned in me. That was a very stressful period in my life. I was a full-time teacher at the University and was doing my PhD as well, and I had to care for twin daughters who were very young. But strangely enough, things started happening smoothly. In six months, I submitted my thesis and I was almost superhuman, doing so many different things, yet I was so happy.'

Alleviation of fear

Fears about the future can destroy your mental state and reduce you to a bundle of nerves. Obsession with such fears takes away from the present moment and although they seem silly and trivial to bystanders, for the person undergoing stress related to fears, their predicament is scary, all-consuming and very real. It is the only reality for them. Sudarshan Kriya moves them into a space of clarity where such fears simply dissipate and an inner strength replaces it. This is because the heart center controls fear and love and when Sudarshan Kriya accesses your true nature which is love, fear simply fades.

Waves of gratitude

The moment you realize how much you have, the hankering after unfulfilled desires stops. When you are in that space of gratitude, the feverishness disappears, life becomes a bonus and everything it offers, a blessing. You are happy for no reason. You are at peace with the world. A sense of comfort and peace dawns deep within and in that instant you connect with everything and everyone around you. For me personally, I write best immediately after Sudarshan Kriya because it clears my mind and paves the way for new ideas to crystallize. Marco DG's experience is similar:

'Sudarshan Kriya helps you to reach your conscience and be happy for no reason. Once I finish Kriya I get many ideas. I feel so grateful. I am so lucky to be able to feel this energy, to be comforted that I am not alone, that I am playing the best game. I feel like a millionaire.'

New sensations

For Pawan Mulukutla: *'My first Sudarshan Kriya, the experience was so strong; I have never before experienced such sensations in my whole life. It's the first time I understood what the word peace meant. There was as stillness in me. I was regular for the first forty days. I kept repeating courses and I finally met Guruji in Miami in 2004.'*

Ravi Pathak was curious about Sudarshan Kriya when he first visited the ashram. He was allowed to participate at Satsang but politely asked to wait outside when the group practiced

Sudarshan Kriya. Swami Sadyojathah, a senior teacher at the ashram, asked him to take a course which was to begin and he agreed only to satisfy his own curiosity.

'I had a great experience with my first Sudarshan Kriya. I spent the weekend in the ashram and I was now in on the "secret happening" that I had not been privy to earlier. From that day there was no turning back.'

Kriya and the realization on opposite values

Lucas Ejchenbaun from Argentina was in his first year of University when he failed a Music exam which was eliminatory, meaning if you passed you were in, else you were out of the program. Naturally he was terribly disappointed and even really angry with himself. A friend at the University used this opportunity to persuade him to take the course. Lucas had some interest in spirituality and practiced Ashtanga Vinyasa Yoga but was not satisfied, as it was very physical and he was looking for something more. His experience with his first Sudarshan Kriya was unique.

'The Panchakosha Meditation was amazing. I felt everything at the same time, opposite values but very strong. I felt I was one of millions but at the same time I realized I was alone.'

Creativity and Kriya

The period of time right after Sudarshan Kriya can often be your most creative. The mind is relaxed and the body energized with fresh oxygen, there is really no stress and the world delusion is minimized. Given this comfortable resting place, you can immediately connect to your source and come up with what needs to be done at that moment. Solutions to problems emerge, writing ideas flow, new and innovative concepts spring to mind and the day is filled with enthusiasm and motivation. For Veena

Narayanan, the period right after Sudarshan Kriya is her most productive time of day. What is even more amazing is her ability to connect astrally with people as powerful thoughts during Sudarshan Kriya. *'Often I get some new recipes or cooking ideas during my Sudarshan Kriya. Creative ideas for decorating my house, gardening and painting come up. Things which I need to complete or things which I have forgotten or things which slipped my mind pop up suddenly when I sit in meditation after Sudarshan Kriya. If I am thinking of someone whom I need to contact, he suddenly calls me after my Sudarshan Kriya. A lot my desires seem to get fulfilled. I am able to attract a lot of people with whom I want to connect.'*

Grace of the Guru

For most, the connection with the Master does not come at first but once they realize that the Grace of the Guru is what alleviates their pain, then the connection becomes apparent. This is why the breathing has to be learned in a course with the Art of Living by a certified teacher. The teachers have undergone a rigorous training process and the Grace of the Master simply flows through them. We are all connected through conduits of energy that permeates the super consciousness and without receiving that blessing no spiritual practice can achieve its true potential. Practices of yoga, pranayama and meditation need the physical presence of a teacher who can guide you, correct your mistakes and ensure that the techniques are learned properly. For Sonia Mehra: *'I felt such a deep connection to the Guru. It was the most amazing sense of belongingness with the Universe; I jumped totally into it and did several courses.'*

Madhu Bhardwaj, a teacher in Mumbai, turned to AOL when she lost her mother, who was diagnosed with cancer, and succumbed to it within two years. Madhu was very brave while her mother was battling the disease, and was in and out of hospitals. Towards the end when she slipped into a coma,

Madhu actually prayed to the Divine to take her away and end her pain. For the first few months afterwards, Madhu was in denial and did not shed a tear. But once the realization hit her, she wanted to end her life. She had no wish to live without her mother and was totally overcome by guilt. She wanted to punish herself by committing suicide. As a result her health deteriorated to a point where she couldn't function normally:

'I was 30 years old and I couldn't sit or stand and suffered with crippling migraines. I made everyone around me miserable. People in my building wondered if I was being beaten up because I used to scream with pain.'

When a friend suggested she take the AOL Part 1 course, SriSri was not that well known and Madhu had not heard about him. She didn't want to do the course but completed it, even though she was in a terrible physical and mental state right through. After the first Sudarshan Kriya, Madhu came home and slept peacefully for the first time in months: *'And the memory of that has kept me going. In the last 11 years I have not missed a single Sudarshan Kriya.'*

It even helps the over-analytical

Timothy Wong like many others who take the course out of curiosity was so entrenched in his corporate world and had such an analytical mind that he was a skeptic from the word go. But the practice is so powerful it changes you whether you like it or not:

'My intention was to go for an hour. After the first day they said we need a four day commitment. I resisted a lot, didn't close my eyes, looked around during Sudarshan Kriya and was amused that some people were having deep experiences. On the fourth day when I woke up from bed something had changed inside me. I could not pinpoint what it was but everything I was searching for my whole life was answered.'

Addictions

Jesica Tirado works with a lot with people who have addictions. When the breathing techniques are used, the need for the drugs and alcohol becomes organically less. They work through their problems much easier. In Europe, drinking alcohol is very acceptable and easily accessible. You can buy beer even in McDonalds. Alcohol gives people the delusion that everything is okay and life is good and they are unaware of their true feelings being masked behind the screen of intoxication. They start young and don't realize when their intake increases or when they cross the border into full blown alcoholism. Says Jesica: *'People are not aware of breath and how it affects them. After Sudarshan Kriya in an instant you get a flash of insight that all the things that were bothering you are really so small. Getting time to do it daily is difficult but you have to take a decision and make the effort in a promise to yourself to feel good.'*

Taking responsibility

Beatriz Goyoaga believes that negativity comes either from bad habits including food and alcohol, or from tensions and stress. Of course if you lose the job you become unhappy. But you can prepare the mind to lose the job and still not be unhappy. Unhappiness is not in society. You put the cause of stress in your boyfriend, in traffic, in your job, your family, your husband. The stress is in your mind. When people realize this and take responsibility for it, then they don't make demands from society and stop commanding happiness from the family or from others:

'With AOL you understand it is your job to clean up the mess and to be happy. Then you start practicing things which give you access to happiness and it is really very simple: Breath and meditation. Both are complementary but not the same. Breath cleanses and meditation deepens your experience. You cannot see through a dirty window.

Ideas, desires and all the bombardment of the mind cloud the vision. The breath helps to clean this so you can go deeper.'

Medical research

All the above testimonials are personal experiences. But what do doctors and scientists have to say about Sudarshan Kriya?

Dr. Neelam Raval lives in Ahmedabad, India and has personally conducted research and presents to medical practitioners about the health benefits of Sudarshan Kriya. (SKY)

'Sudarshan Kriya relieves stress. It has different effects on various parts of the nervous system and releases different hormones. The practice changes cortisol levels, a hormone, the reduction of which promotes good emotions and causes happiness. It has been scientifically demonstrated that it releases stress and causes clarity of mind. This combined with yoga helps balance the cardiovascular, muscular and digestive systems.'

The medical repercussions of stress

Chronic stress can break down the smooth interactions in our mind-body axis and negatively affect every aspect of our lives. According to the emerging medical field of psycho-neuro-immunology, there is a rapidly growing body of research linking psychological and behavioral factors to physiological parameters which predispose us to a broad spectrum of diseases. From the common cold to chronic and life-threatening ailments ranging from cancer to coronary heart disease, asthma and HIV-1 infection, research has shown how the breath can play an important part in preventing and reducing diseases exacerbated by stress.

Effects on Blood Lactate

Blood Lactate levels are another biochemical indicator of stress levels. In a study conducted with a group of Police trainees, there was a fourfold drop in such levels taken after a period of five months as compared to those not practicing SKY.

Antioxidant enzymes

Environmental pollutants and psycho-social stress can cause bodily buildup of toxins which lead to the formation of free radicals. This has been one known contributing factor in diseases like cancer, cardiovascular degeneration and aging. In the same group of police trainees, blood levels of three major antioxidants were measured. After five months SKY practitioners had higher levels present in their blood stream, suggesting that their defense against free radical build up was much stronger.

Cortisol—the stress hormone

In a controlled study, results indicated that experienced SKY practitioners had lower baseline cortisol levels than new practitioners, and new practitioners had lower levels than those simply relaxing while listening to classical music. This indicates that SKY practitioners experience a greater ability to relax and more resilience to stress.

Immune function

NK cells are Natural Killer cells which are part of your immune system, capable of destroying foreign invaders and tumor cells. When compared to a group of non-practicing individuals and cancer patients in remission, it was found that regular SKY practitioners had significantly higher NK cells.

Brain Function and Depression

In one study of the long term benefits of Sudarshan Kriya on brain function, EEG's on 19 practitioners were compared to 16 non practitioners. There was a significant increase in beta activity in the left frontal, occipital and midline regions of the brain in the first group. When looked at in conjunction with studies demonstrating increased alpha, it suggests that regular practitioners have more ability to achieve states of deep relaxation coupled with high alertness. Published studies suggest that Sudarshan Kriya normalizes brain wave patterns increases serum prolactin (well-being hormone) and is effective as standard antidepressant drug therapy. In addition it has no side effects, is cost effective and empowering.

In a study cited in the Harvard Health Publication (April, 2009) on a group of alcoholics in a detox program, at the National Institute of Mental Health and Neurosciences of India, those that were taught SKY had significantly lower levels of cortisol and corticotrophin. Their scores on a Standardized Depression Inventory dropped by 75%. Studies have also confirmed relief from depression in those suffering from PTSD. More detailed information can be found at www.aolresearch.org

Blood Cholesterol and Hypertension

Stress is one of the main contributing factors for coronary heart disease. Studies have indicated a drop in total cholesterol and LDL as well as an increase in HDL. (good cholesterol). For those with elevated blood pressure, just taking your blood pressure before and after Sudarshan Kriya may demonstrate a drop in both the systolic and diastolic readings. (For me the drop is between 20-30 points.)

Sudarshan Kriya and its accompanying practices have reached over two million people, spanning continents. Studies about its long term benefits are ongoing and are nothing other than a revelation of its efficacy.

The Art of Living Foundation is transparent about the results of such testing and information on the benefits is freely available on the internet.

For me personally, Sudarshan Kriya is what keeps me grounded and centered. I did not have a remarkable experience with my first Sudarshan Kriya but in combination with meditation the results have been magical. I only realize the benefits of Sudarshan Kriya if I don't do it for a couple of days. Then the irritation and anxiety comes back and I get reminded how important it is to take time to rest the mind and focus on the breath. Because that determines the quality of the rest of the day.

In my humble opinion, it is Srisri's greatest gift to mankind.

41

Seva—Selfless Service

When you make service the sole purpose in life, it eliminates fear,
focuses your mind and gives you meaning.
— H.H. SriSri Ravi Shankar

The Center for Disease Control and Prevention, estimates that one in ten US citizens is currently depressed or being treated for depression. According to studies conducted and published in the *Journal of the American Medical Association*, the following are true of people with depression.

- Recent statistics suggest roughly seven of every one hundred people suffer depression after age 18 at some point in their lives;

- As many as one in 33 children and one in eight adolescents have clinical depression. Suicide is the third leading cause of death for ages 10 to 24;

- Most people diagnosed with major depression receive a diagnosis between their late twenties to mid-thirties;

- About six million people are affected by late life depression, but only 10% ever receive treatment;

- For every one man that develops depression, two women will, regardless of racial or ethnic background or economic status;

- More than half of all people caring for an older relative show clinically significant depressive symptoms;
- By the year 2020, depression will be the 2nd most common health problem in the world;

These are alarming statistics and one of the main reasons stems from the current definition of success. Success for the modern day man or woman is defined in reference to the world around, which translates to a good job, lots of money and functioning relationships. Failure to meet these socially imposed standards results in lack of self-esteem, which then manifests in dissatisfaction and unhappiness and culminates in depression. As long as we gauge our happiness based on outside influences and forces, over which we have little or no control, depression is going to be a major impediment to progress in a balanced society.

SriSri believes that the sure antidote for depression is to move out of yourself and do something to serve someone else. As Shalin Desai says, '*AOL affects changes in you, from "why me?" into "what can I do for others?" A sure way into depression is asking "why me?" One adornment in all AOL people is the smile on their face. Service grounds you and as life unfolds, things don't shake you because you have that confidence that there is a greater power that always looks after you.*'

Depression is a direct result of internalizing problems, blaming the self, feeling guilt and helplessness in the face of circumstances and feeling victimized. Loss of a job or a loved one, financial difficulties and relationship problems are seen as root causes of unhappiness. Being happy or sad becomes so tied into people and situations that it becomes impossible to conceive of happiness as being part of your nature, divorced from the outside world. There is a whole world out there with millions of people who need your help but when you are so engrossed in your own needs and your own little world of problems, you forget about everyone else and don't want to add to your burden by taking on someone else's sorrow. There is a complete lack of belongingness and as long as you feel isolated you cannot look beyond yourself.

Dr. Alka Ahuja believes that lack of belongingness prevents happiness in people because they place the ego above everything else. When the ego dominates and directs your actions you are on the path to misery. The only antidote for this disease is Seva:

'You need to start giving without expectations; when you do for others and forget about it and don't attach anything to it, this makes you truly happy.'

The problem in today's world is that we don't want to do anything for free. Every service performed has a fee attached to it and in this scenario Seva has no role. The rewards of Seva, fortunately, have no dollar value attached to it; they are intangible. They lie in happiness, in a smile of gratitude, in the sight of a hungry man gobbling a loaf of bread, in the touch of a caring hand. How can one even conceive of quantifying such rewards? The benefits of service are much bigger than your effort. They can be instantaneous or in the distant future. The remuneration is in the internal transformation, it lies in the satisfaction gained from the opportunity to serve, it basks in the higher ideal of serving the divine. As Guruji says: *'When you do Seva, you are not doing others a favor. After doing Seva you are rewarded immediately. The reward of Seva is certain and is always more than your effort. Expecting a reward turns Seva into labor.'*

Gurpreet Singh was told by Guruji to involve himself in Seva projects. He was living in the Bengaluru Ashram at the time and in spite of battling depression he implicitly followed the Guru's direction. *'I would do anything from flyering to organizing courses. No matter what was asked of me I did it, sometimes even before I was asked and the feeling was so good.'*

Ganesh Nagaraj has the enviable advantage of *'getting it'* at a very young age. The whole purpose of Guruji's vision is to inculcate and foster belongingness. At the esoteric level, this is the Brahman concept that there is only one; but at a more practical level, by serving the community, divisions dissolve, ethnicities merge, classes unite and there is only one. Seva is the practical application of the Brahman or 'one consciousness' principle. And it is taught in the very first few minutes of the Part-1 course. For Ganesh, this is the most important aspect of the Art of Living:

'I belong to you. It's the first process in the course. In Hinduism there is no dualism, there is only one. The basic tenet of divinity is to see it in all.'

Now that Ganesh is armed with knowledge he feels committed to share the wisdom and is constantly organizing courses on campus. When he presents the program, he focuses on the utility of the techniques, how to understand, deal and manage emotions, learn to release stress and negative emotions, to use breathing techniques to rest, relax and reenergize. The satisfaction comes from giving to others what is beneficial, and that is the reward he receives.

Lucas Ejchenbaun at the young age of 24 has wisdom beyond his years. *'Save your mind at any cost with any of the tools provided, whether it's Seva or Sadhana. Seva is the most valuable tool in my life. I feel connected to Guruji when I do his job. All the blessings come from him.'*

Seva Opportunities

Nirmal Matella is currently in Togo, where the need for Seva is monumental. In spite of the difficulties, Nirmal is filled with gratitude for the ability to serve and make a difference: *'Opportunity to serve comes from Grace. My only tool and strength to be able to work here is my practice and application of knowledge.*

I am here to be available and serve. At times the pain, poverty and hopelessness that surround me leaves me overwhelmed, but acceptance of the situation brings divine strength within me and leads me to a possible solution. I feel lucky and chosen. In easy conditions anyone can work but tough situations are Guru Stories in the making.'

Dr. Alka Ahuja delved into Seva projects as soon as she finished her first course. Her first project involved opening a school (Sri Sri Sewa Mandir) in a slum in Delhi. Other NGOs helped build the school, and they started classes for small children, tailoring and computer courses for young women, all these to help children from less fortunate sections of the society. *'It was such a beautiful feeling! Guruji has shown us this path of service. Life has become better, our inter-personal relations have improved and we have learned that life is much more than work and home.'*

Even after moving to Muscat in 2003, Art of Living is so much a part of their lives, Seva has become natural and effortless. As faculty of the AOL, she feels the biggest gift one can give to mankind is to show them a path of service and love and to empower people with breathing techniques which bring back the enthusiasm in one's life: *'It is so close to our heart. Even as we serve others, we feel such a sense of belongingness as though we are working for our own family. We do this just like working, eating and other normal tasks. There is no extra effort. Just having a life of Seva has stretched me and shown me that I am capable of so much more. Service just takes you higher and higher.'*

Sameer Desai shares: *'The biggest impact of AOL is moving out of myself and doing Seva, because I know it's what he would want me to do. He is my guide. Reading his knowledge and basing my next step on what he has indicated gives me strength. The spiritual path is tough but Seva eases the way.'*

Preity Thomas an AOL teacher, shares knowledge sheets and has done a lot of work online with live chat. She replies to queries on the AOL website and releases course information via e-satsang. Family responsibilities didn't permit her to work outside and when she could not become a teacher, she found a way to help others while sitting at home. There are many who have real psychological disorders, health and relationship issues, some have questions about the course, others have reactions and need help. Preity has addressed the whole gamut of problems and basically functions as an online counselor.

She recalls a time a young boy wanted to commit suicide. He was failing in his exams and could not tell his parents. Socially inept, his friends did not like him. In addition, he was in a new city and felt isolated. Preity did a number of things. She calmed him down, found a follow-up center near him, made him realize there was nothing wrong with him and that committing suicide was not the answer.

'I asked him to do Kriya and Seva and chant "Om namah shivaya." By the end of the chat this boy was not only ready to live but was prepared to take the advanced course with Guruji.'

Seva: your very nature

Guruji believes that all of us are hardwired to serve others. If this were not so we would not be living in a world with so many people, many of whom need our help and assistance. It is the world delusion that takes us away from this natural need and once we access this untapped reservoir, the Grace just flows in our lives. Jill Smith believes: *'If I look back I have always had the urge to help people, now it has a name; Seva.'*

Ronnie Newman is constantly involved in new research on the various aspects of spirituality and its effects on what constitutes happiness and she believes the world is moving away from a trauma vision to a fulfillment vision. It's insufficient to study and reverse pathology, as that's merely one side of the coin. There are new markers emerging for the Happiness Index: *'There's a whole new field of Positive Psychology, which is the scientific study of what makes people thrive, of what makes a life well-lived. The pleasure center of the brain actually gets stimulated when we perform service for others, so we are wired for service, for Seva.'*

Unexpected rewards

In Bengaluru, India, while doing a course right before the AOL Silver Jubilee celebrations, Meena Krishna joined her uncle on a *padayatra* (walking trip) to promote the event. Volunteers followed the leader who was called Chayanna, giving flyers to pedestrians and putting stickers on cars at traffic lights. Chayanna was a senior member at the ashram and, in his white dhoti and long beard, resembled SriSri. Meena had not met the Master but was happy doing Seva, after which they were to meet SriSri for Satsang at the Ashram.

They walked to the Kanakpura Highway and continued their work. Someone on the street invited Chayanna to enter their home, so she watched him go and continued distributing pamphlets. At the traffic signal Meena asked the driver for permission to put the sticker on his van and he started laughing and asked her to look at the passenger inside. Meena was puzzled and when she looked inside she wondered why Chayanna was in the van. She smiled and said, '*Chayanna, you decided to go by car, is it? You don't want to continue with the padayatra?*' Everyone was laughing and the passenger just smiled. Meena turned around and saw her uncle Chayanna emerge from the house behind her. She was confused. In that moment she realized it was Guruji.

'I touched his feet and tears of joy rolled down my cheeks. Around 700 people were in the padayatra but only I had the opportunity to meet Guruji. If you are really hollow and empty and you do Sadhana and Seva you can meet Guruji, even at a traffic signal.'

Seva projects

The Art of Living has several ongoing Seva projects all over India and around the world. When Anirvachan decided to become a full-time teacher, he was assigned to a group of villages in the Hassan District of Karnataka. It was hard work but Anir remembers that time as the most valuable in terms of the happiness within him:

'Seva is the most valuable tool in my life. I feel connected to Guruji when I do his job. All the blessings come from him.'

Service should never be seen as an act of charity because that brings home the image of dropping a handful of leftover coins at a traffic light. All faiths prescribe charity because it makes you commit to service and, once committed, the natural rewards flow in your life.

Acts 20:35: *'In all things I have shown you that by working hard in this way we must help the weak and remember the words of the Lord Jesus, how he himself said, "It is more blessed to give than to receive".'*—*The Holy Bible ESV*

In Christianity, charity is seen more as an act of love. It lies in giving not what you don't need but that which is precious to you; your time, your effort and your love.

In Islam obligatory charity is called *zakat* and *sadaqah* is voluntary endowments. The Qur'an states: *'And be steadfast in your prayer and pay charity; whatever good you send forth for your future, you shall find it with Allah, for Allah is well aware of what you do.'* *(2:110).*

While you can never belittle generous philanthropy which funds relief and research, the most precious gift to yourself is Seva. If in your lifetime you get the chance to help even one person, that very act tips your Karmic balance and allows Grace to flow.

42

Meditation

Meditating is the delicate art of doing nothing—letting go of everything and being who you are.

—H.H. SriSri Ravi Shankar

Meditation is a higher state of consciousness that relaxes the body and mind while simultaneously refreshing and energizing it.

1. EEGs taken by researchers of individuals, most were not patients but seemingly healthy individuals in meditation, show very few Delta waves. These waves are most prevalent in sleep:

2. The presence of Beta waves is indicative of an active and alert mind. It is more accurately indicative of heightened alertness and sharp focus than activity. Certain types of meditation show periods of Beta activity alone, which indicates attentiveness:

3. There is a greater presence of Alpha waves in the back of the brain, showing restfulness and calm:

4. There is sometimes indication of Theta waves in the frontal area, indicative of deep relaxation, mental imagery and control:

5. Some meditations produce Alpha and Beta simultaneously, an important distinction since not all meditations are the same:

6. A fourth major state of consciousness, sometimes referred to as 'restful alertness,' or 'hypometabolic alertness', when the body is also at rest and the mind is completely awake within itself, is also possible. Not all meditations produce this state.

During meditation the body sinks into a deep relaxed state and the breath slows down. However, it differs from deep sleep, in that awareness is heightened during meditation and you are aware of movement and sensation at a perceptively acute level.

Why meditate?

Meditation is a cleansing process that is the only true rest you can give to the mind. Through the day the senses receive hundreds of images and impressions which get embedded in the brain, revealing themselves as thoughts and emotions during wakefulness and dreams and nightmares at night. While sleep gives the necessary rest for the body, it does not give complete respite for the mind. The mind does get periods of rest during non-REM sleep, according to Guruji and science. However it is an involuntary rest, different from meditation because it is rest with no awareness, whereas meditation is rest with awareness.

In deep-REM sleep, the mind is most active and you are likely to awaken with elevated blood pressure and pulse rate. Meditation is as necessary for the mind as sleep is for the body. It rejuvenates and energizes the body and mind, allowing you to have an active and fruitful day.

Studies have shown that meditation increases the density of grey matter in the brain, which may result in clarity of thought and idea. The period right after meditation is usually your most creative, as concepts originate intuitively from your inner self; and most often those are the best ideas. In memoirs of all great inventors, their groundbreaking ideas were an expression arising from their source. Almost all of them express this spontaneous revelation of truth as sprouting from pure intuition.

Raji Swaminathan is a molecular biologist in Mumbai and believes her practice allowed her to be way more creative than she could ever imagine. *'I was doing experimentation on rice researching techniques for it to grow in harsher environments. After taking the AOL program, I started designing my program differently. I was thinking clearer and was much more productive. The result was an 'out of the box- type' of thinking which had great results.'*

For me personally, writing after meditation requires no effort; ideas just keep flowing, the mind is fresh and the body rested. I know one thing; if I had not learned to meditate I would probably have been stuck in my mental chatter, wondering what to make for lunch and what to buy from Publix Supermarket. Meditation allows you access your true nature so that the path that is right for you just emerges and unfolds.

Meditation eliminates fear

Behind every fear is the fear of death. Meditation gives you that glimpse of what you can expect after death. When you voluntarily drop the body and mind and are able to emerge once again from that state, it implants the idea of permanence, the indestructible quality of the Brahman. In that moment you confront and surpass the death experience. This is powerful medicine for people suffering from chronic disease, awaiting their demise. Meditation removes fear associated with death and replaces it with enthusiasm. It gives you back the ability to smile, knowing that any day it might all end. After all, death can visit any one of us with or without notice. We might as well spend the rest of our days enjoying what we have, rather than lamenting what we are about to lose.

My mother was broken after the loss of her husband, my father. In those first few months we didn't believe she would be able to pull through. But she received *deeksha* (initiation) and a mantra from her Guru Karunamai. It was meditation that brought her back from that dark and hopeless place into the reality of life, giving her the will to carry on, not merely existing but enjoying what was left of her life. Without the meditation she would surely have succumbed to her will to join my father. Meditation changes the quality of your mind, calms your thoughts and realigns your desires. It has to be experienced to be understood.

Meditation relieves stress

The body is so relaxed during meditation that areas of accumulated stress get released. People suffering from severe migraines often find a lot of relief during meditation. Meditation paves the way for better health. Stress accumulates in the chakras and depending on where we hold the stress, symptoms of disease emerge and manifest: sinusitis and bronchitis from the throat (Visuddha Chakra): stomach ailments from the Manipura Chakra, and so on. Meditation aligns the chakras and clears the congestion, thereby allowing free movement of emotions. In advanced courses, after three days of silence and meditation you can actually observe emotions rising and falling within you. The benefits of meditation are too numerous to detail in one book and no matter which path you choose, as long as you meditate, know that you will be taken care of.

Meditation in your daily life

Meditation takes you into the stillness of the self so that you can be more active during the day. When Steve Sperber, our local teacher, once explained why we meditate, he compared it to archery: '*When you string a bow, the more you bend the bow and pull back, the further the arrow travels. Similarly the more you retreat into the stillness of the self, the more you contribute during the day.*'

Meditation does not make you listless and lethargic. In fact it fills you with energy and changes the quality of the day. Kaushik Bhaskaran from Germany, says he only appreciates meditation on days he delays or skips it. *'The effects of my meditation are evident on days that I delay it. Over time, the practice combined with the knowledge has made my world a more beautiful place. It's not that emotions and feelings do not come, it's just that now I have a technique to overcome problems.'*

You only appreciate its value and observe the changes it has affected in your life when you stop the practice, because then you are back in the small mind and the world delusion of problems and solutions. Erjet Malaj says: *'I meditate and if I skip, the day is not the same. You don't feel good, there is something lacking. The mind harps on past incidents that you want to change and you think of things you did well or badly. You get into small unimportant things like what he said or didn't say. So in the end I don't feel good and am not 100 % natural. It's a habit but it's a good habit, it helps me in my daily life, school and relationships. I do have some stress but I am handling it. That's the whole point.'*

Meditation and the scientific mind

Ronnie Newman affirms: *'Science asks the questions "how?" and "why?" and spirituality asks "what is it for?" Whether you talk quantum physics or spirituality and the rule of God, you ask the same thing. Energy is uncontainable; it is pure potentiality. Even Einstein said that the Laws of Nature and the Will of God is the same thing.'*

While several processes are suggested to access a meditative state, the ability to reach that place is a happening. One important sentence to internalize is that *'meditation is not created by any technique or scientific process; it just happens'*. It is important to know that just sitting quietly is not sufficient for meditation. You need the correct instruction in whichever tradition you follow which gives the necessary skill and commitment for meditative practice.

All that science can do is observe what takes place during that process, just like it records other states of consciousness. However, if you can't sleep, a pill can remedy that but there is nothing like a meditation pill; nor will there ever be, because you need Grace to be able to meditate in the first place. In the presence of the Guru you can transcend in minutes. Just the energy and grace flowing from him makes it happen like magic. When you learn from an unbroken link in the chain of a meditation tradition, it brings the Grace of the Master and the entire Holy Tradition to you wherever you are. You needn't be in the physical presence of the Master to have this happen. Guruji gives the analogy of the spoon and soup. Just as you need both these to drink soup from a bowl; you need two things to meditate. If the soup is the grace and the spoon is the mantra, you need the technique for using the mantra properly to get the soup/grace out of the bowl. If you hold the spoon upside down, or stick the handle of the spoon in the bowl, then you won't be able to retrieve the soup/the grace.

My daughter Karunya had learned Sudarshan Kriya but didn't understand why my husband and I were hooked onto meditation after our first taste of '*hollow and empty*' meditation with Guruji at an advanced course. She went to his public talk in Washington D.C. just to make me happy. As usual, Guruji led a guided meditation and my daughter who I have always believed to be an evolved soul, sank into transcendence in seconds. She called me from the Convention Center exclaiming, '*Mom what an amazing experience! I was gone. I was not sleeping, I was not awake; It was unreal.*' That first experience of meditation has converted her into a '*meditation junkie*.' An experience of transcendence converted a skeptic into a believer because the experience was so unlike anything she knew, it left her floating on a cloud of bliss; a sensation that was new, exhilarating and uplifting. This was her first experience and every time she meditates her experience varies, so if you don't find yourself floating on a cloud when you meditate, don't be disappointed. Every person has different experiences and each meditation session varies depending on what you bring into the moment.

Meenakshi Srinivasan did her first advanced course with Guruji. She was skeptical about the hollow and empty meditation and kept her eyes open right through the first meditation. Her scientific mind needed explanation and she doubted everything. She was more a person of action and couldn't think of sitting in one place and doing nothing. The very thought scared her. All her life the mindset had been, *'do the research before you accept anything.'* Guruji kept looking at her, indicating she should close her eyes, but she resisted. But then something happened and she spontaneously closed her eyes. Her second meditation gave her an unforgettable experience: *'I was gone. Who knew where I was? Not on this planet. I lost all sense of time. Since then life has been one amazing experience. Every moment is the Grace of the Guru. I lived so much in my mind; I didn't think that I would be able to meditate. But it is through the meditation that I feel the sense of expansion. I felt the wellness of the world without having to change a thing.'*

Meenakshi wanted to solve the world's problems and the poverty and misery around her made her wonder what the point of life was. Meditation brought about a real transformation of perspective and all it required was that internal shift: *'You feel intensely that all is well in the world even with its violence, corruption and global warming. That expanded sense of consciousness gives you a sense of wellness in this present moment. The Grace of supreme consciousness makes the meditation meaningful. The pane needs to be cleaned with glass plus with whatever you choose to use: your Seva, Sadhana, or Satsang.'*

What happens during meditation?

If you pose this question to SriSri he would probably answer, *'Nothing'*. It is that state of nothingness where you access the deepest recesses of your subconscious, a state nearest to your true self which fuses with eternal consciousness or the Brahman. In this state you lose sense of the body and of time, of the mind and the world. It's a state that has to be experienced to understand and involves discipline and regular practice.

What is the Brahman?

In the beginning there was nothing; just pure consciousness. This is what ancient Hindu seers, in an attempt to understand its enormity at a human level, called the Brahman; space and consciousness beyond the realm of mortal understanding. The absolute is immaterial and no light can be shed on it, yet it is luminous and cannot be actualized by anything else. The absolute is complete in itself. That supreme consciousness, the Brahman, having no part of worldly sensual perception, cannot be completely understood by mortals who rely on sentient measurement.

In that consciousness there is no concept of linear time, time can be comprehended as cyclical, with no beginning or end, where the subtle differences between the present, past and future do not exist. It is pure consciousness, like a magnificent ocean, and from within it crests the wave, which we know as the Universe. Every aspect of the Universe can be seen in the Brahman yet the Brahman is much more than that. And Universes rise and fall in pure consciousness, which is neither created nor destroyed but is ever present. This indestructible quality of consciousness exists everywhere at a subatomic level, where neither matter nor energy is either created or destroyed. Since consciousness is not created and cannot ever perish, it is endless as is an eternal, infinite ocean of bliss. On this ocean of bliss is superimposed our world consciousness, one which loves diversity and separateness, oblivious of its true source that is only one.

The Brahman is neither real nor unreal: it takes on form based on the perceptions of the mind. Just as in a dream persons and things appear to be real and tangible but are distorted images on waking, so also the Universe is like a dream in comparison with the reality of the Brahman.

The Brahman and the meditative state

In the beginning there was nothing; just pure consciousness. Then in a ripple of intention the world as we know it came into being. From that ocean of consciousness there arose a wave of creation and from that upsurge emerged the notion that 'I am.' That momentous instant was when the mind came into existence and from it there arose this notion of duality of 'I vs. everything else'.

The process of going inward to discover one's true nature takes you from the head to the heart: *Manah-namaha*, through the portal of the breath. Practices of deep breathing, pranayama, and relaxation, complemented by meditation, allow you to get a glimpse of the self, of the Brahman, in that elusive 'Present Moment.'

Meditation mirrors the Brahman and over time the practice becomes stronger; very effortlessly you can slip into that state of nothingness. Yet to meditate is much more than just sitting and doing nothing. It requires certain aids to calm the thoughts and allow the mind and body to settle.

Types of Meditation

According to ancient Hindu texts there are over 108 methods of meditating. Different Gurus and schools of thought use different methods. The most common are mantra meditation, chakra meditation and image mediation. It does not matter which one you choose, what matters is that you receive initiation and instruction from a truly qualified teacher of a tradition in the beginning, and then follow it up with daily practice. Initially I used guided meditation tapes and could not find any peace in my practice. I constantly checked my watch, waiting for the thirty minutes to end. I was later initiated into Sahaj Samadhi Meditation, an effortless mantra meditation which works well as my daily practice.

What is Sahaj Samadhi Meditation?

In Sanskrit, the term Sahaj Samadhi translates into 'natural enlightenment'. According to SriSri, it is a practice that is 'simple yet profound.' This becomes important because most often in life, things that are simple are not effective and those that are profound are too difficult to do.

In ancient Vedic times, you had to prove your loyalty to the Guru and after a long period of service, the Guru would grant you '*mantra deeksha*' for meditation. But Guruji has made meditation available for anyone who wants to try it. He doesn't believe you have to be an evolved soul, well along the path to enlightenment, in order to learn meditation. If learning Sahaj takes you one step onto your spiritual journey, then that is a good beginning.

Unlike many other forms of meditation, Sahaj is effortless and needs awareness rather than focus. For meditation to be effective the grace of the Master and the Guru-Shishya parampara (Teacher-student lineage) must flow through you, which is why it has to be received as a deeksha from a teacher for maximum efficacy. It provides the experience of setting up the proper initial conditions that allow the meditation to happen.

Things to remember for good meditation

1. Posture is a very important part of meditation. The spine ideally should be erect so that the chakras are aligned. The most common postures are Sukhasana (Easy pose), Siddhasana (Spiritual pose), and Padmasana (Lotus pose). In AOL Advanced courses they joke about a fourth alternative: Chairasana. Yes, you can sit on a chair with your feet folded or on the floor. What matters is that your spine be erect. If you are lying down you are not meditating. That is called Yoga nidra or Shavasana (Corpse pose) which is a relaxing, restorative pose. It is not meditation.

2. Meditation should be done preferably at the same time each day and in the same place for a minimum of 20 minutes. You can meditate longer but meditating for two hours won't change the quality of your day. It sometimes can lead to more sluggishness. Follow your teacher's directions on this. Each tradition has different requirements.

3. Meditate at a time when you are slightly hungry and rested. Ideally your morning sadhana should be shortly after waking and before eating breakfast and your evening sadhana at dusk. Meditation on a full stomach will put you to sleep and doing it at bedtime might keep you awake. Ancient Hindu scriptures indicate that a half hour of meditation gives you the same rest as four hours of sleep.

4. Ingestion of alcohol and rich food, including meat, affects the quality of your meditation. Not all meditators are vegetarian but a *sathvik* diet consisting of fresh fruit, vegetables and grain gives you the most restful meditation.

5. Expect nothing. Don't think that a light bulb will go off in your brain and the mysteries of the Universe will be revealed to you in meditation. Enter into a meditative state with the innocence of a child. The benefits of meditation do not always

come immediately; they play out during the course of your day and your entire life.

Steve Sperber says: '*There's not one time that I meditated and at the end, when I opened my eyes, I did not feel better than when I started. It's like getting a massage. Even when I'm going through deep emotional challenges, his teachings and the programs he's provided feel like an anchor in my life... It anchors me deeper in my own being so that I'm more rooted in my body, more rooted in my consciousness, so that the winds of change don't blow me away like a hurricane.*'

Meditation is your greatest gift one that makes you truly appreciate life and living, love and loving. I am truly grateful for it.

43

The Guru

In the presence of your Satguru, knowledge flourishes, sorrow diminishes, without any reason joy wells up, lack diminishes, abundance dawns and all talents manifest. To the degree you feel connected to your Guru, these qualities manifest in your life.
—H.H. SriSri Ravi Shankar

On May 13, 1956, the Master incarnated on earth in Papanasam, in Tamil Nadu. Glimpses of his true mission were seen even in childhood when he was able to recite the Bhagavad Gita at the age of four. As a boy of ten he understood his undertaking and is supposed to have declared to his parents that the world awaited his arrival. By age 17 he had completed his studies in Vedic and Modern Science and continued on his spiritual journey.

In 1982, after a ten day silence in Shimoga, Karnataka, the idea of Sudarshan Kriya crystalized and SriSri was ready to give to the world this gift of true joy and eternal bliss.

Ronnie Newman says that Guruji's resume is 17 pages long and that's just the tip of the iceberg. His achievements in the span of three decades are too numerous to detail. She knows in her heart that Guruji is doing this for us; it's the need of the time, it is his nature. Back in 1990 someone asked Guruji why he was here. To which he replied, *'When the yearning in the heart of the devotee is strong, the divine has no choice other than to provide.'*

The qualities of a true Master

The job of the Master is to be your guide as you find your way out of ignorance into knowledge. He is therefore the embodiment of what is known as Guru Tattva, which is that principle that leads you through the maze of intellectual and spiritual enquiry into the verdant meadows of bliss.

The world through the Master's eyes is beautiful: a paradise of love, joy, compassion and pure potentiality. When you attempt to mirror the Master's vision your revelation gets enhanced and the world delusion created by your mind fades into oblivion, leaving you energized and capable, ready to handle any situation.

The presence of the Master is unlimited. It moves beyond the confines of his body because it is pure consciousness. When you become attuned to his frequency, even if it is for one brief moment, then you are embalmed in instant Samadhi, mirroring the eternal presence of the Brahman of which he is the embodiment.

The Master can take away your anguish, your pain and your troubles. You can go to him with any problem and he will never judge you for that. He does that because a true Master is hollow and empty. He holds on to nothing and all that you surrender unto him goes through him and merges in supreme consciousness. Such is the power of the Master.

You have no need to follow him and claim to have the status of a devotee because he is behind you, watching out for you, ready to catch you if you fall.

Having Guruji, a living Master, is a rare fortune, reminiscent of how the apostles felt in the presence of Jesus or the Yadavas in the company of Krishna. That is the fortune you have, a gift so precious that you fear: on opening, it vanishes like a dream. To acquire a Master is a rare grace of fortune, one that doesn't come to you without an inner yearning. Every devotee has a unique relationship with the Master and sees him in a unique light.

The Guru unlocks something in your heart center and when this cap is unplugged, waves of gratitude overwhelm you and tears roll uncontrollably down your cheeks and you know instantaneously that you have found your Master. This happened with Veena Narayanan and the surge of emotion surprised her. She met Guruji for the first time in the Ashram at a Part II course. In that particular session after meditation, when the teacher asked everyone to open their eyes, Guruji was seated on a swing in the room. The sight caught everyone by surprise as they were not expecting him to be there: *'When I saw him, he was sitting there and looking at everyone in the room I was surprised and shocked and tears were rolling down my eyes. I wasn't crying, it was just tears of joy and gratitude. I have never had that kind of joy in my heart before.'*

As God

Amit Kumar Vyaghambare says, *'Guruji is not like God he is God himself.'* Meenakshi knew in her heart after her first silence course that he was the incarnation of Dakshinamurthy. But she wanted to challenge him so she could have proof. A few months later she got her opportunity. After Satsang, she hid in the back of a crowded room and told herself, *'if you are God you will find and hug me.'* He normally never came to that quadrant on his way out, but that day, like the Red Sea parting, Guruji walked up to her and hugged her. Meenakshi recalls that time: *'I was stunned. Then I said, "wait a second" and I put my arms on his forearms. My hand that should have held his biceps collapsed and I touched my fingers; a sensation of being thinner than air coursed through me like a breeze. It was a unique experience. I was sure I was hallucinating. I realized that this person is more than what he appears to be. He has an airy, light quality like the wind. After that I dropped the idea of a physical body and understood the dissolving of the material world into supreme consciousness. It is a phenomenon that can be experienced only in meditation. I stopped the questioning, knowing the experience was authentic and could not be dealt with the mind.'*

Sridhar hails from Kerala and was religious but not really on a spiritual path. Even after taking the first course, many issues bothered him and he had a lot of questions. He had never met SriSri or even heard of him. Sridhar says that in India there is skepticism about Godmen which is why he didn't want to trust him. SriSri was to visit a local temple for a talk and Sridhar decided to go. *'Something happened there. I realized that a divine presence, something unique was here. My breath changed even before he walked in. I saw him so light, almost like a feather and I had tears in my eyes. I just sat. It was a very poignant moment and I looked at my wife and she had tears in her eyes too. I don't remember what he said. As he left, he walked between me and my wife. That was it. I was sold.'* After this Sridhar went on to take the Part-2, Sahaj and DSN courses on his path to becoming a teacher.

Steve Sperber also talked about this 'light as a feather' quality about Guruji: *'I am very athletic and on my first advanced course we were in Canada and up in the mountains with large rocks. He was in a dhoti and sandals and I was wearing Nike running shoes. He starts prancing, running down the mountain and I am doing whatever I can to keep up. He is really wearing a skirt, you can't really stretch your feet out that far. We get to the bottom, I'm out of breath and for him it was like a walk in the park. That's when I realized he was a very special being. To move like that, almost like he was being lifted. It was something I will never forget.'*

The Guru is Love

Guruji is seen by most as the embodiment of unconditional love. But Madhu Bhardwaj takes it a step further and declares that it was plain that she fell in love with Guruji. Then she laughed, confessing that other than her husband she had never told any man she loved him. Guruji has the ability to walk into a room and when his eyes rest on you, you feel that he is there only for you and that he speaks only to you. Many I interviewed said the same thing to me. Madhu says: '*He always comes near me and makes me feel special. I felt at the Canadian ashram he was only looking at me. I am grateful that I tried to commit suicide. If not I wouldn't have come closer to my master. Guruji is the Lord of the Universe. He makes things happen.*'

Steve sees it slightly differently; he certainly loves SriSri but invokes unconditional love through his knowledge: '*He wants us to simply love. Expectations prevent us from feeling that love. There is a lack of unconditional giving and people want to receive rather than give. I immersed myself in his wisdom. The highest wisdom is the love. When you look at him it is perfect example of someone radiating love all the time. I have never seen him when he is not radiating love. They call that enlightenment.*'

When Bhushan Deodhar heard him speak there was an instant connection. He felt that the entire talk was only meant for his ears. For Bhushan, a skeptic thus far, this was a momentous realization: '*I felt like this man doesn't really want anything from anybody, he is just there to share the joy, love and knowledge. His selfless attitude was very obvious. That is the time I became a devotee overnight.*'

The Guru is a mirror

Your Satguru can never judge you. He merely mirrors your own qualities. In return you emulate what you admire and whether you live up or fall short, the Guru is with you anyway. According to

Jill Smith: *'As a teacher you feel so hollow and empty and can switch back into the present moment. Being a teacher is to emulate a guru, to keep learning, falling, and learning to interact with compassion and love. It reflects back onto myself. The guru mirrors your own qualities.'*

He is a presence; Guru Tattva

When Pawan Mulukutla met Guruji for the first time the Master playfully pinched him. Literally. Pawan was shocked but got a feeling as if he was asked, *'Where have you been all this time?'*

A father, a friend...

Guruji connects with his devotees at a deep level. He has an amazing memory and if he has seen you once, he probably remembers meeting you. He always enquires about you and knows what you are going through, sometimes even without you having to tell him. Some teachers say it's uncanny that they go to him intending to ask for help and he then just talks about their problems as if they had discussed its dynamics. It's almost as if he can read your thoughts and know what is going on in your mind. When you are in his presence you feel whitewashed and clean, with nothing to hide nothing to fear. You just feel pure love.

On his first visit to the Bengaluru Ashram, Ravi Pathak had a bag of grapes and was spitting the seeds all over the ashram. Swami Sadyojathah was the teacher in the course Ravi was taking. In the hall everyone was seated when Guruji called from California and told Swamiji that there was a plant on the hills drying out and that he needed to water it. Swamiji shared this with the group saying that Guruji was so caring, he called from Santa Barbara to ask for a plant to be watered. Ravi was aghast! *'He knows everything that goes on in everyone's mind. My first thought was does he know about all the grape seeds I spat all over the ashram?'* He was a little more cautious after that.

Ravi Pathak believes Guruji to be an enigma. Indian immigrants in America always speak of something missing in their lives in the US which you have in India but can't tell what exactly that is. That is how he feels when he tries to verbalize what the Master means to him: *'There is some connection he has that I cannot exactly pinpoint and say "this is it". He is not my father, my brother or friend but he occupies a place I can't define. He has a connection that is deeper that anything in a dimension that is inexplicable.'*

Julia Tang adds: *'He is a father figure, sometimes a friend and sometimes so unbelievably magical. I am so grateful, I feel taken care of. He is such a benevolent person, someone you can totally be yourself with and he loves you more than you'll ever know. When I look into his eyes, I am not hiding any faults or aggrandizing any qualities. It's not that I don't have rough times but it's just that there's faith now and I feel blessed.'*

Pure consciousness

When you have that connection with the Master you feel protected and safe and feel his presence in everything you do. Just a thought can invoke his existence. Someone once asked him if he heard them when they called him in need. Guruji paused and said: *'You have an entire head of hair but if someone pulls one hair can you feel it? Consciousness is like that. It is all connected. I may hear a devotee calling but I don't know everything. Sometimes I forget where I put my cell phone and room key.'*

Umberto Sartori says: *'I feel the presence of the Guru at all times. I don't need his physical presence. He's here no matter what. It's a reality beyond the body. He is the incarnation of pure consciousness. He has taken responsibility for all of us to make sure we are happy and that we grow. He is a friend who never leaves. He is there forever. That relieves me from thinking that I ever have to do this alone. I belong to this life through him and this is an experience not just a thought.'*

Guru Affects change

The Guru changes your perspective. He brings about a positive change in how you see yourself and what your equation is in this complex world of relationships and dilemmas. Marco DiGiano feels the connection: *'At some point I was suffering with dissatisfaction with life but when I met Guruji and started serving the Master, I felt connected and I thought to myself, "Aha! This is life and I want this always." Now it's my time and I can start to live, really live. All this time I merely existed. I am the same person but I see life differently.'*

Once you bury the past and slip into the present moment, your true purpose becomes crystal clear and you move through life with the skill of a sailor navigating a storm, maintaining your composure and centeredness and surging ahead, taking comfort in the knowledge that clear skies lie ahead.

Jakob Lund understands, *'When we connect deep into ourselves we realize that Guruji is always connected and when we realize there is a block between us and ourselves the feeling sometimes can be unpleasant. Meeting my Master has awakened something in me. For me there is nothing bigger than that. My past has been an education to help me do what I do now.'*

No matter what our past contains, whether we have been terrorists or criminals, liars or cheaters or whether we have been mired in ignorance, the Master is always there to forgive us, raise us to a higher level with compassion and give us that chance to make life work. The extent to which we allow him in our lives and the extent to which we connect with him is really up to us. The practices are deep in themselves but the grace of the Master elevates it to another level.

Grace of the Guru

Edina Atic affirms: '*Just being near Guruji is such a blessing, I can't even express it. He leaves me speechless, yet so fulfilled and protected.*'

Anand Kumar knows that the Guru's grace is with him. In Boston, Massachusetts where he lived, there were no AOL activities and as soon as Anand requested Guruji for a center things started moving: '*We cannot make anyone understand it through words; you have to experience the Grace. He is connected to infinity and when he pays just a little attention, things just start happening in most unfathomable ways. It's a reality and a fact of my life. There is nothing you do for it; it comes your way if you are fortunate.*'

According to Camille Abgrall: '*The Grace of the Guru is beyond words. Every moment when you feel connected to Guruji, to higher consciousness, life becomes sweet and devotion and then magical things happen.*'

When you have a Master in your life you are protected and you rest in the confidence that you are not alone. No matter where life's journey takes you and no matter who accompanies you as you make choices, you can rest assured that Guruji is with you all the way. He is here to ease your burden:

- To show you that life is an illusion and the best attitude is one that is lighthearted.
- To be immersed in action in a spirit of dispassion:
- To be so centered in the Self that events and happenings don't buffet you:
- To be able to smile in the face of uncertainty:
- To be fearless as you move out of your comfort zone into unchartered seas:
- To take responsibility and allow the Universe to guide you to achieve your full potential:

- To realize that this moment is all you have in which you can proudly proclaim that you are happy, that you are bliss, and that you are joy.

The path is yours; the Master merely illuminates the way. The choices are yours; the Master merely showers you with blessings. The happiness is yours; the Master merely makes you aware of it. The extent to which you connect with the Master determines his influence in your life.

Your job is to merely repose in the self, enjoy the present moment and rejoice in the happiness.

Epilogue

The choice is clear

If you are reading this then you have followed my journey towards its goal. You are already on the path or perhaps on the verge of stepping onto it and beginning your journey inward.

The purpose of writing this book has been to tell you that you do not need to continue in this world of delusion. It will never give you divine happiness. This is your opportunity to awaken from the deep slumber of ignorance and discover true contentment. This is your opportunity to slip into the present moment and gift yourself a revolutionary infusion of the Divine.

In the Gita, Krishna says that all paths lead to him when the journey is sincere with intention and love. No matter what path you choose make it selfless, filled with compassion for all of nature. You can pick the intellectual by actualizing and making knowledge a part of your daily life. You can rest in prayer and devotion as long as it is inclusive, in a spirit of sharing and compassion. You can choose to serve and in giving you will receive. The breathing and meditation accelerates the process and you can choose one or both or a combination of all the above.

This is my path, which I wanted to share. It has been a great journey so far and I have a long way to go. But I walk in confidence with a song in my heart and a smile on my face, comforted in the protection of the Master and in my belonging to the Brahman.

Each moment is my destiny; each moment is a deliberate unfolding.

The present moment is now my gift to the divine.

A new Beginning

Glossary of Indian Words

Bhajans:
In the Hindu tradition, a religious song of praise to a deity or Guru

Bhakti Sutras:
Important treatise on the aphorisms of love by Sage Narada

Brahman:
A Hindu concept of ultimate reality underlying all phenomena

Dakshina:
A Sanskrit word meaning an offering or fees given to someone in recognition of their gift of knowledge

Deeksha:
A Sanskrit word meaning initiation or consecration.

Dharma:
A moral code based on righteousness for individual and group behavior: The first pillar of the Purusharthas.

Guru:
A personal, religious or spiritual guide in the Hindu tradition

Kailash:
A mountain in the Himalayas considered the abode of Lord Shiva

Kama:
Pleasure, sensuous love, lust or desire: The third pillar of the Purusharthas

Karma:
Action: Often interpreted as the cosmic principle that results from action; good or bad

| Kenopanishad: | One of the earlier Upanishads associated with the Sama Veda, with famous commentaries by Adi Sankara |

Kenopanishad: One of the earlier Upanishads associated with the Sama Veda, with famous commentaries by Adi Sankara

Kundalini: Literally means coiled. It is an unconscious corporeal or libidinal energy coiled at the base of the spine.

Leela: A Sanskrit word signifying the Lord's cosmic game

Maya: A Sanskrit word meaning illusion

Pranayama: A Sanskrit word meaning extension of the prāṇa, breath or subtle life force.

Purusharthas: Four pillars of conduct based on the perceived qualities of the Divine: Dharma—Righteousness, Artha—Wealth, Kama—Desire, and Moksha—Salvation.

Rudram: A collection of Sanskrit hymns dedicated to Lord Shiva

Satguru: A title given to an enlightened teacher/guru who guides the devotee on a spiritual path.

Sadhana: Discipline in spiritual practice. In the Art of Living it signifies daily practice of Sudarshan Kriya and meditation

Sahaj Samadhi: An effortless mantra meditation practiced within the Art of Living

Samadhi: A state of being in harmony: A state of consciousness induced by meditation when the yogi merges with the Brahman

Sanathana Dharma: The original name for Hinduism signifying a way of life.

Sathvik: According to Ayurveda, the purest aspect of the three gunas, (qualities) characterized by equilibrium; responsible for health and contentment of mind and body and associated with the mind, consciousness, or intelligence that maintains health.

Satsang:
A gathering of people in search of truth through knowledge and chanting of hymns and mantras

Seva:
Selfless Service

Shushumna Nadi:
A Sanskrit term used to describe the central channel/ meridian within the subtle body, of energy that flows vertically, along the course of but slightly in front of the spinal column, from the perineum to the crown of the head.

Siddhas:
Masters who have actualized and achieved spiritual enlightenment and physical immortality

Sudarshan Kriya:
Literally meaning proper vision of the Self through a purifying action. A set of breathing exercises, taught by H.H. Sri Sri Ravi Shankar

Sukshma Yoga:
Subtle micro-yoga techniques that facilitate relaxation and release of tension and stress

Sutras:
Aphorisms or spiritual doctrinal summaries

Tantric Practices:
Ancient practices in the Hindu and Buddhist tradition often connected to Shiva and Shakti worshippers.

Upanishads:
A collection of commentaries and philo-sophical texts revealing the essence of life.

Yoga Vashishta:
Recounted by Sage Valmiki this is the conversation between Sage Vashishta and Lord Rama

Kanchana Krishnan Ayyar was born in New Delhi, India, and currently lives in South Florida, with her husband and her two daughters. You can contact her at

www.kanchibooks.com

She is the author of, "When the Lotus blooms," also published by Kanchi Books and "Snapshots," a mini anthology of short stories.

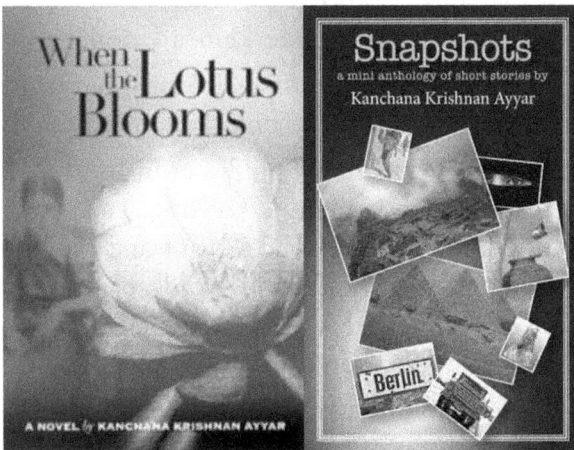

Acknowledgements

This novel represents an important stage in my spiritual journey and could never have been undertaken without the support from my husband, Rajiv and my daughters. I am deeply grateful to Steve Sperber who gave me my first interview and guided me on the right track. I would like to express my deep gratitude to Enrique Ferreira and my Satsang group for their encouragement. My deepest thanks to Ronnie Newman, who has been a beacon of light and helped me every step of the way, ensuring that the information on the research was presented correctly and facilitating the endorsement from the AOL Foundation. Thanks to Janael McQueen for ensuring the accuracy of Guruji's quotes. I am indebted to Timothy Wong, Alka Ahuja, Christine Zambrano, Sushil Nachnani and my husband for their invaluable assistance in the editing process. For the brilliant book cover I thank my dear friend and designer Feroza Unvala.

None of this would have been possible without contributions from all my interviewees and I thank them deeply.

I would also like to thank my publisher in India, Mr. Udayan Singh, for his confidence in me. My deepest appreciation to Dr. Karan Singh, renowned public servant and philosopher, for his enlightening message and kind words of encouragement. My gratitude to Jeff Danelek who took the time to read the manuscript and write the Foreword.

For more information on the Art of Living please visit
www.artofliving.org

www.ingramcontent.com/pod-product-compliance
Lightning Source LLC
Chambersburg PA
CBHW052030090426
42739CB00010B/1854

That should get you by until I get this straightened out." Click. The phone went dead.

Granny would call Child Protective Services— that's what she would do. After all of Mom's deadbeat boyfriends and trips to rehab, Granny didn't care anymore. Mom had promised to change when they moved to Roxford, but she obviously hadn't.

Cassie rehearsed four different ways to break the news, but none of them sounded right. Jenna was too young to understand why this Christmas would be their worst ever. When the bus rattled to a stop, Cassie got off, knowing she would have to make up some excuse why Mom wouldn't be home.

Bam! A cold rush of wind as the front door flew open, followed by the sound of Jenna singing "Santa Claus Is Coming to Town."

Cassie joined her, forcing a happy smile. Sure, Santa would be coming to town, but not to their house. "Hey, Jenna, how was your class party?"

"Great! We had cookies and hot chocolate. Amanda is going to Hawaii for Christmas. How cool is that? Jordan is getting a trampoline."

"Yeah, cool." Time to change the subject. "Mom's not home yet, so we're on our own. What do you want to eat?"

After a quick bowl of cereal, Jenna sat in front of the couch to watch TV.

Cassie unfolded the tattered paper with Granny's phone number. Mom said she shouldn't call, but what else could she do? Why was Mom in jail? Would she go to prison? Cassie didn't want to wind up in foster care again, but she couldn't think of any way out. She was about to dial the number when she heard a car pull into

289

the driveway. Mom!

A knock on the door.

So it wasn't Mom after all.

"Cassie Lansford?" A man's deep voice. "Girls, we know you're home. Come to the door, please."

Cassie cracked open the door, leaving the chain intact. "Yes?"

"I'm Sergeant Collins. This is my wife, Sandy. May we come in?"

The lady looked familiar. Maybe she was a teacher at Crestview High. Cassie invited them in and asked them to take a seat on the couch.

Sergeant Collins hesitated, as if he were the bearer of bad news. "I was on duty last night when the call came in. Girls, your mother has been arrested for motor vehicle theft. She is now in custody at the county jail."

"What? Are you crazy?" Jenna said. "My mom would never steal anything."

Was Jenna right? Maybe not in every situation, but in this case, she had to be. "Sergeant Collins," Cassie said, "Mom didn't steal that car. It was a gift from her boyfriend."

"I don't know about that. We're still investigating. What I know for sure is that the car was stolen, and it was found in your mother's possession. Until we learn the whole truth, your mom remains in custody." His stern look transformed to a smile. "All the news isn't bad though." He turned to his wife.

"Cassie," Sandy said, "I'm the school counselor at Crestview High. "We were aware of your financial struggles before your mom was arrested. I hope she's innocent, but that doesn't change the school's

290

decision."

Cassie felt like crying. She hadn't anticipated being expelled from school just because they were poor.

Sandy was smiling as if she was giving good news. "Your family was selected to receive the Christmas Blessing Basket that the school gives out each year, but after I heard about your mom... Well, we want you to stay at our house until we can contact your family."

"Mom is all the family we have. No aunts or uncles. We don't know where Dad is." Cassie wasn't exactly lying. Truthfully, her grandmother wasn't considered a part of their family, and it was best she not be mentioned.

Sandy's expression said she wasn't going to take no for an answer. "You can't stay here by yourselves. If you don't stay with us, we have to send you somewhere else." She glanced toward Jenna, then back at Cassie. "Please... you don't want that. Just come with us."

When they got out of the car and walked toward the Collins house, Cassie felt like she was entering a palace. Multi-colored lights ran across the roofline and framed the windows. Twinkling white lights made the shrubs sparkle like a million brilliant stars. As she walked up the steps, she thought she would feel like a princess. But she didn't. This wasn't home, and she didn't belong here, not without Mom.

Inside, Jenna twirled the crystal angels and toy soldiers on the tree. She watched them unwind, waiting, as if they were talking to her.

The fireplace warmed Cassie's hands and feet, but not the chill that gripped her heart.

On Christmas Eve morning, Cassie couldn't go to the jail with Sergeant Collins. She was underage. The

Collins had been kind, but she felt like a house slipper at a ballroom dance. She and her sister didn't belong here.

While Jenna sat at the kitchen table helping Sandy decorate cookies, Cassie stared out the window, sipping hot chocolate. Granny really did love them. She was just mad at Mom for making such a mess of their lives. Mom had always said Granny meant to take her kids away, but it wasn't for a foster home.

Cassie was turning to get the phone when she saw a car come into the driveway. She wiped the steam from the window. Sergeant Collins. But who was on the other side of the car? Mom!

"Jenna, quick! Mom's here!"

They both ran out the front door, into their mom's open arms.

"I'm so sorry, girls, but I didn't steal the car. My boyfriend stole it from his landlord. So I've been driving a stolen car for months without knowing it. Now, he's the one in jail." Mom turned to Sandy. "Thank you for everything you've done for us."

"You're welcome." Sandy smiled like a true friend. "We would love you to join us for the evening. We have a big Christmas dinner waiting inside."

"You made it home just in time," Cassie said to her mom. "This is the best Christmas ever."

www.ingramcontent.com/pod-product-compliance
Lightning Source LLC
Chambersburg PA
CBHW052031090426
42739CB00010B/1863